Off the Deep End

Tony Perrottet is an Australian writer and photographer currently based in New York City. After graduating from Sydney University with a degree in Australian History, he headed off to South America to work as a newspaper correspondent, finally coming to rest in Buenos Aires for two years. From his current base in the East Village of Manhattan, he has commuted between Iceland and Havana, from the Galápagos to Tierra del Fuego. His travel writing has appeared in almost all Australian publications, most recently *HQ*, the Melbourne *Age* and *Good Weekend*; in the United Kingdom, the *Independent* and *Sunday Times*; and in the United States, *Esquire*, *Outside*, *Escape* and *Islands* (as a Contributing Editor). His black and white photographs — taken with a $15 plastic camera made in China — have appeared in several New York exhibitions.

off the

DEEP END

Travels in forgotten frontiers

Tony Perrottet

f l a m i n g o
An imprint of HarperCollins*Publishers*

This project has been assisted
by the Commonwealth Government
through the Australia Council,
its art funding and advisory body.

Flamingo
An imprint of HarperCollins*Publishers*, Australia

First published in Australia in 1996
by HarperCollins*Publishers* Pty Limited
ACN 009 913 517
A member of the HarperCollins*Publishers* (Australia) Pty Limited Group

HarperCollins*Publishers*
25 Ryde Road, Pymble, Sydney NSW 2073, Australia
31 View Road, Glenfield, Auckland 10, New Zealand
77–85 Fulham Palace Road, London W6 8JB, United Kingdom
Hazelton Lanes, 55 Avenue Road, Suite 2900, Toronto, Ontario, M5R 3L2
and 1995 Markham Road, Scarborough, Ontario, M1B 5M8, Canada
10 East 53rd Street, New York NY 10032, United States of America

National Library of Australia Cataloguing-in-Publication data:

Perrottet, Tony.
  Off the deep end: travels in forgotten frontiers.
  ISBN 0207 189773.
  1. Perrottet, Tony — Journeys. 2. Voyages and travels.
  I. Title.
910.4

Cover photograph by Tony Perrottet
Cover and internal design by Paula Marchant
Printed in Australia by Griffin Paperbacks, Adelaide

9 8 7 6 5 4 3 2 1
99 98 97 96

Contents

Prologue

CABIN FEVER

It had been a tough winter here on Tenth Street.

The island of Manhattan was encased in ice — a thick protective layer of it, sparkling in the brilliant sun. Icicles hung in daggers from every window. Pedestrians skated along the footpaths, trying not to break their necks. Cars were lined up under giant piles of snow, like pagan burial mounds.

When it got this cold, Les agreed, it was best not to go out. For days on end, we ordered in Chinese noodles, pizza, Ukrainian soups. It was claustrophobic, sure, but we could normally have managed. Our one-room apartment is organised as efficiently as a NASA space shuttle: every inch serves several purposes, from the fold-down futon/couch, to the shower closet that doubles as a photo darkroom. Les has her easel and canvasses out the back; I've got my laptop and negatives in the front.

As I say, normally we could survive the long dark winter. Unfortunately, this year, cabin fever was getting to us.

It all started in December, when new tenants moved in overhead, a charming pair we soon referred to simply as 'the Scum Upstairs'. We quickly learned that they were club kids, and that they liked to come home dancing in their snow boots at 4 a.m. By about 5.30, they'd start a screaming argument and throw the furniture at each other. These old tenements work like echo chambers; their stomping and tossing shook the foundations and brought rotten plaster showering down on our heads. We'd bang the roof with a broom and bellow out the window; they'd stomp and bellow back. When things got too violent, the police would turn up — sirens, crackling radios, the whole 'NYPD Blue' regalia.

Things took a turn for the worse when the Scum bought a dog. It happened at precisely 6 p.m. on Christmas Eve, when we heard a pitiful howling echo through the corridors. It sounded as if the animal was being exquisitely tortured — ritually disembowelled, perhaps, or burned alive on a spit — and the sound went on all night. From then on, the Creature woke up every morning at dawn, then went into an epileptic fit on the bare floor above our heads; all night it would bay like the Hound of the Baskervilles.

I won't deny that we had some forms of revenge. The hot water runs up through our kitchen, so when we heard the Scum having a shower, we'd turn on the sink taps full bore. We could take a mirthless pleasure in their curses as the water ran ice cold. It was petty, but strangely satisfying.

But then — no sooner had the Scum Upstairs bought their dog than the Scum Downstairs brought in a piano. It was placed by the air-shaft window, where the building's acoustics are better than Carnegie Hall's, and a German music student practiced religiously at the machine for eight hours a day. Scales, old Broadway show tunes or modern jazz — pretty well anything calculated to drive the average person insane. We imagined this character poised over his piano like Schroeder, a bust on the mantelpiece, pounding the ivories until his fingernails bled. 'He never even goes to the bathroom!' Les noted bitterly.

Between the show tunes and the dog and the lunatics fighting upstairs, we weren't getting a lot of work done. Living on Tenth Street was like being part of a sleep-deprivation experiment. And in winter, there was no escape. We lived with earplugs in, even during the day. We bought a device called a 'white noise machine' to put by the bed; it was round and plastic, and we soon referred to it as the Orgasmatron. Every night it hummed away next to our heads, putting out this 'white noise', slowly giving us brain tumours.

I found myself lying awake in the dark, wondering how much it would cost to hire a hitman. It wouldn't be much, judging from the movies. Fifty dollars, even. Or what if I bought a shotgun? I could walk up and down the apartment, blasting away randomly through the ceiling until I quietened them all forever.

That's when I realised: God help me, I'm turning into a New Yorker.

To pinch a line from Melville's Ishmael, who once lived on this 'insular city of the Manhattoes':

> Whenever I find myself growing grim about the mouth; whenever it is a damp, drizzly November in my soul; whenever I find myself involuntarily pausing before coffin warehouses, and bringing up the rear of every funeral I meet; and especially whenever my hypos get such an upper hand of me, that it requires a strong moral principle to prevent me from deliberately stepping into the street, and methodically knocking people's hats off — then, I account it high time to get to sea as soon as I can.

As for me, at times of stress, I call a few editors. Les arranged a couple of weeks' break at a friend's studio, to do some painting in peace.

I went to dig up an assignment.

There are three things that get me worked up about a place:
* it should be as obscure as possible
* it should be some sort of former colonial frontier
* it should have some kind of weird literary association

I started thinking about desert islands — and one in particular, the archetypal escape, the definition of remoteness, the very antithesis of the isle of Manhattan.

Crusoe Slept Here

To reach the Juan Fernández islands with your nerves intact, it helps to have a religious nature. I learnt this early, at the small private airport in Santiago de Chile, where a twin-engine Cessna was about to take off directly over the Pacific. The only other passenger was a fifteen year old island girl, who took me by the arm, nodded towards our blond Italian–Chilean pilot and said, 'Don't worry about anything. I have *absolute faith* in Mario.'

It wasn't long before I saw what she meant. We had barely left Santiago when the cabin was filled by a thunderous gasp of air: the cabin door had popped ajar, flooding the plane with freezing cold air. 'It won't open up completely,' Mario yelled over the din, and as I clutched onto the armrest, my fingers slowly going numb, I thought to myself: *Absolute faith. Yes, all will be well.*

Mario was right — we didn't get sucked to our deaths — yet my faith was tested again when the tiny Juan Fernández islands finally appeared some three hours later. Three serrated specks of earth poked from the sea like the rusted remains of a wreck. They looked as tall as they were wide, with the only clouds in the whole blue Pacific settling menacingly above them. 'Engineers said it was impossible to build a landing strip here,' Mario screamed out, as we hit the air turbulence. 'But the islanders, they did it!' We plunged towards a strip of red dirt carved onto a cliffside; it was built in an arc, like a gigantic ski jump. 'Great for taking off. Not so good for coming down. We might have to try a couple of times.'

But absolute faith protected absolutely. It was a flawless landing, and perhaps the ideal way to arrive on what may actually be the most famous island on earth: the Isla Grande of the Juan Fernández archipelago. Few people might be able to locate it on a map — it lies half-way between Easter Island and the South American coast — but this corner of the South Pacific holds a permanent place in our imaginations. It was here that a rather obnoxious Scottish sailor, Alexander Selkirk, was marooned for more than four years at the beginning of the eighteenth century — an experience that his contemporary Daniel Defoe turned into *The Life and Strange Surprizing Adventures of Robinson Crusoe of York, Mariner.*

Eventually rescued from his island, Alexander Selkirk became a minor celebrity on his return to London. Defoe took up the basic elements of the story, tidied up the more debauched side of Selkirk's character (he suffered from all the classic sailor's vices, and was usually interviewed in seedy waterfront taverns) to create the beloved figure of Crusoe, goatskins and all. In the process, the largest Juan Fernández island became our popular conception of a desert isle: lush and green, with plenty of food, water and game, completely unlike the barren rocks where most shipwrecked sailors actually washed up.

I decided to make the pilgrimage to this Edenic prototype to explore the physical roots of the myth, and see how history has taken over. Of course, there was the risk of fracturing the romance. Some 600 people live on the archipelago now, and they obviously weren't shy about their claim to fame. My air ticket was emblazoned with a drawing of Crusoe ambling along with a parrot on his shoulder; in the seventies, the name of the main island was officially changed to 'Robinson Crusoe'. But this brand-name endorsement hadn't exactly turned the archipelago into a tourist trap, for one good reason. Reaching the islands today is about as difficult as it was for Selkirk to leave them 300 years ago — and the air strip was only the start of it.

No sooner had we scrambled out on the ski-jump runway than Mario leapt out to tie down the Cessna; its wings had to be secured by metal cables or it would simply be flipped over by the gale-force winds. There was no sign of human habitation, so I asked the island passenger, Josefina, where the town lay. She laughed ominously and waved into the distance. '*Lejos, lejos, lejos.*' Far, far, far. 'We have to wait here for the *chicos.*'

'This island,' Mario added cryptically, 'is an adventure from beginning to end.'

Rambling towards us was a broken-down jeep, looking like it was made of scrap metal and packed with half a dozen gangly fishermen in jeans and terry towelling caps. The islanders are all descended from European immigrants who came to the islands via Chile a century ago, and some had the slurred expressions that suggested an economical gene pool. They ran out giggling and falling over each other, embraced Mario and Josefina, then each came toward me with mock-ceremony, shook my hand and introduced themselves. Perhaps it my imagination, but at least two of them were called Robinson.

The next stage of the journey began when we all piled into the jeep, with Mario sitting on the hood, and slowly backed it onto a narrow gravel pathway that wound at a forty-five degree angle down the sheer cliffside. 'We've got to fix these shitty brakes,' muttered the more sober leader of the pack, Robinson Schultz, as he craned his neck out the window, and everyone roared with nervous laughter. Bobbing in rough seas at the bottom of the cliff was an open longboat, like something taken from the decks of the *Pequod*. This was obviously for stage three.

'You're lucky it's sunny!' Robinson #2 told me as he pulled the motor and we took off into the spraying waves. The weather on the islands is actually fairly autumnal all year round; the wind was chilly and damp. But Robinson Schultz was merrily setting up a makeshift metal drum to smoke succulent lumps of cod that had been caught on the way over. He turned to Josefina. 'Hey, *hermana* — what did you bring us to drink?'

'Oy, chicos. Already?' She resignedly pulled out a bottle of gin, to general disappointment. 'Gin? Gin? And you didn't bring any tonic?' He looked about despondently, until after lengthy discussion everyone agreed it was potable straight.

Mario the pilot was beginning to relax; he would have to stay on the island for four days, until the next scheduled departure. I asked him whether he liked being away from his family for so long. 'For me, this is like a release from prison,' he grinned. 'No telephones. No mail. No work. I don't have to worry about anything at all. Except maybe drowning.'

The engine stalled after about an hour, and nobody could get it going again, so we all stretched out for a siesta as the boat bobbed about in the afternoon sun. It was like being in *Fantasia*, with everything around us glowing fresh and clean and blissfully harmless. The cliffs towering up above looked like they were rippled with petrified tree roots; schools of fish zigzagged in formation through the crystal green water below; obese sea lions sunned themselves on the rocks or coolly appraised us from the water. After a few swigs of gin, I was ready to believe that this was something of a paradise myself.

Needless to say, that hadn't been Alexander Selkirk's first reaction.

When planning this trip to Juan Fernández, I'd packed my copy of *Robinson Crusoe*, to be sure, but also an eccentric history book-cum-literary critique from 1930, by the British poet Walter de la Mare, titled *Desert Islands*. It turns out that the real-life Crusoe was hardly the stuff for an edifying moral tale.

Selkirk was just the sort of seaman that no self-respecting captain would want on his crew. Loud-mouthed, foul-tempered and stubborn as a mule, the Scottish-born mariner always spoke his mind with a hail of baroque curses. Meanwhile, Thomas Stradling was the sort of captain with whom no sailor would wish to serve. As quarrelsome as Selkirk and an incompetent to boot, he had an English bloody-mindedness about admitting his mistakes. The two loathed each other on sight, and when circumstances forced them together on the *Cinque Ports* during a privateering expedition to South America, it wasn't long before they clashed head-on.

Whereas the fictional Crusoe was shipwrecked in a tropical storm (and so, in his more meditative moments, could see the hand of God at work), Selkirk only had himself to blame. After some unsuccessful raids on Peru, the confrontation between the two came over some repairs to the hull that Selkirk felt were dangerously shoddy. He announced that if the ship were to go down it could go down without him, and asked to be let off at the nearest dry land. Stradling was only too glad to set course for the uninhabited islands of Juan Fernández.

Selkirk stuck to his absurd plan until the very last moment. It was only as he was sitting on the rocky beach, watching his former shipmates row back to the ship, that the enormity of his decision struck him. Selkirk later admitted that he plunged into the ocean and chased after the departing rowboat, screaming madly that he had changed his mind. 'Well I have not changed mine!' spat the captain (according to Selkirk). 'Stay where you are and may you starve!' It was early in 1704.

We finally chugged into the bay where this indecorous scene took place — now the site of the only human settlement on the archipelago, San Juan Bautista (St John the Baptist). Despite the brisk weather, the village looked dreamily sub-tropical, backed by a verdant fist of rock whose peak was permanently wrapped in clouds. Along the rocky shore, tiny fishermen's huts were lined up like turn-of-the-century changing rooms.

Waiting at the dock was Josefina's brother; of the five cars on the island, he had the only one that worked. Accommodation for the *extranjero*? No problem. He took my bag and gunned it at top speed along the only 300 metres of roadway through the village, then up a dirt path to their mother's house.

Señora Green was stocky and stern, the descendant of English settlers from the South American wars of independence; she had a little guest house in her backyard that was designed like a Swiss chalet. Planted before me was a dinner of fresh lobster empanadas — the crustaceans breed by the thousands in the shallow, cold waters around the islands — and a bottle of Chilean wine.

'You're not Chilean are you?' she asked as I sat down. 'Chileans are hateful. All they do is eat. I like all other foreigners, just not the *chilenos*.'

'No, no, no,' I assured her. '*Australiano*.'

It's usually the safest answer on earth, but Señora Green's face darkened. '*Not* Australian!'

'Uh, I'm afraid so.'

'Here on the island, we are not fond of the Australians.'

'I'm surprised you give us much thought,' I said.

She filled her glass with white wine and gulped it down in one go. 'Why did your countrymen want to destroy our island?' she demanded. 'Destroy it from top to bottom?'

'My countrymen? Are you sure?'

Then she spat out the name: 'Bond. *Alán* Bond.'

The story began back in the late eighties, when Bond and the Pinochet government were wheeling and dealing together. They came up with the idea that the Juan Fernández islands could be an off-shore banking haven, just like the Bahamas, complete with skyscrapers and a casino complex. The islanders violently opposed the plan, and with the world's changing fortunes, nothing ever came of it.

'Well, in my country, *El Señor Bond* has not been doing too well,' I told her. 'Bankruptcy, sickness, divorce, jail ...'

The news did not surprise her. 'Here, Pinochet has also come to no good,' she snorted proudly.

Bond's hair-brained scheme was one of the few times the islanders have needed to rouse themselves against the outside world. Before that, it was probably 1915 — when three British battleships chased the German rogue *Dresden* here; it gave them the slip in the fogs, but shells from their exchange are still embedded ten feet into the cliffs just outside of town.

Next morning, I strolled down to the waterside to try and imagine how Selkirk must have felt watching his ship the *Cinque Ports* sail away that day in 1704. The fictional Crusoe set furiously about improving his lot with Protestant zeal, but by his own account, Selkirk was thrown into utter despair by his predicament, wandering up and down the rocky beach, bewailing his cruel fate, gnawing on shellfish and staring at the empty horizon. As De La Mare suggests, 'It is indeed one of the charms of Defoe's book that we can compare its fiction with at least a fair number of the facts on which it was founded.' Selkirk simply could not believe that his crewmates would really leave him here alone. At night, he was terrified by a deafening chorus of sea lions — 'monsters of the deep,' he thought — whose cries were 'too terrible to be made for human ears'. This paralysing despair continued, he said, for eight whole months.

Today, the sea lions were gone from the stony beach; the only sound was the wind slashing through the trees. There were a few tidy bungalows; a soccer field where a white crane sat on the back of a mule; a cemetery with ship's anchors over many of the graves. Two or three people usually sat down by the pier and watched fishermen bring in the lobsters; in the afternoon, a few would gather at the Bahia Bar, where a well-fed man with a pencil moustache attended. A goat's skull with horns was mounted on the wall and a model sailing ship on the bar.

Chatting idly with people, I was expecting a certain amount of dissatisfaction and restlessness in this Pitcairn-like isolation. But although the islanders were all reasonably well-educated, they maintained an almost total indifference to the outside world. Thanks to the rich lobster trade, everyone had the means to visit the mainland. 'It was so damn noisy!' explained one of the more energetic fisherman, rolling his eyes. 'It stank! Everyone running around like lunatics. Now look at me. I've got enough money to make a visit if I want to. I could go five times. But why would I bother?'

Apart from Señora Green, who felt it was her civic duty, nobody asked me any questions about where I was from or what I was doing here. And the little black and white TV in the Bahia Bar was snapped off as soon as the news came on — even though a national election had just been held throughout Chile.

'Oh, the sons-of-bitches made us vote,' explained the rotund barman. 'If we don't, there's a thousand peso fine. Otherwise, nobody gives a damn.' He stroked his moustache and gestured at the great beyond. 'What's it all got to do with us?'

It's a satisfying irony that these latter-day hermits should have inherited the island on which Alexander Selkirk was so mortified to be abandoned.

It hadn't been long before the Scotsman's tea-chest of supplies gave out, and the real test of survival began. He soon realised that he'd been fairly lucky in where he ended up. Most marooned sailors faced a slow death by starvation or dehydration; they were usually put ashore with a pistol and one ball, and tales abounded of sea parties finding a lone skeleton on the beach, with a shattered skull and a rusting firearm clenched in hand. But here on Juan Fernández, life could be sustained. There were fresh streams and shady ferns, and a ready supply of food in the form of wild goats. Selkirk shot them at first. When he ran out of ammunition, he had to chase them barefoot with his knife. Bounding around the island's rocky coasts, kept on a rum-free diet, the Scotsman became quite an athlete. Sewn together with sinews, the goat skins also made warm clothes — Crusoe's legendary uniform — and a fine lining for the two wooden huts Selkirk constructed in the forest.

The months dragged on without a single passing ship, and to stave off boredom Selkirk even started reading the Bible, the only book he had with him. In desperation, he took to chasing goats for sport, marking their ears as a record. This diversion had its dangers: once Selkirk caught a beast just as it was leaping off a precipice. He used its body to cushion his fall, but was knocked unconscious for at least a full day, possibly three. After this debacle, he turned from hunter-gatherer to cultivator, raising goats in a compound. Sea lions made safer prey than goats. Overcoming his fear, Selkirk learned to climb up behind the ponderous beasts and clock them with his hammer. Their whiskers were so stiff, he said, they made fine toothpicks.

In fact, the only island animals that posed much threat to Selkirk were the wild rats. They invaded his hut by night to nibble his feet and gnaw on his clothes. The mariner's solution was to tame feral kittens — which had, like the rodents, escaped from passing ships many years before — and lay them in a ring around his bed. Apparently he also taught some of the cats and kids to dance. 'Thus best do we picture him,' intones Walter de la Mare, 'praying aloud, singing and dancing with his kids and cats in the flames and smoke of his allspice wood, and the whole world's moon taunting and enchanting him in her seasons.'

Diverting as these bestial balls must have been, Selkirk did not allow his hopes for escape to flag. Every morning, at the crack of dawn, he jogged up from his hut to the top of the square mountain behind him — the one point on the island where the horizon is visible in every direction.

His trail on El Yunque, the Anvil, is still in use today. Señora Green told me I'd do well to get cracking at dawn myself: Selkirk got up so early because the clouds always rolled in by mid-morning. And so I set off in the bone-chilling half-light, with the wind crashing menacingly in the trees above. Bond aside, Australia's most significant contribution to Juan Fernández is the eucalyptus — whole forests of gums line the rugged coast, and in my half-awake state it all looked eerily familiar. Higher up, the trail plunged into the temperate rainforest, full of prehistoric ferns with leaves the size of radar dishes. Most of the plants looked like they were plucked from the pages of a Dr Seuss book. Tiny red hummingbirds darted in and out of their exotic flowers.

Wheezing and gasping — I would have been no match for Selkirk — I followed the path onto a razorback peak. This was El Mirador, the Lookout, with sweeping views over both sides of the island — one green and gentle, the other brown and sharp, like dried icing on a chocolate cake. A plaque had been placed by one of Selkirk's descendants from Largo in Scotland, and another by a British naval ship last century. But nothing else had changed since the mariner bounded up here every morning, squinting at the concave horizon and praying for a passing ship. It was both majestic and discouraging to see the ocean sparkle in every direction without the slightest hint of movement. It was here that I could most vividly imagine Selkirk's plight: if nothing else, his loneliness must have been as deep as Defoe described.

Once, poor old Selkirk actually saw two ships approaching and ran down to greet them — only to find to his horror that they were Spaniards, who would have taken him as a prisoner to the mines of the Andes. The crew fired on this strange apparition and chased him into the bushes, but they were no match for his superhuman speed. The maroon hid up a tree until the danger passed.

After only a few days in San Juan Bautista, I was beginning to fall for this desert island idea. An unnatural calm had fallen over me, and I'd picked up some of the islanders' more sedentary habits, like taking a seat by the foreshore at dusk to watch the lobster catch being brought in, then nursing a beer at the Bahia and chatting about dogs with the barman. And the disturbing thing was that I didn't feel bored.

The daily rhythm was varied on Saturday, when a soccer tournament took place. The whole town huddled around the dusty field to watch the matches, beside the cemetery where so many of their ancestors resided. Nobody seemed bothered that the wind kept blowing the ball over the sidelines and into the sea. That night, a small disco was set up in a waterfront shack, lit by kerosene lamps. Soccer players, fans and families with their pets all downed their potent pisco and Coca-Colas and danced to a live band playing a mix of salsa and sixties

American rock. After the town's generator was turned off at midnight, a battery-operated ghetto blaster continued to belt out music until dawn.

Sitting in the moonlight at 4 a.m., some players and their girlfriends wanted me to admit that Juan Fernández was indeed the earthly paradise. Sure, there were none of the swaying palm trees or golden sands of other South Pacific islands, and it was a bit cold and damp. 'But look here,' said the bushy-haired goalkeeper, listing the reasons on his fingers. 'Nobody is poor. There is no crime. No pollution. No social tensions. No drugs — except for pisco, which doesn't count. What more do you want?'

It's the sort of thing you often hear from people on other islands, but with a sly betraying look, a gloss of self-irony. Here they sounded serious. And it may have been the pisco bubbling in my brain, but it seemed foolish to disagree. Every other so-called paradise I'd been to, from Tahiti to the Caribbean, had seemed secretly hellish: there was always some wretched colonial past, an oppressed native culture, a destructive tourism industry. But Juan Fernández was uninhabited when it was settled. Its people seem to take what they want from the twentieth century — medicine, music, radios, TV soap operas — and leave the rest. Maybe that was why their island was so beguiling: it created a groundswell of nostalgia for a lost way of life that was still completely familiar. I felt like I was back in 1910, say, in some remote rural town. But while it's pleasant enough to contemplate, you have to be born into such a paradise to belong there, or even seriously care to live in it.

'So what do you want?' the goalkeeper challenged again.

'I don't know,' I shrugged. 'I guess I want everything.'

And they probably thought I was joking.

As for Alexander Selkirk …

Who can imagine his feelings when, after fifty-two months of isolation, the maroon spotted the English *Duke* and *Duchess* lowering anchor on the island with fifty scurvy-ridden sailors? Brought on board, the delirious, ratty-bearded, skin-clad Selkirk cut an extraordinary figure; he couldn't get any words out, croaking rather than talking. The captain was inclined to shoot the wild man, until an officer named William Dampier — who had twenty years before led the first English visit to Australia — stepped forward to recognise Selkirk and confirm his incredible tale.

Selkirk certainly made himself useful to his saviours. With his intimate knowledge of the island, he was able to provide fresh water, meat and fruit to nurse the battered crew back to health. But Selkirk had few qualms about returning to his old life of privateering and debauchery. Appointed as mate on the voyage, he took part in the pillage of various Spanish–American ports before returning to London to blow the profits on spectacular bouts of drinking and whoring. The Scotsman was no doubt gratified to learn that his nemesis Captain Stradling of the *Cinque Ports* had been captured by the Spaniards soon after marooning him. The boat had foundered, just as Selkirk had predicted, and the crew had spent the last four years rotting in a Lima jail.

Back in London, the great eighteenth century metropolis, Selkirk's adventures made him a hero. But high living and celebrity took its toll, sapping his preternatural fitness. It was said that he built a mud hut in his father's backyard in Largo, to escape the unfamiliar crowds. Occasionally, when inebriated in sawdust-floored taverns, Selkirk even waxed sentimental about his Pacific island home. Confessing that he had spent most of his time reading the Bible, he told one journalist that he had been a better Christian while in solitude than ever he was before, or than he was afraid he would ever be again. 'I am worth eight hundred pounds,' he said, 'but I shall never be so happy as when I was not worth a farthing.'

It was this idea of the redemptive power of solitude that Daniel Defoe developed in *Robinson Crusoe* — changing the location to the Caribbean (never mind that goat skins wouldn't exactly be needed there), extending the time period to twenty-eight years and throwing in Man Friday as the imperialist's bonus. Of course the real-life story was less tidy. Selkirk's remorse apparently dissolved with the hangover. He ran away with a milkmaid, dumped her, signed up for another privateering expedition, caught fever in the tropics and died on board in 1723 — never dreaming that he would be the model for one of the world's great literary figures.

The fishing boat began its journey back to the airstrip just as the afternoon clouds broke, dousing us with freezing rain for the next three hours. All along the way, Robinson Schultz plucked fish from the sea with his red cotton line and homemade lures. Mario untied the Cessna, packed its hold full of lobsters thrashing away in wet cardboard boxes, then revved onto the ski-jump runway.

In the air, ocean mists blurred the horizon line so that the earth and sky seemed a pale open shell. Straight ahead in the dusk rose a bright full moon. I could easily dream that we were drifting into the ether, until the doors creaked open and I was awoken by the harsh taste of pollution.

A Room

in the Village

Of all New York neighbourhoods, the East Village always seemed the perfect address — a place where rootlessness isn't just a normal condition, it's considered a positive human virtue.

Transience has always been a part of its fabric. The rows of tenement houses were thrown up in the 1890s to extort Jewish immigrants from Eastern Europe, one family per room; Puerto Ricans got the same treatment after the Second World War. In the 1960s, artists and writers began moving in; by the 1980s, the East Village had become fashionable, but, thanks to the rigid rent laws that protect long-term tenants and a certain ingrained seediness, it has only ever been partly gentrified.

These days the neighbourhood is a fermenting compost heap of humanity. If you took Sydney's Darlinghurst and Kings Cross and dumped the whole population in one spot, along with its restaurants and artists and winos and drug dealers and prostitutes, everyone piled on top of one another in these small apartment buildings, you'd probably fill half a dozen blocks of the East Village. It's always been the most heterogeneous part of New York, where America's diversity is taken to the nth degree: our small apartment building is divided equally between white, black and Hispanic tenants, with an old Polish family, a hat-designer from New Jersey, the German pianist, students from Argentina, clerks, cleaners, actors, a gay psychiatrist couple, two drag queens, a book editor, a sculptor, a Texan New Age computer whiz and 'John the Super', who's from Puerto Rico. A pair of itinerant Australians fit right in. When everyone comes from somewhere else, you never feel particularly alien; or more precisely, you feel just as alien as everybody else.

The East Village is also the perfect home for anyone easily bored. Its streets are a medieval pageant, a place of endless distraction, where you can remain in a state of permanent adolescence. All the world, and every time period, converges here. Take a five minute stroll, and you'll see the eighty year old babushkas with their canes and hoods beside fifteen year olds with crew-cut hair dyed into green leopard spots; there's the grimy Russian restaurants with their pasty-fleshed regulars, Orthodox churches and Jewish delis next to nightclubs in decaying thirties dance halls, leather bars, black magic shops, art galleries, sculpture gardens in overgrown lots, acres of garbage, the old guy with the huge white beard who dresses like Father Christmas, a small army of panhandlers, hippies, punks, yuppies, skinheads, rockers, magazine models, aspirants, failures, poseurs of every stripe and description, the twenty-four hour cafés, Allen Ginsburg reading poetry at the church around the corner, Jim Jarmusch in the next booth, Chrissie Hynde hiding without make-up at a Morphine concert, Philip Glass frowning in his doorway, bars that look like junkyards, Tompkins Square Park full of bums and Senegalese guys playing bongos all summer so that you're ready to strangle them, bars that look like motels, restaurants set up in gas stations, the Pyramid Club, Save the Robots, CBGBs, a street of Indian curry-houses, kitchens for Tibetan noodles, Burmese curries, Cuban sausage, Brazilian beans, the Asian Lucky Cheng's where all the waitresses are gorgeous transvestites, gloomy Irish pubs, a pseudo-London tavern, Mexican tequila bars, Gus the flower vendor, the Chinese laundry people working from dawn till near midnight, De Robertis café with its cracked tiles and pastries and cigar-puffing mafiosi, the party throngs at the Clit Club and Jackie 60, the Polish bars with their torn pool tables, the used clothing shop selling golden capes from the Met production of *Aida*, the smell of chicken fat, the rats that sit on the doorstep and stare you down, the rollerbladers being pulled along by three dogs like huskies, Woody Allen scurrying along St Marks with his fishing hat over his eyes, Spike Lee being followed by hordes of adoring fans, Hunter S. Thompson cruising in the gutter (not even bothering to look at the stars), the Hell's Angels HQ, the ancient Italian who wanders around singing perfect snippets of opera, a restaurant like a Roman bath house where the drunken diners eventually fall into the pools, the strange German inscriptions on the buildings, the old Yiddish theatres on Second Avenue (once the 'Jewish Rialto'), the second-hand bookstores, the Rastas selling stolen volumes on the sidewalks, the screaming lunatics in the otherwise eerie silence of 5 a.m., the desperate huddled figures as winter approaches, the evening market of torn clothes and broken watches and mix-masters that never worked, the cardboard boxes quivering with homeless people at dawn ...

Sometimes it all becomes too much, and you have to get out.

Cuba: The Old Man and the Macho

Getting from New York to Havana all depended on Lionel. I'd never met the man, but in a telephone call from the Bahamas he gave me my instructions: I should fly to Nassau, casino capital of the Caribbean, and meet him in the 'Old Airport' with five hundred American dollars in cash. He'd take care of the rest.

I felt like a character in an old John Le Carré novel, which I suppose was appropriate for a journey between the world's last two Cold War enemies. Private travel from the US to Cuba has been effectively banned since Washington began the trade embargo back in 1963, but there has always been a trickle of individuals who have evaded the State Department and gone via third countries. Exactly how this worked wasn't easy to find out, until a journalist friend from Miami gave me Lionel's number. When I called, Lionel explained the rendezvous in his lilting, Creole baritone: 'You'll recognise me, Mr Tony,' he said. 'I'll be the fellow with the cigar.'

I spent the week worrying whether Lionel would show, and listening to rabid local news reports — the Special Period was provoking massive shortages and unrest; Fidel was about to fall in a Ceasescu-like bloodbath, according to Miami exiles, as they have been predicting every year since he came to power in 1959 — before I took the plunge and flew to Nassau. Everyone else on my flight filed straight into the 'New Airport', where a live calypso band was thumping away and rum fruit cocktails were being given away beneath posters of golden beaches. In the Bahamas, it was obviously carnival time even at the baggage ramps. But when I asked for the 'Old Airport', the guards' happy faces fell, and they pointed warily down a shabby grey corridor. It looked like something out of a Wes Craven movie, a ghost terminal with no lights, cracked windows, electrical wires hanging from the ceiling. A long row of old airline counters were dark and empty. The place obviously hadn't been in use for years — except by Air Cubana, whose dusty desk was manned by two gaunt, haggard pilots. Either they could do with a square meal or they'd been taking some rough flights.

Lionel was three hours late, but then again, he knew that Air Cubana's flight timetable was largely fictional. I didn't, and I was a nervous wreck before a portly, bearded figure, chomping on a huge cigar and looking like a Caribbean Arthur Daly, swept imperiously into the terminal and produced a satchel of documents. Tickets, visas, boarding passes and vouchers for a Havana hotel were duly produced, before Lionel bowed, shook my hand and said, 'Oh, mon, you gonna have one hell of a trip.'

It was time to enter the Cuban time warp. Sitting on the tarmac was a small Russian-built propeller plane that might have seen service in the siege of Leningrad. Frilly pink curtains covered the windows, and the cramped seats were all askew; the dozen other passengers were mostly lanky Bahamans, so the aisle became a forest of tangled arms and legs. When the air conditioning was turned on, thick white mist poured from the ceiling, along with sprinkles of icy water. There was a stewardess on board, but she had given up trying long ago, settling herself into a back seat and slugging down shots of the in-flight Coca-Cola.

As the plane lurched off over the Straits of Florida, I closed my eyes and tried to remind myself just why I was doing this.

I was going to Havana to immerse myself in the broken Communist dream, to visit the last place on earth with a Lenin Park, Carlos Marx Theatre and memorials to the Rosenbergs. I wanted to see Cuba before it all changed, before Fidel died, retired or was thrown out, before the McDonalds stores started appearing on the Malecón. On the way, I planned to dig up the memories of Ernest Hemingway, once the island's most glamorous expat resident.

It was hardly an original idea, but a pilgrimage was inescapable: the writer's love affair with the island has taken on a fantastic dimension given the enmity that has developed since between Cuba and the USA. From the early 1930s to just before his death in 1961, Hemingway lived in and around Havana, drinking in its bars, fishing for marlin off its shores and using Cuba as the background for some of his most famous writing. His macho antics captured the world's attention, with Hollywood stars, famous literati and US senators vying to visit him in his sumptuous Havana mansion. Cubans, by all accounts, worshipped him (cries of 'Papa! Papa!' followed him around the watering holes in later life). As a sign of his esteem, Hemingway donated his Nobel Prize medal to the Cuban people in 1954, and today he is still the island's favourite *yanqui*. Even Fidel has sung his praises: while he was in the Sierra Maestra during the Revolution, Castro read *For Whom the Bell Tolls*, Hemingway's epic of the Spanish Civil War, to learn about guerilla warfare.

These days, with Cuba desperate to earn hard currency from tourism, the writer's life has become a minor industry, and in Havana a 'Hemingway Trail' has turned his hangouts into plastic literary shrines. But somewhere outside the city, I'd heard, lived a man named Gregorio Fuentes, who for nearly three decades had been the writer's fishing guide, skipper, cook, bartender, confidant and drinking pal — and who, thanks to his role as one model for Santiago, the ancient fisherman in *The Old Man and the Sea*, was as famous in Cuba as Hemingway himself had been. I thought that if I could meet Fuentes, who was now ninety-six years old, I could make some connection between the mythic, pre-revolutionary Cuba, dreamed of by exiles in Miami, inspiring a whole genre of nostalgic literature, and Castro's Cuba — now at the nadir of its fortunes, desperately out-of-kilter with the rest of the world and wallowing all but forgotten in the Caribbean.

Looking down from the AK–24 plane, the island looked deserted. On all the roads stretching across the sugar-cane fields, there wasn't a single moving car or truck. This sense of a past apocalypse grew stronger as a dollars-only 'turismo-taxi' sped me into Havana: although a few overcrowded buses trundled along the streets belching black smoke, most of the population seemed to be on bicycles imported from China. Cuba's supply of 1950s American Dodges, Chevrolets and Buicks was parked by the curbs, all polished to perfection but without the petrol to fuel them. Still, the icons of Caribbean Communism were proudly littered around the city. El Che gazed down mystically from the monolithic flanks of the Ministry of the Interior. Mounted in a glass case in the middle of the city was *Granma*, the yacht Che and Fidel landed in to start the guerilla war. And facing the office windows of the US Interests Section was a cartoon-style billboard, showing an enraged Uncle Sam growling across the sea at an armed Cuban *compañero*, who gamely replied, *'Señores imperialistas!* We have no fear of you at all!'

In the airy foyer of the Hotel Plaza, where Lionel's coupons were good for a room, Mozart's greatest hits were being pounded out on a grand piano next to a gurgling Spanish fountain. Exotic birds skipped about in the rafters above, and over in the bar, women in miniskirts winked at me knowingly. The hotel was a foreign island cut off from the rest of the city. At 8 p.m., the apartments across the street were blacked out, while the bulbs blazed on in the hotel twenty-four hours a day. When I went up to the dining room to look at the dollars-only smorgasbord, it was full of Germans swilling Heinekens and singing beer hall songs.

That night, I was woken up by a telephone call to my room.

'Hola! Hola! You want to marry me?'

'Oh, uh, no thanks. Who is this?'

'Me llamo Marita. You do not like me?'

'I don't know you.'

'Y eso que me importa?' Basically: so what? I obviously wasn't getting the point.

There are no official restrictions on foreigners' movements at all in Cuba, but in the rarefied half-world of the Plaza Hotel, a siege mentality seemed to have developed amongst the guests. Most seemed to look with some dread at going outside except in the government-run tourism buses. Even the Cuban doormen, who kept the local populace at bay, looked at me with confusion when I headed off for a stroll next morning to see what was left of old Hemingway's haunts.

Down Calle Obispo, past the former Bacardi Rum building, sprawled the festering embroidery of Old Havana, the city's colonial centre. This maze of rococo buildings, with their looming oak doors, stone curlicues and wrought-iron balconies, was built when Havana was the jewel in Spain's crown; beneath the golden fortress walls, vast Armadas took on supplies for their long voyages to Castille. These days, the whole extravaganza is in magnificent decay. Most structures haven't had a lick of paint in over thirty years, and are falling apart from generations of tropical rain. It's also the most crowded real estate in Cuba; neighbours screamed at each other from the windows, kids in shorts played soccer in the street, teenagers bopped to distorted salsa. Every step of the way I was approached by an exhausting stream of hustlers selling black market rum, cigars, drugs and Che Guevara ten peso coins. (The person who puts Che's face on wristwatches will become Cuba's first millionaire.) There was a neurotic, almost hysterical edge to the air; I didn't know if it was coming from me or everybody else.

I thought I may as well get into the Hemingway spirit by picking up a bottle of Havana Club rum, so I fell into conversation with a gangly, serious character named Leonardo, whose baggy blue jeans, stove-top haircut and sneakers made him look like a rapper from South Central LA. To close the sale, we slipped into his family's house, on the first floor of one of the tenements. Leonardo's extended family of twelve were all sitting around in the same windowless room, and his mother was cooking up a nauseating mash of maize and rice in rancid fat. Noisy grunts came from the darkness; there was a huge black hog being kept in the bathtub, which the family planned to sell to a restaurant for dollars.

Once away from the street, Leonardo relaxed: he had just finished three years of university, he said, leaving him with an easygoing fatalism about politics I'd continue to hear from Cubans. 'Nothing's going to happen in this country,' he announced breezily, 'fear and apathy will keep the system going.' I gave him ten dollars for two bottles of rum, and he counted out the bills carefully. Greenbacks were everything in Cuba now. 'When people fled to Miami, we sent them off with stones and called them *gusanos*, worms,' he mused. 'Now anyone who is even distantly related to them is getting dollars sent back and doing fine. The worms, we say, have turned into butterflies.'

Gasping for fresh air, I lurched back outside and kept wandering. The magnificent plazas and cathedrals were connected by streets full of garbage (including packages of human shit wrapped up in newspaper and tossed from above, since most buildings have no sewerage). But despite the Hogarthian squalor, the fresh sea breeze still drifted up from the harbour, and you could feel the tropical caress that Ernesto found an antidote for his uptight Midwestern upbringing. I called in at the Hotel Ambos Mundos ('Both Worlds') where he finally moved in full-time on his return from the Spanish Civil War and wrote *For Whom the Bell Tolls*. The hotel is now a fleabag, but Ernesto's light and airy room on the fifth floor was maintained as a sacred site. One of the harassed hotel staff took me inside, extorted $2 entry fee and $1 for every photo, then stood about impatiently as I looked around. The room was tidily kept, with an antique typewriter (not Ernesto's — it would have been sold long ago) and American 1930s magazines (likewise). His view across the rooftops was marred by a new, Soviet-style construction block.

Within staggering distance of the hotel was Hemingway's favourite bar, El Floridita, a simple *bodega* that was rated with the 21 Club in New York, Ritz in Paris and Raffles in Singapore as one of the world's best bars by *Esquire* in 1953. You can see old photos of Ernesto in his cotton shirt, scruffy khaki shorts and moccasins, listening to the three-piece bands, playing dice, knocking back double frozen daiquiris. But the atmosphere was shot, thanks to a brutal renovation: a dozen waiters in crimson tuxedos hovered around empty tables, the menu served lobster thermidor for $40, and except for the wooden horseshoe bar with its little Ernesto bust, it was all but unrecognisable.

The mood was looser at the nearby Bodeguita del Medio, where Hemingway used to drop by for a *mojito* (a potent mix of rum, mint leaves, ice and sugar). The walls were dark with thousands of autographs, like a cave full of Indian petroglyphs; at the bar was a famous sign supposedly written by Hemingway: *My Mojito in La Bodeguita, My Daiquiri in El Floridita.* According to the American writer Tom Miller, it was probably a hoax made up by one of his Cuban drinking pals to attract customers. If so, it was certainly working: the barman couldn't pour out the *mojitos* fast enough for a boisterous French tour group.

The 'tourism apartheid', as it's bluntly referred to, was getting me down. Once the hangout for Havana's intellectuals and Bohemians, the only Cubans in La Bodeguita were now the waiters. (A popular Cuban joke: a mother asks her son what he wants to be when he grows up. 'A tourist!' he says. Another joke: Castro's brother goes to Miami to check out the economic situation. When he comes back, he tells Fidel not to worry. 'Things are just as bad as here,' he says. 'You can't buy a thing without dollars.') But they had you trapped — the only other place I could get a meal was my hotel smorgasbord, with the beer hall Germans. So I ordered a small plate of barbecued pork for $25, resignedly sipped on a sickly-sweet *mojito*, and wondered if Leonardo's great black hog would one day end up on La Bodeguita's tables.

If Havana by day was bizarre, by night it became truly surreal.

As the blackouts descended on the city, I hopped into a tourist-taxi for the Tropicana, an old nightclub that has stayed open through the austere years of the Revolution. Clouds of sea spray drifted across the curving Malecón; the streets looked glum and forlorn. Apart from a few Chinese bicycles wobbling along in the darkness, my taxi was the only thing moving.

But when we pulled up out of the gloom, the Tropicana was lit up like Coney Island. I'd never seen anything like it outside of old Hollywood musicals. In the spotlit gardens, statues of naked nymphs peeked from the bushes. Tables in the open air amphitheatre spread out like sunbeams from a golden stage, the stars twinkling above a crown of frangipanis; amongst the luxuriant foliage, blazing neon signs recalled the names of Latino musical greats from Benny Moré to Carmen Miranda.

The show kicked off with a blast. As a twenty-piece orchestra, all in gleaming white tuxedos, pounded out the salsa beat, women in gold lamé swung above us on trapeze and row after row of *mulattas* burst from the bushes in a blur of pink feathers, sequins and bronze legs. In one act, the dancers strolled out wearing giant chandeliers balanced on their heads, all blazing with light as if in mockery of the blackouts in the rest of the city. It was hopelessly crass and sexist, but you couldn't help but be impressed by the sheer brazen kitsch of the spectacle. And the crowd of Cubans at the back of the auditorium was lapping it all up: despite all the progressive social legislation, Caribbean Communism has always had room for its tit-and-bum shows.

At around 2 a.m., I hopped another taxi to the million-dollar disco at the Comodoro Hotel. Modelled on some nameless club in Miami's South Beach, the circular dance floor was packed with holidaying Spaniards, Germans and Canadians; no sooner had I stepped in the door than a stream of barely pubescent prostitutes, known as *jineteras* — literally 'jockeys'; not for some exotic carnal rite but the Cuban word for anyone trying to get ahead in society — appeared around me cooing in Spanish baby talk, 'Why aren't you dancing? Do you want to dance with me?' Hands kept groping me from the darkness, and I retreated in complete disorder to the bar, where I'd spotted a Canadian I'd met on the airplane from Nassau — a middle-aged former oilman named Frank.

Frank was feeling right at home — chomping on a cigar, knocking back $11 Cuban *libres* (rum-and-Cokes) and trying to deal with a petite blonde *jinetera* who had wrapped herself around his leg and was slowly gyrating against his thigh. 'Just look at this place!' he drawled in my ear. 'I've never seen anything like it. You go to some place in the Bahamas, and there are only one or two pretty women, the rest are dogs. They're *all* beautiful here. No wonder the other Caribbean islands are scared shitless of when Cuba opens up.' While we were talking, the girl kept putting Frank's hand between her legs, then sat on his lap and showed him her black lace underwear. 'Jesus,' he sighed, 'it'd sure help if I could speak some Spanish.' A few drinks later, he decided conversation was beside the point and led her off to the connecting hotel.

From the Comodoro bar, it looked like Cuba had come full circle back to the 1950s — not the detached, expat-filled world of Hemingway, with its cold daiquiris and American bars and hearty fishermen, but the decadent island of Graham Greene's *Our Man in Havana*. Back in the Batista years, the American Mafia ran the casinos, the 'Jewish godfather' Meyer Lansky had a permanent suite at the Riviera and poker machines were flown in from Las Vegas; after hopping from nightclub to nightclub, you could watch the famous gigolo called Superman measure his spectacular erection on stage with a silver ruler. Havana was the prostitution centre of the Western hemisphere: businessmen could choose their *mulatta* for the weekend from photographs at the airport, and the Casa Marina specialised in thirteen year old girls and boys from the provinces (virgins $2 extra).

Reaction against the excesses of those days helped fuel the revolution — at least amongst the middle class — and Cubans have since considered the fifties to be the country's lowest ebb. But now the hotels and discos are part-owned by the Cuban government, and tourism is supposed to be the saviour of the Revolution. I started talking to two people at the bar you could tell weren't foreigners by their cheap polyester clothes, wide eyes and gaping mouths: they turned out to be professors from Havana University who, insanely enough, were here because they had won a prize for political correctness. Using Party coupons, they were able to get in to the disco, buy a couple of drinks, and hoard two cans of Coca-Cola to give to their kids.

'So what do you think of the Comodoro?' I asked delicately.

'You've got to understand, this is only a small slice of Cuba,' smiled Rosa, a botanist, trotting out the party line with every appearance of conviction. 'Of course, it's a shock to see so much wealth, and worse to know that the girls here can make more in one night than I do in an entire year. But we all know it's a historical moment, and necessary for the country.' Her husband Pedro, who taught the History of Imperialism, chimed in. 'Cubans are highly educated. We're all prepared to accept a few years of hardship for a peaceful transition to a more capitalist economy. Look at Russia! We don't want to end up like that.' Despite the fighting words, Pedro blanched when the imported beer I bought him turned out to cost US$5 — about six weeks' wages at the current exchange rate.

The disco was winding down, so the couple offered me a lift back to my hotel in their Russian-built Lada. It took ten minutes to start, but eventually we were rattling through the dark, misty streets, looking for a moment like Brassai photos of twenties Paris. As I got out, Rosa proudly brought up another point. 'We may have prostitutes in Cuba, but it's well known that Cuban *putas* are the most beautiful and cleanest *putas* in the whole world!'

Havana was starting to seem like a very mixed-up place.

Next day, I decided to get back on the Hemingway Trail and try to find the old skipper Gregorio Fuentes. It wasn't hard to establish that he still lived in the tiny fishing village of Cojímar, some twenty-five kilometres east of Havana, where

Hemingway's yacht had once been moored; en route, I could visit Hemingway's mansion, Finca Vigía, now a museum. The problem was that twenty-five kilometres was a very long way in a country without public transport and where rental cars cost a small fortune. I could pay someone with their own auto to give me a lift — but even the idea of an 'informal taxi', the lowest peg on the evolutionary scale of capitalism, had barely caught on in Havana.

Still, I had some names of friends of friends, who might be able to find someone with both a working car and access to black market petrol. I liked just dropping in on these people: everyone in this decaying, hermetic city had their own story.

My first call was to Sandy Waterman (not her real name, at her own request) — a sweet, grandmotherly American woman who first came to Cuba in 1960 burning with the fire of the revolution and was now entirely disillusioned. She would have left years ago, she said, but for her husband; he was a former Black Panther activist, who'd done the classic 'Take-Me-To-Havana' hijacking of an airplane thirty years ago. The Americans had gotten their plane back, but he couldn't go home: he had stayed in Cuba, worked in the sugar fields and taught English in the literacy campaigns. Looking like a former heavyweight boxer, with huge meaty arms and a polished bald head, Ted moved carefully around their tiny, potplant-filled apartment as if trying not to break things. He didn't want to talk about his past: it was all going into the autobiography, which he was writing to convince the US government to regard the hijacking as a political act and let him return. (When I last spoke to them, the book was done and en route to the publishers.) They said they'd call an acquaintance who *might* have a car, but that I should keep looking ...

The second number I had was for Carla, a young artist from one of Cuba's few traditional Bohemian families that hadn't packed up for Miami; after a dozen attempts on the telephone, I got through and offered to drop around at dinner time with some food from the dollar supermarket, open only to diplomats and foreigners (the monthly food ration had just been reduced to two kilos of rice and one of beans with a handful of maize, coffee and sugar thrown in; the only meat was a single frankfurter sausage).

Carla's ancestral home was a Spanish version of *The Addams Family* mansion, rotting amongst the foliage of a once-affluent Havana suburb; she herself was wafer-thin and pale, like a nineteenth century consumptive. I was late, so we had to rush to cook the tuna and pasta before the blackout. Joining us was Lina, a speedy woman in her mid-forties, who had been thrown off the official arts magazine in 1970 for running an article that mentioned both exiled writers and homosexuals, and had spent three years in prison. Since then, she has been unable to find work or have her poetry published in Cuba, although it is well known in Spain and Latin America. 'It's the psychological climate that destroys you in Cuba,' she said flatly, as she laid out the cracked crockery on the table. 'It's still like living in prison.'

The meal had a neat García Márquez feel: we ate by the light of a kerosene lamp in the close, stifling atmosphere of the old mansion, with mosquitoes biting our ankles. I felt uncomfortably like Father Christmas pulling out Spanish wine and English chocolate biscuits to looks of utter amazement. 'We eat worse than the slaves did under the Spanish,' said Carla, more with wonder than resentment. 'At least the slaves were given dried cod every day.' It was no wonder that Havana had that neurotic, semi-hysterical edge: Cubans are the best educated paupers on earth, a sophisticated bunch who had become used to an almost middle class standard of living and, suddenly, with the collapse of the USSR, had the rug pulled out from under their feet. Perhaps it shouldn't have been, but this fall from grace was harder to block out or rationalise than your average Third World poverty, and I had become an easy touch in the streets, peeling off dollar bills to elderly people and handing out shampoo and soap, which nobody had seen in months. I didn't know what good it would do, but it made me feel less guilty about being there.

More friends dropped by Carla's place in the course of the evening, all artists looking straight out of the sixties. I presented Leonardo's bottles of black market rum, the first drinkable stuff anyone had tasted in years, and the homespun entertainment, the only kind available, began. One by one, each guest pulled out a poem and orated theatrically by the lamp. A guitarist played a few of his own compositions, satirical songs about food shortages and problems with the bureaucracy. The digs at the system were mild, but as the rum started flowing everyone attacked the regime roundly, particularly the all-consuming censorship. Still there was the fatalism. 'We've always been dependent on someone,' declared the guitarist sententiously. 'First it was the Spanish. Then the Americans. Then the Russians. Now Cuba depends on tourists. Nothing changes.'

The fiesta suddenly died down when Carla's brother-in-law came home — he was distantly related to a member of the secret police. I whispered that, given the obvious chaos of Cuba, it was difficult to believe that the Government could manage any omniscient presence. 'Believe me,' Carla muttered, 'the secret police is the only thing that's efficient in this country.'

The bottles of rum were finished, so someone pulled out a homemade brew, nicknamed *chispa de tren*, train sparks. It smelled like floor-wash, but I took a swig or two anyway. All I remember is wandering out to the garden and looking up at the stars burning closer and closer in the black velvet sky. Next thing I knew, Carla and Lina were leaning over me, saying, 'Tony, Tony, wake up, it's time to leave, it's already dawn.'

It was an ignominious end to the evening, perhaps, but at least word was spreading that I wanted a car. The day after, a shy, sixtyish fellow named Hector turned up at my hotel in a battered red 1955 Chevrolet with tail fins and tan leather seats that felt like they could fit five people across.

For $50, Hector said he would get me to the village of Cojímar and back. At last, I could go in search of Fuentes.

As we cruised regally through a river of bicycle riders into suburban Havana, Hector began to slowly unwind, explaining the mysterious selection of wires, rubber and tin cans he used to keep the Chevrolet going without American spare parts for thirty-five years. It turned out that Hector had been the director of Cuba's first television station before recently retiring and going into the taxi business, and he had a few well-pondered opinions of his own. Within a few minutes, he was lashing out at the new policies that had handed over Cuba's most famous beach, Varadero, to Spanish companies. It was as if, bowing to investors, the Australian government had turned Bondi into a Japanese-only resort. 'Do you know what it's like to see the hotels where you have been going for your annual holidays since you were a child, where you have been taking your family for years, and to know you can't go inside — even to buy a lemonade? Do you know what it's like to be forbidden to walk on the sands, or go in the water?' But Hector saw himself with a certain ironic distance: 'When Cubans are alone, we endlessly complain about the lack of food, the travel restrictions, the censorship. But nobody does anything about it. When Fidel decides to give a speech, we all go and listen, we all cheer! I'm no different. I'm no better.

'Besides,' he added, 'Fidel still has his attraction. He can't just disappear! *La situacíon*, the situation, is not all his fault!' He imagined Castro as an avuncular, Mitterand-like figure on the fringe of Cuban politics, protecting society from the depradations of returning Miami exiles.

Before long, we pulled up at the iron gates of Finca Vigía — the house on the outskirts of the city that Hemingway bought with his third wife, Martha Gelhorn, in 1940, with money from the film rights of *For Whom the Bell Tolls*. Although Gelhorn later divorced him, Hemingway stayed on for the rest of his life, luring his buddy Gary Cooper, Ava Gardner and countless other stars to his tropical refuge. Hemingway may not have always been the most gracious host (one sour biographer describes him as 'boastful, lying, obscene, boring, overbearing, ill-tempered, touchy, vindictive and self-righteous'), but he must have had something going for him. Not many refused an invitation.

I'd read that Finca Vigía still contained a library with 9,000 volumes, Hemingway's original Royale typewriter and animal heads on every wall, trophies from African safaris. ('Don't know how a writer could write surrounded by dead animal heads,' sniffed Graham Greene when he visited.) And connected to the main house was a four-storey tower, home to the writer's sixty or so cats, where Hemingway would get up before dawn and hammer away on the typewriter while standing up, barefoot on a lion's skin.

The mansion lay at the end of a long, leafy driveway — but the gardener refused to open the gates. We argued; he got a museum official. She was terribly sorry, she said, but she couldn't let us in, even to look at the house from the outside. I produced journalist's passes, press clips, letters of introduction; she shook her head. No exceptions could be made. No reasons could be given. I begged, cajoled, pleaded, abused: 'Ernesto would be turning in his grave if he knew!' Hector looked on at this display with pity. He knew what the outcome would be, and it was too hot a day to get worked up with a bureaucrat.

So we headed off for Cojímar, driving briefly along one of the six-lane highways built to cater for heavy traffic a decade ago: as usual, this was the only car on the road, and we picked up as many hitch-hikers as would fit in the voluminous seats.

Finally, the village appeared. It was bleached and barren; a squat Spanish colonial fortress, now run by the Cuban navy, looked over the dusty promenade where half a dozen sickly palm trees were withering in the blinding sun. Hector knew the place (thanks to the ocean currents, it was famous as a jumping-off point for people floating to Miami in homemade rafts and inner tubes) and took me straight to the Hemingway monument — a bust of the writer, surrounded by Grecian columns, made by local fishermen using their melted-down boat propellers.

Thanks to years of over-fishing, not many in Cojímar made their living from the waters: two young ex-fishermen sitting on the sea wall sold beer when there was any (and there hadn't been for nine months). They were almost dead from boredom, and asked me the most detailed questions about Australia, and how precisely they could apply for an immigrant visa. Both nodded sagely when they learned I was searching for Gregorio Fuentes.

'You'll find him in La Terraza,' one advised, 'but you'll have to wait until he's finished with the New York *Times*.'

I thought he was joking, but when I arrived two American journalists were indeed plying Fuentes with questions at the bar; I'd have to wait my turn, so I took a seat in the restaurant. Hemingway hung out here when it was a tiny hole-in-the-wall, but it too had been lavishly restored (supposedly on orders from Castro himself — El Lider Máximo was aghast to find it nearly collapsing during a visit a few years ago). Unlike La Floridita, the job had been done well: a cool breeze wafted in through the windows that opened out over the Straits of Florida, on the walls were black-and-whites of Ernesto and Fuentes fishing in Peru (where they went to film *The Old Man and the Sea*).

I was the only guest, and the maitre d' hovered around my table excitedly when I ordered not only a rum but something to eat.

'Yes, yes, you must talk to Gregorio,' he said, delightedly. '*Periodista australiano*, Australian journalist, from the land of the *kanguros*!' At least I was something different. Finally, after I'd scoffed a plate of fried snapper, the maitre d' clapped his hands and announced theatrically, 'El Señor Fuentes!'

A fragile figure ambled up to my table and politely introduced himself. His face was scorched, and as finely cracked as an antique canvas; his teeth were gone and his hearing was not what it used to be; but Gregorio looked extraordinarily sprightly and shrewd for his ninety-six years, happily puffing away on a Havana cigar and knocking back a bottle of German beer. Along with the traditional Cuban linen shirt, he was wearing a baseball cap and wristwatch both emblazoned with marlins. I gathered straight off the bat that Gregorio wasn't quite the stoic Santiago: the *Times* reporters had started him thinking about the US trade embargo, and no sooner had he sat down than he brought his fist down on the table, sending two forks flying. 'When I think about the American blockade,' he shouted feistily, looking after the reporters, 'I almost can't breathe, those sons of bitches!'

Calming down, Gregorio apologised for his busy schedule: apart from the *Times*, Japanese TV was expected that night. But he handled his celebrity like a veteran. Leaning back in his chair (at Ernesto's favourite table, of course), Gregorio gladly trotted out the anecdotes. They might have grown formulaic, like any repeated patter, but I didn't mind. His life — with its career trajectory from obscurity to celebrity and back again — made as compelling a yarn, in its way, as Hemingway's own.

Like the fictional Santiago, he was born in Spain's Lanzarote Islands and emigrated to Cuba as a child. For his first forty years, Gregorio explained, he was just one more fishing guide working the Straits; highly respected, to be sure, but unknown. Then, in 1928, a squall off Dry Tortugas forced him to take shelter with an American yacht, captained by the young, moderately successful Hemingway. 'I heard a loud voice say in Spanish: this is a Cuban boat, and all Cubans are friends of mine,' Gregorio recalled. He must have told the story a thousand times — how he laid out wine and onions for the famished *yanquis*, how he invited them aboard — but he still took relish in the moment, stabbing the air with his cigar as he spoke. 'I told Ernesto: here is my boat, here is the food, lunch for everyone. I told him: come aboard, you are my guest.'

It was the beginning, as they say, of a beautiful friendship. In 1934, the now-famous author chose Fuentes as master of his custom-made luxury yacht, the *Pilar*, and for the next twenty-seven years Gregorio was plunged into the writer's heady circle (although always as a servant, not a participant). The cream of international society vied to go marlin fishing under his stewardship, and Fuentes did everything from maintaining the boat to cooking lunch (often crab sautéed in lemon, Hemingway's favourite dish, he pointed out). Last but not least, Gregorio attended to the 'Ethylic Department', whipping up whisky sodas, highballs and daiquiris for Ernesto and his guests. Working for Hemingway was no picnic, and the two developed a volatile relationship, arguing regularly and threatening to split up, but always reconciling like a pair of feuding lovers.

So what did he most remember about his famous boss? Knocking back his second beer, his face glowing, Fuentes told me scattered stories from 1942, when he and Hemingway converted the *Pilar* into a gunboat to scour the Caribbean for Nazi submarines (luckily for them, they never found one). He remembered how he bought Hemingway his first cat (he famously gathered over sixty to live with him at the Finca) and talked about Hemingway's biggest marlin (1542 pounds). Gregorio was very concerned at Ernesto's current reputation as something of a drunken boor. 'I've never met a more intelligent man in the world,' he rasped, fixing me with his yellow, glutinous eyes, 'nor one more humane.'

We were twice interrupted by an official from the Hemingway Museum, who had come to clear up some abstruse details relating to Ernesto's life in Cuba. But Gregorio was too good a showman to let this spoil his flow. Soon he started in on the taller tales: how he once cracked the skull of a Frenchman who insulted Ernesto's literary ability in Havana; how Hemingway looked the other way when he found Gregorio running guns for Fidel.

I wanted to hear more about this. Hemingway stayed in Havana after the Revolution triumphed on New Year's Day, 1959, but his attitude towards it is still hotly debated. Having been famously vocal about the Spanish Civil War twenty years before, he remained publicly silent throughout the guerilla war in his adopted home. I asked Gregorio if Hemingway supported the Revolution. 'Of course,' he replied, surprised that there was any doubt. 'Why would he not? But we never discussed it. I never asked his opinion, and he never asked mine.'

In the 1950s, there seemed an odd symmetry between the two machos, Hemingway and Fidel: the writer growing older and sicker in his Havana house, the guerilla leader slowly gaining power and fame. In private, Ernesto was attracted to the romantic side of the war ('This is a good revolution,' he wrote to one friend, 'an honest revolution'). They only met once, during a fishing tournament in Havana in 1960 — Fidel won an armful of prizes, Ernesto awarded the trophies — and had a long conversation, which historians have always been eager to learn about. Finally, an eyewitness was found: they talked about marlin.

Hemingway left his island home soon afterwards, unaware that it would be for the last time. Violently depressed, diagnosed with a rare form of diabetes, high blood pressure and a host of alcohol-related illnesses, he checked into an American clinic — only to be given a radical course of electro-shock therapy. The loss of his memory only worsened his depression, and in mid–1961 in Idaho, he killed himself with his shotgun.

The Cuba Hemingway knew would soon disappear, too: within a couple of years would come the botched Bay of Pigs invasion, the Missile Crisis, American trade blockade and Castro's declaration that he was, and always had been, a Marxist-Leninist.

News of Hemingway's suicide shocked Fuentes, because the writer had seemed perfectly healthy when he left Cuba the year before. 'I feel the pain still,' Gregorio said, his eyes welling with tears. 'He was like a brother.' Almost as shocking was the news that Hemingway had left him the yacht *Pilar* — all $500,000 worth. Gregorio tried to maintain the treasured boat in Cojímar, but found he couldn't afford to; he soon donated it to the young Revolutionary Government. That gesture earned Fuentes a personal visit of thanks from Fidel Castro himself, perhaps the man he admires most after Ernesto.

Today — like the Cuban Revolution itself — Gregorio was surrounded by ghosts. He has not only outlived Hemingway, he has outlasted his wife and all of his fishing companions in Cojímar. Although four daughters have brought him a bevy of grandchildren, he still lives alone in the simple house he bought with his first wages on the *Pilar*. But celebrity had its compensations: when we were finishing, a busload of Italian tourists piled into the restaurant, all begging to pose with Gregorio for photographs. The ancient mariner readily agreed — provided he could sit the prettiest women on his knee. All this, he insisted, was only his patriotic duty. 'I should rest at my age,' he confided *sotto voce*. 'But I do this so that Cuba can earn tourist dollars.'

Speaking of which, he mentioned in passing, his own financial situation has become grim. A painful skin disorder on his leg needed expensive medicine, which could now only be bought on the black market with dollars ... There was an awkward moment when I gave him some of the soap I'd bought, as well as a small amount of cash, broken only by the waiter offering us an afternoon coffee — 'Cuban or American?'

The choice set Gregorio off again about the US blockade. 'What has Cuba ever done to the US to deserve this?' he thundered, thumping the table. 'If I was in an airplane, I'd kill every last one in the government of the United States!' But like all Cubans, he drew a clear distinction between the government and its people. 'There are good Americans and bad Americans,' he said, 'just as there are good Cubans and bad ones.'

Gregorio grew sentimental again. 'And Mr Hemingway was one of the good Americans.'

Hector was waiting patiently outside the restaurant, ready to take me back to Havana just as a tropical downpour hit. Not far from the Plaza Hotel, the Chevrolet crossed a flooded roadway and stalled; Hector waved me off to walk home as he leapt into the knee-deep water, trying to do something to the engine with an empty can and a long piece of wire.

'Of course, the situation, it's grim,' Hector sighed, by way of farewell — sounding as if he was the archetypal Cuban fisherman lost at sea himself. 'But,' he smiled wanly, 'one must endure.'

The Tenth Street

Drug Circus

We found our apartment from a classified ad in the *Village Voice*. It was shaped like a railway carriage with polished wooden floors and bare brick walls, plus the original window mouldings from the turn of the century. It was sunny. It was cheap. It was in the heart of the East Village. There was only one problem: it was also right in the middle of Manhattan's longest-running drug war.

We discovered this fairly quickly — on our first morning there, in fact. I went downstairs to buy some milk at the corner store, and found the street full of crew-cut gorillas, all wearing blue windcheaters with 'FBI' emblazoned on the back in big white letters. They were crouching behind cars with complicated rifles and telescopic sights trained on the building three doors down; a van blocking the street said 'NYC SWAT' on the side. So naturally I walked up to one — like everyone else, he had a Burt Reynolds moustache and a mass of gold chains around his neck — and asked if this was a film shoot.

He didn't bat an eyelid, or even turn to face me for that matter. Just kept looking through the sights and said flatly, 'No. This is not a fucking film shoot.'

After lunch, the FBI guys were still down in the street, but looking much more relaxed. I saw the same cheery officer I'd spoken to before, so I asked him what the problem had been.

'We thought there was a bomb,' he said in the same flat voice. 'There wasn't.' Trying to sound more heroic, he added, 'We got some automatic weapons. A fair cache of drugs. You'll see your street on TV tonight, if you're lucky.'

'Great,' I said uncertainly.

'Welcome to the Tenth Street drug circus,' threw in Marion, a hard-bitten, fortyish woman from our building who was the head of the Tenth Street Block Association. 'Didn't know you'd moved into a famous street, did you? We're on the front line here, man.'

To be honest, when we first checked out the apartment, we did notice that rather a lot of swarthy young Latino gentlemen seemed to be hissing at us *Smoke? Smoke?* when we walked by, but it didn't really bother us. Laura, who sub-leased us the place, was completely up front about it all. 'From a renter's point of view, the dealers are a *definite* plus,' she confided. 'They make the street much safer for the people who live here.' According to her, they didn't want to attract attention from the police. Hence there were no muggings allowed on the block. No burglaries. No car thefts.

The safest street downtown, she insisted.

Summer was just descending on the city when we moved in, and so we had the chance to observe the dealing at its annual crescendo. The street turned into an open bazaar, with about two dozen dealers lining our sidewalk, chorusing one after the other *Smoke? Smoke? Coke? Smoke?* to every passerby. At peak hours, from around 6 p.m. to 2 a.m., they'd get a sale about every couple of minutes, and they'd whip out their stashes hidden inside garbage cans or above the tyres of parked cars. If they were feeling cautious due to a recent bust — or if there was an unusually exotic order — a package would be dropped by friends from the windows above.

Friday and Saturday nights were busiest. We used to make a pot of tea and sit on the steps, just to watch the hordes come by. You'd get these shiny white stretch limos pulling up; the front window would glide down, a uniformed driver would place the order, there was a quick exchange and the window slid back up. It was all so open and efficient you had to wonder if they took Amex.

Marion soon filled us in on the history of the block. Some time in the 1970s, she said, two 'drug supermarkets' began working on opposite sides of the street. The Blue Door, as it was known, specialised in soft drugs; the Black Door, hard stuff. Everyone knew about these places — the lines of customers went down the street — and it was assumed the police were paid off. Eventually the trade became so flagrant that City Hall closed them down in the early eighties. But by then the block had been fixed in New Yorkers' imaginations as the place to buy.

There was still a division on the street. Our end, near Second Avenue, was run by the Colombians. 'They're the businessmen,' Marion assured us. 'They only deal in grass, they're only interested in money and they don't want trouble.' (One of our neighbours, Min from Melbourne, got on very well with them; 'Oh, the Colombians are lovely,' she said. 'They always hold the door open for me and carry up my groceries.') The First Avenue end, however, was being taken over by a black gang selling a lot of crack. And the buyers were more volatile and unpredictable, especially when they were out of cash.

Marion had started the Tenth Street Block Association to lobby the police to clean up the street. (Most downtown blocks have their own residents' association, although they mainly worry about cleaning and street fairs.) 'I take no moral stand on drugs at all,' she explained. 'But I do object to the crime and the violence that's coming with them. They're making this block unlivable.' Little Marion was a tough cookie. You'd see her screaming at dealers in the street. Once she got into a brawl with one of the women, falling over into the garbage with her. As for us, we just kept a low profile as summer went into fall.

The police weren't completely absent, although their scattered busts were more theatrical than effective. You'd be sitting upstairs writing when someone downstairs would shout, 'Hold it right there! Hold it right there!' Police would have some suspect up against the wall, then whisk them into a car. Once I was buying a toothbrush at the corner pharmacy, trying to avoid two characters who looked for all the world like the sickest, seediest, weediest junkies in New York City, when they suddenly pulled out badges and handcuffs and jumped a suspect. Within seconds, three police cars roared up outside to take him away.

Less successful was 'Hawaii Five O', as the more cynical street wits dubbed them — a car full of Latino undercover policemen and women wearing bright pink singlets and shorts. They kept cruising the streets at night in a beaten-up Ford looking for action. The fact that they kept pulling out their two-way radios at street corners did little for their disguise.

These flurries of police activity would stop trade for about twenty minutes; then it was business as usual on Tenth Street.

Things turned nasty in winter. The black and Hispanic gangs started fighting. There was some shooting in the street; one of the Colombians was killed. A bullet actually came in the window of one of the downstairs flats in our building and lodged in the ceiling. Then one of the crack dealers had his throat slit. The blood was in the gutter for two days; it looked thick, like scarlet glue.

There was a groundswell of support for the Block Association; even we were broken out of our trance enough to go along to one of the neighbourhood meetings. To be honest, it was becoming a drag just walking down our street. The gauntlet of dealers really hadn't bothered us at first, but to hear that hissing of *Smoke? Smoke? Coke? Smoke?* from twenty different people every single time you went outside really did get on our nerves.

Then it was election time, so we saw some action from City Hall. Our street was closed off to traffic. We'd look out the window and see a police car going backwards and forwards, backwards and forwards, over this 100 metre stretch all night. And the patrols went on for months. Soon people did stop coming to buy drugs here. By the next summer, Marion was tentatively declaring victory. For the first time in twenty years, new businesses started opening: a bar, a Japanese restaurant, a furniture shop.

And the dealers? They're all still working — around the corner, over on Eleventh Street. I recognise them when I go past, every one. The residents over there have organised a Block Association and are lobbying the mayor. But the police can always say that they finally did clear up Tenth Street.

Deepest South

They don't get a lot of travellers down in the Deep South. Folks at the Mississippi Tourism Authority sounded delighted, even touched, to hear that we were going to visit and write a few stories; their state ranks fiftieth in the US for numbers of visitors, and neighbouring Alabama comes forty-ninth. Still, it seemed a bit excessive when we drove up to the Clarksdale Comfort Inn and saw the huge glowing sign outside the hotel: WELCOME TO MISSISSIPPI MR PERROTTET AND MS THELANDER.

We pulled up in front of it, somewhat dazed. The sign dominated the whole six-lane highway running into this decrepit Delta town. It was quite a sight after staring at flat monotonous cotton fields for eight hours. They'd even spelled our names right; the 'Ms' for Les was a nice contemporary touch.

Feeling inflated, we spilled into the reception and introduced ourselves.

The pimply clerk, who was dressed like a Baptist choirboy, smiled blandly. 'Why, welcome. D'y'all have a reservation?'

'I guess so.' I thought he was joking. 'We're the ones you've got on the sign.'

The clerk looked puzzled.

'That's us,' Les repeated. 'The ones on the sign.'

The clerk looked at her as if she was mad, then looked over his register. 'How do you spell the last name?'

Perhaps he didn't understand our accents? Les pointed out to the parking lot and repeated forlornly, 'That's us on the sign ...'

But the poor kid was starting to look panicky, so we decided to spell out the names for him. Then he looked even more confused.

'I'm very sorry, we don't seem to have a reservation.'

Entirely deflated, we took the cheapest room. Maybe it was just as well. It would have been almost disappointing if Mississippi was a model of corporate efficiency.

'Thanks anyway,' I mumbled.

He was still looking after us nervously as we shuffled off.

'We aim to please.'

1 THE DELTA BLUES QUEST

It was Saturday night when we slipped into Clarksdale, so we decided to go hear some blues. Not that we're exactly passionate blues fans. But this was where Robert Johnson sold his soul to the devil, where Muddy Waters and B. B. King got their starts in the thirties and forties; in Clarksdale's tin shack bars, the juke joints, the Delta blues kicked off as one of the great musical influences of the century. It was a bit like going to a Mozart concert in Salzburg or listening to tango in Buenos Aires.

Unfortunately, we weren't having a lot of luck. One blues bunker just off Route 61 was full of potbellied rednecks listening to ragged country and western. The promising 'House of the Blues' was actually a discotheque. We tried a couple of other places without any success. When I asked one of the bartenders where people play the blues these days, he just looked at me blankly. 'Ain't nowhere really. Not here in Clarksdale.' You could say we were getting them 'looking-for-the-Delta-Blues' blues.

What was going on? There was supposed to be a 'blues revival' around the United States. But maybe there was a reason why B. B. King and friends moved to Memphis and Chicago. 'Ironically,' bemoaned one Mississippi academic study on the blues, 'the indigenous people lack an awareness, understanding and appreciation of their heritage.'

Next morning, we found that the indigenous tourist industry was trying hard anyway. There were a few kitschy tributes to the blues scattered about between the burned-out buildings and vacant lots (the Delta, with its seventy per cent black population, is the poorest corner of the whole United States). The 'Delta Blues Museum' had a ghastly, life-size dummy of Muddy Waters in the foyer. Stackhouse record shop was shaped like a riverboat, where almost every blues recording ever made can be found or discussed. In Wade's Barber Shop, where 'blues legends' used to hang out and play, you could order a singing telegram. And around the corner was an old hotel where great musicians once stayed. It still costs only $15 a night, although it's nicknamed the Roach Motel. It was so bad that tourists who survived a night were interviewed by the local newspaper to describe their experiences.

'You're more likely to hear the blues played by white musicians in New York City than black musicians in the South,' had warned Willy, curator of the Blues Archive in Oxford, when I'd talked to him a few days before. The archive was in a huge concrete cavern. Willy himself had been born in Germany; he had a long moustache and cowboy hat, and talked with evangelical enthusiasm.

'But what is the blues anyway?' he mused on. 'You can say technically that it's a certain number of chords and every line repeated twice, but that doesn't mean anything any more. The blues is a feeling, it's a state of mind, not a type of music. It was born out of the repression of black people in the 1930s, and a lot of those conditions haven't changed.

'You know what the blues of today is?' he asked, in a flash of inspiration. 'It's rap, that's what it is. If Muddy Waters was starting off today, he'd join a rap band.'

'So blues lovers shouldn't come to the Delta?' I asked.

'I say: forget about finding the blues. I say: go drive around the countryside. Go take a seat in the park; listen to people talking. Listen to the rhythms of life here. I guarantee that when you listen to a blues recording again, one of the old greats, it will be with a whole new understanding.'

We were walking back from Wade's, in the most bombed-out stretch of Clarksdale, when a scrawny figure lounging against a street post grabbed my arm.

'Hey, homey. Use some chitlins?' He nodded at a hole in the wall, PJ's Place, where his enormous wife waved; she was tossing squares of fat into a bubbling vat of brown oil.

'Uh, maybe,' I said. 'What are they?'

PJ rolled his head. 'You don't know what chitlins is? Chitlins is guts, y'know. *Hog* guts.'

'Deep fried pig guts?'

'Sright. Comes from the substantive, *chitterlings*. Chitlins.'

We got out of it by buying some beer instead.

'Where y'all from, anyway? Aw-stray-lee-yah?' He let out a low whistle. 'Dang!' For a while we pondered the fact. Then he asked, 'What the hell you doin in a borin ole town like this?'

'Just passing through.'

'That's as well. Ain't nothing to do here but sit around an talk, talk, talk.'

We told PJ about our failed attempts to find the blues. He shook his head after the name of each bar. 'White club,' he sniffed. 'White club.'

Then a car pulled up, a souped-up black Ford with the silver engine protruding from the bonnet. The driver snaked smoothly out of the door. He was wearing reflective glasses, a fistful of rings and a dazzling tigerskin jacket.

'Now this man is a *musician*,' said PJ. 'Ain't you, Chop? *You* play the blues, don't you, Chop?'

'Hell, course I play the blues,' he said proudly, before qualifying it a bit. 'Kind of the blues. More like funk.'

It turned out Chop was playing that very night. A special event in a juke joint just outside of town. A little wooden place thrown up in the thirties. Musicians were coming from all over the United States. Chop was from Memphis himself.

'Ah'd like to invite you,' he flashed his gold-capped teeth. 'But it's a closed shoot, y'understand?'

Turned out the whole thing was organised by a French film crew, for a documentary on the South. They wanted a genuine Delta blues bar in action, but had to import musicians from wherever they could. There just weren't enough bluesmen in Clarksdale any more. 'Sorry you cain't see it,' Chop shrugged again. 'But it's gonna git crowded with all them cameras and lights and microphones and shit.'

'Oh well,' we said, not too disappointed. 'We've got to move on anyway.'

2 THE EUTAW SUPPER CLUB

We got lost trying to find Eutaw, Alabama; we got lost again trying to find the antebellum house where we were supposed to be staying. We did run across a cemetery, which had several hundred Confederate soldier graves — rusting metal crosses poking from the rich green grass. One old stone marker was facing away from the others. It read: *Murdered by Ku Klux*. It was the town's biggest tourist attraction.

Darkness was falling by the time we pulled up at 'Brentwood Manor'. We couldn't quite believe it: a Greek Revival plantation house, with huge Doric columns, was set high on a rise. It loomed from the surrounding oaks like a palace or a film set. More than that: it was the Acropolis.

'We're staying here?' Les asked.

I double-checked the address. 'Yep. Brentwood Manor.'

The Southern gentry were like English aristocrats in at least one respect: to pay for the upkeep of their huge mansions, they often opened them up as bed-and-breakfasts. Staying in one had seemed a fine idea … but this place was a bit too magnificent for the way we felt. We'd been driving all day. We were unkempt and exhausted. Maybe we could slink in and lock ourselves in our room. But that's the problem with b-and-bs. You're in someone's house. You have all the disadvantages and moral duties of a house guest, and you're paying for it too.

'Maybe we should just go get a motel,' Les said.

But before we could escape a short woman bounced down the driveway in a tizzy.

'Ah was expecting you a deal earlier!' she flapped. 'We're already late for dinner!'

'We are?'

'Oh yes. The Supper Club's on tonight!'

She pushed us into the back of her car. Apparently the Eutaw Supper Club met once a month — as luck would have it, the only night we were in town — and everyone was *delighted* to hear that two Australians would join them. There was no chance of getting out of it; no time to change or shave. Mrs Slater — Mary — was dressed up in her evening best, but she insisted we'd be passable as we were. Les ran a brush through her hair; I glanced at myself in the car mirror. I looked like a convict.

No matter. As Mary drove us through the Eutaw backstreets, she explained one extra detail. The hostess' husband had only recently passed away, so we should be aware of that. This was her first social engagement since the funeral. Mary knew what she was going through: her own husband had died only recently. 'But you know, I told her at the funeral, you just have to keep on living now that he's gone,' she said, cheerily. 'You just have to *decide* to keep on living.'

We pulled up beneath another wall of Greek columns and shuffled like Union prisoners up the stairs. The other dozen guests were waiting expectantly; they were all in their fifties and sixties, mature professional folk. Lawyers, doctors, people of property. Their faces fell a little when they saw us — they had expected us to be a little older, obviously, a little more *dignified* — but they were Southern, and good manners are part of the code. The bejewelled hostess was named Sally, and she was obviously trying hard to bear up for the event. As tradition dictated, she dropped everything to give us a quick tour around her huge, immaculate home, which had just been built in Old South style.

'This was our dream for thirty years — my husband's and my dream, that is — to move into a house like this,' she said, more in wonder than bitterness. 'We spent every waking moment planning it. Every spare dollar. But my husband only lived here for one year before he passed.'

She showed us every detail, obsessively, as if to deliberately delay her return to the party. In the master bedroom, she opened the closet doors. Rows of men's coats were lined up; men's shirts; men's shoes.

I glanced at Les, and she asked how long had it been … ?

'One week,' Sally pulled herself up straight. 'One week today.'

'Since the funeral?'

'No, since he passed. The funeral was yesterday.'

No wonder the atmosphere was a little oppressive. Back downstairs, the men were standing about on the porch in their perfectly pressed Brooks Brothers slacks, their expressions smug and self-satisfied; the women, in their Laura Ashley frocks, were less self-important and thus easier to bear. Soon the food was ready, Sally smiled valiantly, and we all shuffled into a large empty salon, where a long side table had been laid out with the evening buffet. Everyone stood in a vague circle, hands clasped before them, staring at the food in respectful silence. I was famished. What was everybody waiting for?

But Sally was poised to address us. 'I want to thank our new friends from Australia,' she said graciously, 'for joining us here tonight. We are always happy to have new friends at the Eutaw Supper Club.'

It was the man's job to reply, it seemed, so I said how delighted we were to be here, all the time glancing at the table.

'And now — Miss Lesley?'

Les stiffened as if she'd received an electric shock. 'Yes?'

'Would you like to lead the buffet?'

'Sorry?'

'*Lead* the *buffet*,' she bowed towards the food with a flowing arm gesture. It was evidently a Southern ritual that the woman guest should go first. Les timidly crossed the circle while the rest of us stood there in silence, watching intently as she moved from dish to dish. Only when she was finished could the other guests start.

It was all getting too much; we were exhausted; what other embarrassments did they have in store for us? I began to plan excuses. But we had no car, no idea where we were. And to be honest, I was too hungry to leave — I was starting to see spots.

Les was already sitting at the dining table when I staggered out with my plate. She was ashen-faced from the ordeal of keeping up bizarre conversation, and had started gulping down wine; not one to enjoy being put upon, she was likely to lash out if things got worse. I was about to join her for moral support when Sally clutched me by the arm and placed me between the two most oafish of the men. So that was their technique, I thought, a bit delirious now — like separating accomplices during a police interrogation, to see who would crack first.

I got one mouthful of fried chicken down before it stuck in my throat. All hands were coming up to the table, locked for prayer ... heads were bowed ... Les was looking about like a trapped animal ... and then she seemed to realise that it might be easier to cut our losses and make a show of it.

'And now we can say grace,' said Sally. 'Perhaps our new friend Tony ... ' — no, I thought; this isn't possible — ' ... can show us how grace is said in Australia?'

All eyes turned towards me expectantly. I went blank; froze completely. Finally, all those years at a Christian Brothers school kicked in. I dredged my distant memory and stammered a garbled line, which had the words 'food' and 'thanks' in there somewhere. Everyone looked a bit perplexed, but what they didn't quite make out I hope they blamed on my accent.

Back at Brentwood, we spent the night in a vast four-poster bed, sweltering in the ninety-nine percent humidity; the room was crowded with old furniture, lace, throw pillows and prints from before the Civil War, which induced feverish dreams.

I woke up early, and slipped downstairs to have a look around. The place was a living museum, with its porches and shutters and open rooms with silk curtains flowing in the breeze. Every stick of antique furniture had been lovingly restored; a pianola graced the drawing room; portraits of Southern gents looked possessively from the walls. A plaque showed that Nancy Reagan had given the house an award for the restoration work, and put it on the National Register of Historic Homes. But splendid as it all was, I felt a creeping guilt about staying here. There was something perverse about relishing this Temple of Beauty from the Old South, built on the plantation system; I didn't think too many African-Americans would be hurrying to stay here.

But there was one odd element in Brentwood Manor: a portrait of Abraham Lincoln was hanging on one wall.

'I put that up there,' came Mary's voice behind me. She was bustling about cleaning, ever cheery, ever energetic; she seemed to have forgiven me for various *faux pas* the evening before. 'You know why? The family owners here used to be related to Mrs Lincoln. Course, nobody ever admitted to that during the war. It was a dark, dark secret.'

When people talk about the 'war' in the South, they still mean the Civil War.

'Course, we're glad the South didn't win the war,' she went on briskly. 'We wanted the United States to be whole and democratic, didn't we?'

It was an almost sacrilegious remark from a white Southerner. In most of these plantation houses, a picture of Lincoln would be as welcome as Charles Manson in Hollywood.

'I take it you're not from the South yourself?'

'Originally from Utah. Been here for twenty years, but that doesn't count, not to Southerners.' She dusted under a pot. 'I consider *myself* a Southerner, even if they don't.'

Mary had moved to Eutaw with her husband, she said, and bought the house when it was nothing but a ruin. Just like Sally and her husband, they had spent years renovating — repaired the foundations gnawed by termites, patched the holes in the wooden columns made by woodpeckers, chased chickens from the back rooms. Then, just when the work was completed, her husband up and died.

The very next year, her daughter's husband had been killed in a car crash. I met the daughter briefly — she was round and straggly-haired, 'not all there,' Mary said bluntly. The granddaughter was running about in the backyard naked.

'There's four generations of women in this house, can you believe it?' Mary sighed.

'Who's the fourth?' I asked, and immediately regretted it. Mary was going to show me.

She opened the door to a dark back room. Her mother-in-law was laid out like a waxwork. About three feet long. No hair. No teeth. Her mouth was a perfectly circular hole, through which a loud rasping breathing could be heard.

'She had a stroke,' Mary whispered. 'I think it's better keeping her here than in a nursing home. I don't believe in that.'

I was beginning to imagine all the mansions in Eutaw, all those silent houses, saturated with family tragedies; all owned by widows, a matriarchy of the South.

Les crept down the staircase to breakfast, having been looking over the antiques. 'What else have you got hidden away in here?' she said to Mary. Oh God, I thought; don't ask.

But Mary volunteered her *pièce de resistance*. When she and her husband first bought Brentwood Manor, they found fourteen trunks stored in the attic. Turns out they belonged to the original owner from the Civil War days. They were now upstairs in the hallway, and would we like to have a look?

We felt like a couple of grave robbers opening the ancient casks, going through these people's private belongings. The first contained a slender pistol from the war, some round shiny bullets, a Confederate soldier's uniform, campaign buttons, a great wad of Confederate bills. The second was the lady of the manor's: a silk dress, still bright white; some china dolls; little blue bottles for perfume. A 'flirting fan', with a tiny mirror on the tip so that some nubile Scarlett O'Hara could glance at her admiring beaux.

There wasn't even a hint of mustiness; the clothes were untouched by moths or damp, neatly pressed and folded. Finally, we opened a trunk that had a whole ponytail of blonde hair laid out on top, tied neatly by a bow. I held it up in the sun; it was golden and fresh, as if it had been cut yesterday.

In the silent, stifling hallway, it was just too eerie. We lay the ponytail back on its bed, and slipped back downstairs.

✳

After one last iced tea — now rocking fiercely in our porchfront chairs — it was time to go. Mary seemed unwilling to let us leave. She had no more guests scheduled, and had no inclination to go visiting for company. She had hosts of friends, she said, although she still felt like an outsider.

'I've been here twenty years and they still don't accept me,' she said, cheery as ever. 'They like me well enough, but they don't accept me. Not really.'

But she shrugged and brushed the thought away.

3   WATCHING THE KLAN

Three days later, we mentioned to a woman in Montgomery that we'd been to Eutaw.

'You're going to put Eutaw in a story on the South?' She was shocked. 'We're right particular about what we consider the South. There's too many Yankees in Eutaw!'

The capital of Alabama was like something out of the 1950s — inexplicably wide and empty streets, down which vast Buicks slowly rumbled; a domed State Congress building; a soda fountain serving hot dogs and chilli beans. It had opened in 1917, said the sign, providing 'fast food before it was fast'.

Given Montgomery's unfortunate past, I decided to drop by the office of the 'Klanwatch' program of the Southern

Poverty Law Centre. It was in an almost jarringly modern building, with a circular fountain outside commemorating those who had died in the Civil Rights movement. Getting in was like entering Fort Knox. There were surveillance cameras and speakers. The door was one-way, bullet-proof glass. Back in 1983, the former building had been arsoned by Alabama Klansmen who came up through the sewer system; since then, there had been regular bomb threats.

The director of the Klanwatch program was a relaxed lawyer from Montgomery, Daniel Welsch. The corporate design was like any other law office, except that on the walls were photos from the 1920s, when 40,000 hooded Klansmen marched in Washington (there were five million members America-wide); a poster from the W. B. Griffith movie, *Birth of a Nation*, which glorified the Klan; and some modern snapshots of burning crosses at Klan ceremonies.

The Klanwatch program was begun in 1979; now it monitors about 300 different white supremacist groups in the US. These days, Welsch said, the Klan — well, actually, there are lots of little Klans, no national organisation — was definitely no longer the most dangerous hate group. 'The Klan has only five to six thousand members now, nation-wide,' he said. 'A lot of younger people have left it. They don't want to get about in these hokey Halloween bedsheets. They go for neo-Nazi groups like the Aryan Nation, where they get to wear paramilitary garb, or they join the skinheads.'

I asked how things were in Mississippi and Alabama these days.

'Truth is, the South is no longer the hot-bed of white supremacist activity,' Welsch admitted. 'Over the last decade, there has been much more violence in the north-east and

California than any other part of the United States. We've done a lot of work on this, and we find that in the South the races actually get on a lot better than in other parts of the country. Even the poorest neighbourhoods of Montgomery are integrated somewhat, which is something you didn't see twenty years ago.

'The real tensions today are in the big American cities like Detroit and Chicago, where black and white people rarely even see each other.'

4 GRAVEYARD OF THE MYTHIC SOUTH

This whole journey to the South had really begun, symbolically at least, in the orderly outskirts of Oxford, Mississippi, where at the end of an oak-lined driveway another white plantation house had been glistening in the afternoon rain. It was like a scaled-down Tara, with chandeliers shining through the French windows, and there were slightly disordered grounds that you could imagine extended forever. The air was thick with the fantasy of a pre-Civil War world — a place where dashing young blades and hoop-skirted women drank iced tea on the porches, chatting about cotton prices and waiting for the next evening ball.

But this was Rowan Oak, home of William Faulkner — whose passionate, Byzantine novels helped undermine the romantic view of the South. From here, Faulkner changed Oxford and the surrounding Mississippi Delta ('my little postage stamp of native ground') into the mythic domain of Yoknapatawpha County. Instead of a chivalric *Gone With The Wind*-style dreamland, Faulkner described a rather more decadent place, with lavish helpings of racism, incest, murder, madness and suicide.

Since his death in 1962, Faulkner has been turned into a minor tourist industry here in Mississippi. Inside the portals, we shook off the rain and flicked over the guest book. That morning, a Paris-based Faulkner Appreciation Society had passed through; clearly marked from many years before was the signature of Gabriel García Márquez, who claims that reading Faulkner convinced him to be a writer. The curator was a plump, jolly fellow; he proudly showed off the house, which has been painstakingly preserved, down to Faulkner's battered metal typewriter and favourite pipe sitting on his desk. Still scrawled onto the bedroom is the original outline of his Pulitzer Prize winning novel, *A Fable*, divided into chapters. The curator pressed a little map upon us: it showed which parts of Oxford can be identified in Faulkner's books.

'Do many people in town remember him?' I asked.

'Oh, my yes,' he chuckled. 'You see, people here used to be able to recognise themselves in the stories.' He dropped his voice cautiously. 'That didn't make Mr Bill too popular — people called him a good-for-nothing loafer.'

'Even after he won the Nobel Prize?'

'Well, consider his, uh, subject matter ...'

'Too much incest?'

'That and the rest.'

Over on the bookshelf were a few of the volumes I'd read a while back. In *As I Lay Dying*, a half-witted in-bred family drags a rotting corpse for weeks to bury it in the provinces; in *Sanctuary*, a drunken son of a fallen aristocratic family abandons his girlfriend, a young socialite, who ends up kidnapped in a Memphis whorehouse; in *The Sound and the Fury*, a brother and sister carry on a tempestuous affair; and in *Intruder in the Dust*, the whole town of 'Jefferson' is ready to lynch a black man for a murder he clearly didn't commit. I suppose this was where I'd gotten a lot of my own images of the Deep South …

The curator raised his eyebrows. 'See what I mean?'

Downtown Oxford was affluent and well-scrubbed. Its tidy plaza had the inevitable statue remembering the Confederate war dead, next to a 200 year old courthouse; stately mansions lined the streets; and all roads led to 'Ole Miss', the University of Mississippi — whose campus, when the first black students tried to enrol in the mid–1960s, erupted into violent riots. Oxford was then one of the most conservative towns in the Deep South, a bastion of white privilege on the fringe of the impoverished, black-populated Delta; more recently, it's become one of the South's most liberal centres, although still noticeably white. I headed off to the campus café to meet with Bill Ferris — the soft-spoken, intensely lucid director of the Centre for the Study of Southern Culture, which hosts a 'Faulkner and Yoknapatawpha Conference' every year.

'Faulkner is *the* greatest American writer,' Ferris enthused patriotically. 'He's our only writer whose influence has reached all around the world. The only other candidate would be Mark Twain, but his reputation is based on only two novels, *Tom Sawyer* and *Huck Finn*. Faulkner has over a dozen truly great works.'

I asked him if he thought the South was keeping its identity, its sense of difference from the rest of the United States.

'I think the *past* still has enormous influence in the South,' he explained. 'Everywhere else in America has a total future orientation. The South is the opposite. That's reflected in its writers, who constantly examine their tortured relation to our history. The rest of the world relates to that.' He decisively broke open a corn muffin. 'American culture is an *aberration* in the world, an aberration that the South is not a part of ...

'Faulkner said: *The past isn't dead ... it isn't even past.* And that's the key to the South.'

Wandering around Oxford, you could feel as if Faulkner himself was still around — and still resented. Over the next couple of days, we were regaled by a canon of derisive Faulknerabilia, trotted out by everyone from shopkeepers to restaurateurs — in low gossipy voices, looking over their shoulders as if the writer might walk in. The stories usually came in the following order:

* Faulkner and his wife Estelle were both famous drunkards. On their honeymoon, Estelle became so inebriated that she tried to drown herself in the sea.
* Faulkner was a miser. When guests came to visit, he would serve them cheap bourbon, while secretly pouring top-notch Jim Beam into his own glass.
* Faulkner hated noise. Whenever he went out to dine in Oxford, he brought an 'Out of Order' sign to put on the jukebox. If anyone played anything, he would walk out.
* Perhaps worst of all, Faulkner publicly squabbled with his wife over money. On one occasion, Faulkner took out an advertisement in the local paper announcing that he would no longer pay for any purchases that she might make.

In other words, the stories were all saying, the man was not a Southern Gent.

The rain showed no signs of easing, so I went back to Rowan Oak to take some photographs. The mansion was packed; the curator clapped his hands in delight.

As I was snapping away in the impressive parlours, Rowan Oak began to seem a fairly ambiguous literary shrine. Faulkner's writings may have depicted the decay of Southern rural society, but in his personal life all he really wanted was to join the same land-owning aristocracy — as a 'gentleman farmer' in the patriarchal tradition of his great-grandfather 'the Old Colonel' and grandfather 'the Young Colonel'. One step to this end was marrying his childhood sweetheart, the Southern belle Estelle Oldham; another was to purchase Rowan Oak in 1930, along with the extensive lands around it.

Both arrangements were fairly disastrous. The marriage was a failure. And Rowan Oak required massive funds for its upkeep. To make money, he churned out film scripts for Hollywood, where he began to spend time and have short affairs while drinking himself to death. Faulkner ended up with a bevy of black servants, more land, two cars, fine clothes and even a small airplane. But despite his efforts, he was never accepted in Oxford. Townspeople still referred to him as 'the Count', 'Count No-Count', or just 'the queer'. He could never really be more than a 'scalawag' — the Civil War term used for a Southerner who sympathised with the North. He was holding the South up to ridicule, and anyone who broke ranks was a traitor, Nobel Prize or not. He died in 1962 from an alcohol-induced heart failure; at least the townsfolk let him be buried in Oxford cemetery.

Another bus pulled up outside Rowan Oak; there was going to be afternoon tea and a violin recital. The obsessively private Faulkner would have been horrified by the fossickings of recent biographers, appalled at the hordes now tramping through his home, coming to gaze at his pipe. But maybe even more irksome would be the idea that people are more interested in the residue of his life than his actual writings: Faulkner is becoming an author more admired than read.

Yet even here in his shrine, Faulkner is not entirely secure. The last word on his reputation should go to the jovial curator.

'You know, I'm doing my Ph.D. in literature next year,' he confessed conspiratorially as I was leaving, 'but not on Mr Bill. He's just too much hard work.'

5 A TOWN CALLED SPROTT

We went for a drive down the back roads of Perry County, just to see what rural Alabama was like. To be brutally honest, we were looking for sick America — not just Faulkner's version, but *Deliverance* and *Easy Rider*. There were forests everywhere. Hillbilly shingled shacks. More deserted towns with their Civil War monuments and soda fountains and American flags and once a flashing neon sign outside a church that mysteriously promised EVANGELICAL THRUST NIGHTLY. Every time we turned on the car radio there'd be an anti-abortion rave or plugs for a restaurant where guests could 'dine in a totally Christian environment'. It was starting to freak us out a little.

And then it appeared — the Sprott P.O. It's the only building still standing in the town of Sprott, Alabama. Decaying at the empty crossroads, it was squat and lonely, like a wart.

This obscure edifice figured in the copy of *Let Us Now Praise Famous Men* we'd been carrying as a sort of unofficial guide, published in 1936. The book was a collaboration between the photographer Walker Evans and writer James Agee. They were sent on assignment by *Fortune* magazine of New York to document the gruelling lives of Alabama's tenant farmers at the tail end of the Depression. They did too good a job. *Fortune* killed the story when they got back to Fifth Avenue, but the material soon made the basis for a book. It's now regarded as a classic of American social history.

Since 1936, Sprott P.O. has had a new façade, and the petrol pumps are automatic. But it was still recognisable as the same lonely building on the same empty highway.

We got out of the car — almost knocked down by the forty degree heat — and peered into the dark interior. Jars of pickled pig trotters sat on the greasy wooden counter. A red Coca-Cola refrigerator throbbed in the shadows. Wooden fans creaked overhead. Every piece of furniture was an antique, from the battered old postal scales to the built-in shelves to the steam-driven coffee machine that has been churning out industrial-strength brews for decades.

'Y'all seen the funeral?' came a voice from the back. An ancient attendant waddled out, shaking his head in disgust; he was wearing denim overalls and a yellow baseball cap.

'Old post-mistress in the next town's got shot. Robbers shot her dead last week. They're buryin her today.'

The murder made him jumpy, he said, being out here in the middle of nowhere as he was. Sure wouldn't be the first time this place had been taken, though. He showed us the back room: surrounded by piles of rotting paper documents were two metal safes whose doors would no longer properly close, ruined in Dillinger-style hold-ups decades ago. Virtually the only modern addition was a small printed white sign showing a dejected prisoner silhouetted behind bars. It read: THINK FIRST — ARMED ROBBERY — TEN YEARS TO LIFE.

'Only trouble is' — his near-toothless mouth broke into a vampire grin — 'them robbers cain't read.'

We ordered a couple of sodas and sat on the porch. The postmaster settled behind the counter, wheezing thickly as we checked out a Pepsi-Cola thermometer dating back to the thirties. It no longer worked — the heat might have blown the mercury — but it would have been worth a lot in a New York op-shop.

'People come round all the time want to buy that thang,' he gurgled. 'But we always says no. Pepsi-Cola offers to give us a brand new one if we hand it over, but we says no.'

He dragged himself up and nervously scanned the road. 'They shouldn't have shot her,' he said. 'That post-mistress.'

He'd bought this P.O./grocery store/petrol station only a couple of years before, he said. Before that, he had another store in Perry County, but it was burned to the ground during a night robbery. 'If I'd have been around, they would've shot me too.' He pondered this for a while, before adding matter-of-factly: 'It's blacks that do it.'

He wasn't the only one who thought a hold-up was inevitable. The insurance company wouldn't cover him. Fire yes. Robbery no.

As we were sitting there, a red pick-up truck with two teenage rednecks in it hooned by (white, as it happened). They shouted some abuse and threw a beer can at us before disappearing down the highway. The heavy silence returned, menacing now. Backwoods Alabama was starting to feel like *Mad Max*.

'Just hope I'm not here when them robbers come,' the old guy shrugged, before retiring back to the comforting half-light of Sprott P.O.

Art Frenzy

When I first visited New York, I used to stay in SoHo, Manhattan's art world ghetto — in my friend Dick's loft. Dick's a sculptor who bought his space in the 1960s for $10,000, when SoHo was just a seedy wasteland of abandoned warehouses. Everyone thought he was throwing his money away. Then the art boom hit, SoHo was declared a historic district for its cobbled streets and cast iron façades, and the address became the height of chic; soon Dick's place was worth at least fifty times what he paid for it. But while other artists had turned their lofts into spotless white-cube boxes, indistinguishable from the 300 galleries that now packed the twenty-block neighbourhood, Dick still kept the faith. His loft was entirely unrenovated, just a huge space smelling of clay and turpentine. Sculptures filled every inch of furniture space. Abstract watercolours covered the walls. There was a big silver kiln where the kitchen stove should be.

I used to wake up in the mornings and find Dick at the back of the loft, sculpting away in clay from a naked model. Usually they were dancers trying to make some extra money, and their spread-eagled poses could be truly gymnastic. It was all a bit distracting while you were trying to make your morning cup of tea and read the paper. Every night, Dick would clean up the clay and start gathering some of his friends together for dinner. Usually there'd be a dozen or so people who'd never met before and never would again, all from completely disparate walks of life, crowded around a table in Chinatown. It made for some interesting conversations. Dick was a rare breed — a New Yorker born and bred — and he knew the best cheap restaurants in the city. We never spent more than $7 a head for those feasts. He's fiftyish now, with this shock of silver hair, silver beard and new silver glasses; you can't miss him in a crowd.

In any case, the very first time I visited Dick was just before the Wall Street Crash. The art world was in a frenzy. Money was being thrown about like confetti. You used to just wander out anywhere in SoHo and drop by a dozen art openings. There'd be free wine and food, perhaps a little performance or fashion show. Then the word would go out about the party afterwards, with more free food and drink. Adding a frisson to the decadence was the knowledge that this couldn't possibly last forever. Like the Weimar Republic, perhaps.

There were even 'professional party-givers' — of whom the most ambitious was a guy called Baird Jones. Baird would waft into gallery receptions and pass out special invitations to 'Art Happenings' in a nightclub called the Tunnel — an enormous dance hall built in a disused stretch of the subway. Naturally, I took a handful of these, and turned up at midnight with some friends. There was already a line of a hundred or so people to get in, but as soon as we showed our passes we were ushered straight past the velvet rope, through the sea of gyrating dancers into the V.I.P. Lounge. In this elevated bar, surrounded by giant statues of angels, a motley mix of Avenue C auteurs and Wall Street brokers were being besieged by waitresses bearing trays of free cocktails. Music throbbed, chandeliers sparkled. Behind it all, the subway tunnel continued on into the darkness: a light flashing in the distance suggested an oncoming train.

Baird was there, ready to greet us personally. He may be New York's preppiest nightclubber — slightly balding, bespectacled, in his thirties, he got about in a rumpled tweed coat and baseball cap. But he was clearly wired. 'Welcome to my Art Happening!' he announced grandly, clasping my hand. When I asked about the art we could look forward to, Baird clapped his hands and shouted, 'Biceps, *please*!' Out of the darkness bounced a short, muscular figure wearing black leather and studs — a sort of leprechaun gladiator — who went on one knee and flexed his right arm before my nose, an idiot grin on his face. 'Double biceps!' Baird clapped, and his underling obeyed like a circus clown.

'I want you to meet *Davide*,' Baird explained. 'Davide is into performance art.' He proudly pointed out some of the other exhibits. There was Roy the Human Wonder-Pony, who had saddled himself up and was riding lady guests about on his shoulders. A few ageing 'Superstars' from Andy Warhol's old 'Factory' of the sixties, with names like Penny Arcade, Ultra Violet and Cherry Vanilla, had been resurrected for the event. And the guest of honour — surrounded by an admiring entourage — was a wraithlike impersonator of Warhol himself, his straw hair and pink eyes glowing above a black tuxedo. This was Allen Midgett, whom Warhol had hired back in 1967 to replace him on a lecture tour of American universities. The double received thousands of dollars from student groups before he was discovered to be a fake.

It was all pretty silly, but what the hell? We stayed till dawn and came back twice a week thereafter, getting drunk for free in the name of Art.

Nobody could ever quite work out how this whole party system worked — somebody had to be paying for it all. Then one day I ran into Baird in SoHo while he was delivering some of his invitations. He was still wearing his baseball cap and crumpled tweeds, although in the daylight his face had a shiny, alabaster quality. He'd heard that I wrote for Australian magazines, and so invited me along in his limousine, to explain all.

I think he saw himself as a latter-day Jay Gatsby, and maybe in some weird way he was. As we sped around lower Manhattan, Baird explained that his party-giving career had begun while he was in college, studying fine art. That was when he had his key revelation: nightclub owners would let him use a space in their venues for free, if he brought in a cool art crowd and got them a few mentions in the press. 'You see, in New York, people will always *pay* to be near other people more interesting or famous than themselves,' he said, in his clipped, rapid-fire delivery. 'That's what makes a club hot.' Baird then convinced liquor companies to sponsor free drinks — also for the publicity.

Soon he had an elaborate mailing list, with 5,000 invitations going out a week. The fact that few turn up didn't trouble him in the least. 'If I get 100 people out of 5,000, I'm happy. As long as they're 100 *good* people.'

The precise number of good people at a party was how you gauged its success, at least in the eyes of the 'competition'. There were many other professional party-givers at work in the city, Baird muttered darkly, all furiously trying to show one another up. 'It's the personality of the party-giver to compete with others,' he said. 'For someone to tell me that there has been a better party elsewhere makes me agonise for hours.'

And who exactly were good people? Artists, successful or not. Socialites. Anyone rich. Anyone mentioned in the press, for any reason. Heck, when you got down to it, good people included anyone living in Manhattan — as opposed to denizens of the outer boroughs or, worse, the 'tunnel people' (New Jerseyites who surge in Morlocklike hordes every weekend from the Lincoln Tunnel and PATH trains). '*Australians* are good people,' Baird added reassuringly. 'Sydney is closer to Manhattan than New Jersey is. At least you've got an art scene.'

The real Andy Warhol even came to a few of Baird's parties, just before his death — a fact that Baird never fails to mention, although he holds the late megastar in low esteem. 'Warhol wasn't a great artist,' he sniffed. 'He was just an ageing gay with a bad complexion who nobody would give any publicity to. That's what finally killed him: the lack of publicity.' Baird was thriving on it, however. His invitations now included a small drawing of himself, and the notice: *In Recent Years, More than One Million People Have Come to Baird Jones Parties!* He had set up a phone message service, which included a speedy resume (Baird's Ph.D., books he had authored) followed by precise details of his parties. He was stepping up the tempo, he admitted, and hoped to have a party every night.

Every few minutes, Baird leapt out of the car and deposited a few invitations at key locations: fashionable bars, restaurants, galleries. I had to ask what was in it for him. 'I just love to give parties,' he beamed. 'I love to greet guests as they arrive, and have that thirty seconds of contact, and then watch them disappear into the darkness again.' (Rumours were always flying that Baird has somehow made a fortune from his parties — that nightclub owners kick back a fee every time he gets their name in a newspaper. Someone else swears that Baird drunkenly admitted at a dinner party to have made half a million ...)

The invites were delivered, and Baird drove me back to Dick's place. As I was about to get out, he said: 'Sometimes I think I'm working in a total fantasy world.' But then he quickly dismissed the thought. 'On the other hand, I provide a service.'

The SoHo frenzy went awry as the art market collapsed in the early nineties. As one critic put it, SoHo suffered a Manhattan version of the London blitz: some fifty galleries closed their doors. At openings, the shower of free champagne gave way to cheap white wine in plastic cups; the trays of canapés born by black-tied waiters disappeared. To murmurs of horror, some galleries began serving beer. But everyone knew that a great art era was over — never mind what was hanging on the walls — when one well-known gallery actually started charging for its drinks.

Even Baird started going down-market. His invitations were printed in newspapers, and the clubs he courted became far from exclusive. I went with Les to one event: the crowd was mostly fifteen year old Puerto Rican kids, who looked like they were packing heat, standing around and staring at each other morosely. The only drink was a toxic vodka punch. We decided to skip any future invites.

Adding insult to injury were accusations that New York had simply 'lost it' as the world art centre — passing on its mantle, won from Paris in the fifties, to either Barcelona, Berlin, London or Prague (depending on who you listened to). Even the New York *Times* magazine announced that SoHo had ceded its cultural hegemony to — of all places — the small industrial city of Cologne in Germany. *That* was where the most challenging artists were congregating, the most interesting work being done, and (most importantly) the highest prices being paid, not in recession-ridden SoHo.

In the spirit of nostalgia, I did a story on SoHo's decline — mainly because it gave me the chance to talk to a few people I'd wanted to meet.

Leo Castelli, the legendary, octogenarian dealer who nurtured the careers of Jackson Pollock, Jasper Johns, and Roy Lichtenstein, was particularly vitriolic about the Cologne story. 'That's just sheer nonsense,' he said. 'The woman who wrote that is out of her mind. That is my considered opinion, and the opinion of art experts all over the world — including those in Cologne.'

Robert Hughes had long argued that the quality of SoHo's art suffered dramatically during the over-priced, commercialised boom years of the late eighties, when artists were more highly regarded as celebrities than for anything they actually produced. Now, some art aficionados were hoping for a sorting out of the dross — or even a new fin-de-siècle epoch. 'People have been really bored to death with seeing the same artists promoted, the same artists shown,' said Dooley Le Capellaine, a Tasmanian-born dealer who ran a small experimental gallery. 'Now a new generation of artists is coming up to replace them, working in a way that is entirely different — the kind of thing that happens once every twenty years or so at the most.'

Hughes himself, while unable to hide a certain satisfaction at the reaction against the eighties SoHo hype, was less optimistic that survival-of-the-fittest principles applied to art. 'The crash will knock an awful lot of overrated artists out of the market,' Hughes remarked, 'but the question of New York versus Cologne — or Barcelona, or wherever — is fantastically over-simplified. Basically, there is no longer a single pulsating G-spot in the world; the idea of an imperial capital is very convenient, but between them, the fax and the 747 have made it redundant.'

Meanwhile, artists took solace in history. Long-term resident Virginia Cuppaidge remembers being told that New York had 'lost it' when she first arrived there from Australia in 1969. 'Everyone said to me, "You've come to New York too late! Pop Art's all over; New York's finished. You should go to London." So whenever people tell me that the art world in New York is dying on its feet, I don't pay much attention.'

Iceland the Brave

Every visitor to Iceland has a moment of doubt, a time when they ask themselves what on earth they are doing there. Mine came early, on the scorched black lava field of a volcano called Krafla. Wherever I looked, piles of twisted rock were spouting steam into the cold, sub-arctic air. The stench of sulfur was so thick I could hardly breathe, and the brittle volcanic ash crunching beneath my feet was actually hot, making my feet sweat.

The other people picking their way across the lava field looked like they loved it. As for me, I just couldn't seem to relax.

Maybe it was the battered old warning sign that had announced this existential wasteland: VOLCANIC HAZARD ZONE — DO NOT ENTER. Or maybe it was because, a few days before in Reykjavik, I'd seen the 'Volcano Show' given by Villi Knudsen, an Icelandic filmmaker who specialises in eruptions. Knudsen, whose hulking frame and ginger beard would have impressed his Viking ancestors, had said that he was prepared to fly to Krafla at a moment's notice because underground pressure has been building there for years, and a blast is now expected at any time. The warning sign I'd seen had been put up at Krafla during the last series of eruptions in the early eighties, when hundreds of tourists had flocked to the spot to watch the natural pyrotechnics.

'If Krafla had gone up,' Knudsen intoned, 'they would all have been blown back home without a ticket.'

Krafla was a vision of the earth in its formation, at once impressive and vaguely horrifying. All around were the signs of Iceland's endless evolution: in some places the ground had warped into enormous egg-shaped bubbles and volcanic vents, spraying constant fountains of steam out into the air. The earth here rises and falls several centimetres a year, like an enormous geological lung. And although the volcanic magma is a mile and a half underground, I kept imagining that the earth's surface was only three feet thick and could crack open like an eggshell.

Still, I'd come all the way to the fringe of the Arctic circle, and I wasn't about to turn back now. So I went out wandering over the lava field like everyone else, thinking that if Nature wanted to blow me away, there wasn't much I could do about it. Which is, of course, an Icelandic state of mind.

Over the ten centuries since the first Norse settlers arrived in their longships, Icelanders have learned the hard way to live with their hyperactive island — one of the most volcanic places on earth — treating it with a mix of respect, dread and black humour. Iceland's most famous volcano, Mt Hekla, was so active in the Middle Ages that it was considered by theologians to be the gateway to hell. Another volcano, Snaefellsjökull, was the passage down which Jules Verne sent Professor Liedenbrock in *Journey to the Centre of the Earth*.

Fully one third of the earth's flow of lava during recorded history has come up through Iceland. In 1963, a completely new island, Surtsey, burst from the sea off Iceland's south coast. In 1967, another island, Heimaey, had to be evacuated because of an eruption, and rescue workers turned back a 100 metre tall wall of lava using sprays of sea water, while rocks the size of television sets fell from the sky.

After visiting Krafla, I went over to Namafjall, an orange plain full of gurgling mud pools stretching up to a cleft mountainside, where Icelandic peasants once mined sulfur for gunpowder, fuelling Europe's wars for centuries. The notices at Namafjall didn't say I might be blown up, at least. They said not to walk on the light coloured clay or I'd fall through and be boiled alive ...

It may sound like Iceland would only be visited by certifiable masochists. But in high summer, this island on the edge of the Arctic circle is perhaps the ultimate nature trip, a haunting, sodden journey into a landscape of fairytale greenery. These dreamlike shores have inspired poets ever since the first Vikings took time off from their self-destructive feuding to pen the sagas, considered the greatest literary achievement of the medieval world. A little more recently, in the 1930s, W. H. Auden and Louis MacNiece wrote a famous travel book called *Letters from Iceland*. A good part of this loony volume is in the form of an ode addressed to Lord Byron. Trying to figure out what on earth *he* was doing in Iceland, Auden mused as follows:

The reason for hereness seems beyond conjecture,
There are no trees or trains or architecture,
Fruits and greens are insufficient for health
And culture is limited by lack of wealth.
The tourist sights have nothing like Stonehenge,
The literature is all about revenge.

And yet I like it if only because this nation
Enjoys a scarcity of population.

Today, Auden would be pleased to know, Iceland is still empty; the island's mix of ice and fire has protected it, forcing Icelanders to huddle in a few corners of the coast. (Living Icelanders, that is — since every corner of the forbidding countryside is saturated by folk tales about witches, ghosts and elves. A census was made of Iceland's ghosts, and it was found that they outnumbered the humans two to one.)

Even the simplest things in Iceland are appealingly weird. The first time I smelled sulfur, for example, was in the hotel room in Reykjavík. I'd decided to run a bath, and the room was filled with the powerful scent of rotten eggs. The water was perfectly clean — as pure as bottled mineral water — but it was coming ready-heated from somewhere beneath the surface of the earth.

That first morning, it was brilliantly sunny — a fact hardly worth noting anywhere but Reykjavík, where it usually rains. Buckets down, in fact. On this cloudless day, every one of the blonde, statuesque Icelanders seemed to be out promenading. German and Swedish tourists, all donning the latest designer sunglasses, preened in open air cafés as if this was one long après-ski party. Most of Reykjavík had a spare East European feel, its half-formed streets lined with concrete apartment blocks and monolithic public sculptures that looked like giant spanners or can openers. But there's money everywhere: high-tech fishing methods have given Icelanders a higher per capita income from the sea than Saudi Arabians earn from oil. Icelanders now have the longest life expectancy on earth, and pay the world's highest taxes; Iceland is also up there with Japan as one of the world's most expensive places to visit.

'Icelanders love to collect statistics about themselves to prove how eccentric they are,' chortled a ghostly white photographer named Páll I had to work with. We met up at Reykjavík's duck-filled Tjorn or pond, now thronged with families in the dazzling sun. Páll was so pale and blonde that he seemed to have no eyebrows. And like most Icelanders, he had a stone-like expression for the first five minutes of conversation, which switched without warning to effusive friendliness.

'Consider the following,' Páll said excitedly, reeling off a few favourite figures. With only 260,000 inhabitants — less than, say, Wagga — Iceland had more chess grand masters per capita than anywhere on earth (six of them), and more beauty queens (two Miss Worlds in the last decade); it had the first democratically elected woman head of state (President Vigdis Finnbogadottir, elected 1980) and produced the first feminist political party to gain parliamentary seats. Icelandic is Europe's oldest living language; Icelanders publish more books per person than any other nation; they own more videos per capita, more cellular phones …

On those long, dark nights, Páll went on, the home-bound Icelanders had time to cultivate their obsessions. It was an Icelandic priest, for example, who wrote the first dictionary of the Basque language, and an Icelandic farmer who wrote the most famous epic poem about an obscure Balkan revolutionary.

'If *you* lived in Iceland,' Páll challenged, 'or even lived through one Icelandic winter, believe me, you'd be acting pretty strange yourself.'

'If you like eccentricity,' I suggested, 'you should try a summer in Darwin.'

'You know,' he said in deadly earnest, 'one day I *shall*.'

I soon found that Icelanders are as fascinated by Australia as Australians are about Iceland: it's as if the two countries were opposite twins, mirror images, true antipodes. Páll quizzed me for hours about the Outback deserts, the habits of snakes, the Queensland beaches. Later, in an isolated northern village called Olafsjodur, I ran into a student from Sydney named Fiona, who had come here to scale fish in a factory for $7 an hour. Visiting Iceland had always been her dream, she confessed.

And there has been more historical traffic between the two countries than one might guess. Consider the adventures of Jorgen Jorgensen, 'the Viking of Van Dieman's Land'. As captain of a British merchant ship in 1808, this florid, visionary character weighed anchor in Reykjavík harbour, only to find that the Danish colonial powers would not let him trade with the wretched, mud-covered Icelandics, who looked like they were barely out of the Middle Ages. Jorgensen promptly locked the Danish governor up and declared Iceland independent, with himself as 'Protector'. This sub-arctic revolution was short-lived. The aristocratic captain of a passing British gunboat cancelled the whole putsch and brought Jorgensen back to London in disgrace. He went on to an exotic career as a secret agent and entrepreneur before being framed for theft — which resulted in his transportation to the furthest corner of the globe, Tasmania.

Jorgen Jorgenson — now known as 'John Johnson' — earned his ticket-of-leave and worked for the Van Dieman's Land Company as an explorer (it is said that he discovered Lake St Clair). He became a policeman in Oatlands, and was one of the few settlers sympathetic to the doomed Tasmanian Aborigines. Jorgensen died in 1841, still occasionally mocked as 'His Icelandic Majesty'.

On that first day in Reykjavík, I wasn't sure that Iceland's eccentricity was enough to make the place bearable. At 6 p.m., shops closed, people vanished and only a few nervous foreigners like myself were left wandering about, like characters in a Bergman dream sequence, trying to find somewhere to eat.

I finally found a pizza bar which was full of beautiful blonde women dining out together. (Leaving the men at home is an old tradition amongst the independent-minded Icelandic women, I was told). I ate some expensive pizza, very, very slowly drank a $14 beer, and listened to the guttural sound of Icelandic flowing around the bar in a smooth, incomprehensible stream.

There was one statistic my pal Páll had neglected to mention: on Friday nights, Icelanders probably guzzle more alcohol per person than any place on earth. They don't drink a drop all week, work like dogs, then go out and get totally plastered — turning law-abiding, genteel Reykjavík into something (as one Icelandic writer has observed) straight out of Hieronymous Bosch.

Things kicked off with the *runtur*, the teenage coming-of-age ritual. By 11 p.m., the still-sunny footpaths were littered with inebriated adolescents. Afraid I'd have a bottle cracked over my head, I ducked into Reykjavík's most famous 'pub', Gaukur a Stong, named after a Viking farmer whose house was buried Pompeii-style by the great volcano Hekla. The bar was just getting going. A local band dressed in black leather belted out some heavy metal chords, singing in English to a crowd that looked full of twenty-five year old fashion models. The beers were $17 a glass. Nobody else seemed to mind: they were paying for their drinks over the bar with personal checks and credit cards, running up bills that must have easily hit the hundreds.

I ordered a rum and the barman automatically asked, 'Double?' Any less was considered a waste of time. It soon became obvious that nobody was drinking for the taste.

'Getting drunk is idiotically expensive in Iceland,' declared a woman at the bar named Birna, 'you have to save up all week, then do it all at once.' Like most Icelandic women in their early twenties, Birna was already married with two kids, but this didn't stop her from knocking back a cheap Icelandic firewater known as *Brennivin* — Black Death. 'You know the English expression: blow off steam? That's Friday night in the Icelandic duck pond.'

Her husband loomed from the darkness, baring his teeth like the figurehead from some Norse longboat. Thorgeir was a nurse, and he had his own pseudo-medical opinion on Friday nights. 'It's much healthier to drink hard, once a week, and then finish!' he slurred. 'It gives your liver a chance to clean out the alcohol. It's your English and your French, with their three glasses of beer every night, who get cirrhosis.'

The place was packed by midnight, and the booze was flowing like water. Drunken lovers fell writhing on the floor; men passed out with their heads on the bar; one drunken kid knocked over his double vodka and orange and looked like he was about to cry. (No wonder, I thought: it had cost $25.) At 2 a.m., I left with Birna and Thorgeir for another bar across the street, where an American guitarist was on the stage and turning the place into a frenzy. Dancing arm in arm, the whole bar started singing along to old Beatle songs in perfect English; but then came the real favourite, making the audience link arms and scream along:

How much is that doggy in the window ... ?

'Do you know this one?' Birna shrieked maniacally.

The one with the waggly tail … ?

The swaying movement was too much for some, who fell howling to the floor. Thorgeir staggered off to the bathroom to be sick, and Birna shook her head.

I do hope that doggy's for sale!

'The problem with Icelanders,' Birna shouted over the din, 'is that we take everything to extremes.'

I realised nobody comes to Iceland for the urban life. My plan was to hire a car and spend three weeks driving around the island, staying in remote farmhouses and hiking. I was ready to leave Reykjavík when it started raining. Not just normal rain, but Icelandic rain, which is driven by eighty-kilometres-an-hour North Atlantic gales, making raincoats and umbrellas next to useless. A mechanic at the car rental agency told me not to worry.

'Do like the Icelanders do,' he said. 'When it's raining in the South, go to the North. When it's raining in the North, go to the South.' The whole time we were talking, this guy Hrafn ('raven') just stood there in the deluge, getting soaked to the skin. He said he didn't even notice. 'I grew up wet,' he shrugged, by way of explanation.

It seemed like nature was already taking control of my actions, so what could I do but obey? The Ring Road runs around the green and misty Icelandic coast, dotted with sheep farms and red-roofed wooden churches. I passed black sand beaches, broken fields of lava, twisted cairns that looked like the perfect home for a family of trolls. The only thing missing were trees, nearly all of which had been cut down by the Vikings and have never grown back. At regular intervals came Iceland's spectacles: the hypnotic waterfalls, glaciers oozing down between mountains like rivers of blue putty, lakes filled with masses of ice.

It turned out that being regularly doused in rain and lacerated by wind only added to the purgative effects of Iceland, like having a sauna then diving into a freezing pool. The island is almost completely unpolluted: nearly all energy is geothermal or hydroelectric, the water 100 per cent glacial, the food deliciously pure. Fish are plucked from clean seas or crystal rivers, vegetables are grown in greenhouses and sheep graze in fields untouched by fertiliser (the wild herbs make their meat taste of rosemary). After a week in Iceland, my skin was clear, my eyes sharp, and the extra hours of daylight had given me boundless energy. After four weeks, I felt like I had been stonewashed clean.

I was also bankrupt. Because of the high cost of food, I'd packed a huge suitcase of processed ingredients in New York — nothing fresh, to get it through customs controls — and had been cooking it up in farmhouse kitchens. In supermarkets, the only cheap deals were on smoked salmon and frozen cod. You could occasionally buy a tomato or a piece of fruit — just one, weighed out like a nugget of gold.

One night, after crossing the Arctic Circle, I decided to celebrate in a restaurant in Akureyri. At 8 p.m. on a weeknight, the dining room was entirely empty, and as bright and sterile as an operating theatre. The elderly waitress gave me a menu and stared at me without expression as I perused it and slowly blanched. The main courses started at $60. The taxes on that would be another quarter ... I hoped she wasn't expecting a tip.

'Ah, do you have any specials tonight?' I asked desperately.

'No specials.'

I was trapped. I resignedly ordered the cheapest dish, salmon.

'Wine list?' She pushed it forward with pursed lips. The cheapest bottle was about $100. And that was Romanian.

'I don't drink. Had to give it up. Very tragic.'

The old lady looked at me askance — she was onto my game — and gave me a tiny bread bun and a wafer-thin slice of butter. Since she was just standing there looking at me, I made an attempt at small talk. 'It's an expensive place for foreigners, Iceland.'

Her stare didn't waver. 'If people cannot afford it, perhaps they should not come.'

When the meal appeared, it was four tiny slices of salmon in sauce. A sprig of parsley. Three slices of potato. It was the opposite of eating in America, where you get piles of food, usually bland, but in grotesque quantities. Here in Iceland, food was precious. There was a single perfect slice of cake sitting on a tray, rotating under lights as if it were a piece of the true cross.

'Any chance of some more bread?'

'Bread is extra,' the waitress said sadly, turning up her palms. She was growing almost sympathetic. 'We cannot grow wheat in Iceland. Everything is imported.'

Five minutes later, the chef stuck his head out of the kitchen door and beckoned her over. They re-emerged with a small plate and three glasses, both suddenly animated and friendly.

'We will offer you an Icelandic specialty,' they announced. 'You know *hakarl*?' From this tiny square of grey paste on the plate wafted an amazing stench. As if a sack of dead fish had been crossed with an Indian railway station latrine.

'It is no charge,' encouraged the chef. The paste was divided onto the three wafers; they downed theirs, munched it quickly, then knocked back the glass of Black Death. I followed suit, and my mouth exploded. The detergent burn shot up my nose, up behind my eyes; I forced the substance down and quickly gulped the spirits, scalding away the taste, like acid.

As I gasped away, the chef happily explained what *hakarl* was. By Icelandic tradition, shark meat would be wrapped and buried in the sodden earth. Wait for three months and dig it up. The decomposing, cured remains were *hakarl*. 'It's so strong,' he noted proudly, 'even the carrion birds won't touch it!' Apparently I should be here during the Great Feast in winter. I could dine on ram's testicles in aspic; roast puffin breast; or another dish called 'slaughter', which was bits of random offal sewn into a sheep's stomach.

'Does everybody here get into *hakarl*?' I asked.

'Eating *hakarl* is like surviving the Icelandic winter,' pronounced the waitress. 'It's not exactly pleasant — but you are happy to survive. Life begins again.'

In Iceland, obviously, whatever doesn't kill you makes you stronger.

With its three winter months of Stygian gloom and landscapes that are always playing with the imagination, it's no wonder that the island has produced so many writers (including a Nobel Prize winner, Halldór Laxness). But no Icelander would disagree that the greatest stories of all are still the Old Icelandic sagas — bloodthirsty little tracts that were once described by Jorge Luis Borges as medieval prototypes for the modern American

'Western'. Instead of cowboys chasing one another across the prairies, the sagas are full of wandering Vikings and strong-minded Norse women with ringing names like Thorsteinn Cod-biter, Ketill Flat-nose, Hallgerdur the Long-legged and Audur the Deep-minded (with the odd shield-biting berserker thrown in for good measure), all battling it out for the classic themes of love, honour, greed and revenge in the shadow of glistening glaciers. Still avidly read, and even hotly debated by Icelanders, the sagas are loosely based on the historical events of the island's first Norwegian settlers. Unlike most writings of the Middle Ages, which are eye-glazingly dull, these are actually fun to read.

I hoped there would be some of this history left over in Iceland, relics of the Viking days that fitted in with the sagas. But whenever I tried to find anything, I ran into the all-new, high-tech, metamorphosed Iceland of the present. One day, I tried to follow the course of *Njáls Saga*, a widely read tale of a fifty-year blood feud in southern Iceland. The saga's gory climax occurs at a farm called Bergthorshvoll, where the hero Njál orders his family to barricade their house against a horde of enemies — thus signing their death warrants, because the house is burned to the ground. I managed to find the farm still called Bergthorshvoll, but it was a tiny box-like house from the sixties, straight out of suburban Lakemba. A polite middle-aged woman showed me about the property, but there was nothing there. Even the site where archaeologists had found the eleventh century remains of a burnt house had been filled in long ago and looked like a manicured golf green.

Almost nothing in Iceland, it turned out, was older than about fifty years. Rural towns are even blander than Reykjavík, with a few jerry-built houses thrown up around an Esso station, whose fast food bar would be the social hub for whole regions.

There were a few old turf farmhouses, with grass growing over their dirt roofs like hobbits' homes, and some wooden chapels dating from the last century, but that was about it. With little wood and nothing but volcanic stone to work with, Icelanders built none of the cathedrals or fortresses that are the staple of history-lovers in the rest of Europe.

Instead, the sagas stand alone. They give every part of the Icelandic landscape a meaning far beyond the purely visible: here on this headland is where the warrior Grettir overcame an ancient ghost, only to be left forever terrified of the dark; this pile of stones is where the heroine of *Laexdela Saga* forced her husband to murder her former lover; here at this creek one of Iceland's first settlers was ambushed by the Irish slaves he used to tether like cows to a plough.

For Icelanders, in fact, words are the most exciting historical artefacts, more evocative than any collection of ruins or Viking helmets could hope to be.

Back in Reykjavík, I visited the sanctum sanctorum of the Icelandic soul, a concrete building called the Arni Magnusson Manuscript Institute, where the original vellum manuscripts written by twelfth century scribes are kept. Magnusson, who died in 1730, was a great collector who devoted his life to tracking down the writings. On occasion, he found priceless scraps of manuscript that had been turned into shoe leather or waistcoats.

'The Icelandic language goes back ten centuries without change,' enthused an aged, bushy-eyebrowed scholar from the folklore department as we wandered around the glass display cases. Inside, the priceless vellums were magnificently illustrated with warriors, monks and ghosts. 'In Norway, Sweden and Denmark, the Old Norse tongue evolved into new languages, but here in far-away Iceland, it stayed intact.' Today's Icelanders can basically pick up the medieval sagas and read them as easily as they read the weekly newspaper. It's an appealing idea, as if we could suddenly speak the Old English of Malory or Chaucer.

This mind-bogglingly complex language is still at the core of the Icelandic identity. Possibly no other nation is so obsessed with linguistic purity. Next to the Icelanders, the French look like cultural wimps. Institutions make sure that no foreign words creep into Icelandic, even in technological and medical fields.

In the same vein, medieval customs are kept up. Thanks to the ancient Scandinavian patronymic system, everyone in Iceland calls one another by their first names and is so listed in the telephone book: children's surnames are taken from their father's first name, so Olaf Jonsson's son will be called Thorgeir Olafsson and his daughter, Greta Olafsdottir. According to surveys, most Icelanders still believe in all those ghosts and elves. (Roads are built around knolls said to be occupied by the 'hidden people'.) And Icelanders still snack on dried cod instead of Mars Bars. But despite these holdovers, foreign television, foreign music and foreign videos are pressing against the cultural floodgates. ('The language is slipping,' the Institute scholar lamented. 'Young people simply cannot be bothered with some of the syntactical rules, which are admittedly rather convoluted.')

And if the language goes, I wondered, then where does that leave the Icelanders? Just another bunch of very rich, very blonde Europeans occupying a spectacular but empty national park. Seen like that, the Icelanders' struggle to save their culture started taking on an oddly heroic — or quixotic — dimension.

On my last day in Iceland, eating one more hamburger with fries in an Esso station, I was beginning to have my doubts about Icelanders' chances. But then, on the way to Keflavík airport, I stopped off for one last swim in a place called the Blue Lagoon.

I was directed through the change rooms to a steaming open air spa, whose waters were indeed a pale milky blue. A geothermal heating centre loomed over the whole scene like a giant silver spider, its organ pipes pumping steam into the freezing air: swimmers looked like they were wallowing in chemical waste from some horrifying twenty-first century nightmare. But it was too cold to stand there naked, so I carefully slid down into the sharp lava basin. Not only was the whole thing natural, I reminded myself, swimming here was actually good for you, thanks to the minerals rising from beneath the earth. People with rare skin disorders travel to Iceland from around the world just for a chance to bathe in the Blue Lagoon's Lourdes-like waters.

Floating on my back in the hot blue milk, I looked up at the swirling mists and felt the gentle brush of a cold, light drizzle on my face. No matter how much Iceland changes, I had to admit, it would never be quite like everywhere else.

1 – 8 0 0 - L a w y e r

Nothing gets a New Yorker's blood pumping quite so fiercely as the prospect of litigation from a personal injury case. Health care is so outrageously expensive, and the legal system so out of control, that there is a rare satisfaction in having your medical bills paid by somebody else *and* collecting a little something for yourself (enough to buy a small penthouse, say).

I was walking with Les past Union Square one evening, just before dusk. Maybe I was glancing up at the skyscrapers too often, the way you do when you're back in Manhattan — the silver spire of the Empire State Building can just be glimpsed from 14th Street — or maybe I was distracted by the gathering storm clouds. But I don't think so. In fact, I doubt any non-native New Yorker could have predicted what happened next. There was a sudden thud — I felt like I'd been hit in the guts with a baseball bat — and my legs were dangling in space. I'd plummeted down a trapdoor that had opened without warning in the pavement; one of the upright doors had caught me in the midriff.

These metal service hatches are such a natural part of the landscape here — used by every shop in the city to connect underground basements to the footpath — that most New Yorkers sidestep them instinctively. To prevent accidents, the law says that they can only be opened from above (a few even have sirens and bells as warnings). But some half-witted busboy at the Union Square Pizza Parlour had decided to take out the garbage just as we were strolling past, and he opened one from below.

It must have been a spectacular fall. Les let out a scream and pulled me off the gaping trapdoor. As I lay doubled up on the ground, gasping for air, all hell broke loose in the Pizza Parlour. The owner was out in a flash, jabbering in Spanish at the top of his lungs; he was followed by the customers, who'd seen the whole thing through the giant plate glass windows. Soon there was a small crowd standing around me, all yelling and waving half-eaten slices and calzones.

'I'm a witness!' I vaguely heard one guy bellowing. 'I saw it all, the whole frigging thing.'

'Take my name and address!' somebody else had Les by the arm. 'Here, look, take my phone number!'

The owner looked terrified. An accident was obviously a bond in New York. Suddenly it was the People versus the Pizza Parlour.

'I'm an attorney,' proclaimed a balding type in shorts and glasses. He pushed forward a piece of paper with another number. 'Gimme a call tomorrow. *You can't lose this case.*'

Later Les told me that he had taken her aside. 'Listen, I'm not really an attorney, I just said it for the owner's benefit. But even if your friend's not badly hurt, ask them for a few hundred bucks. Everybody does it,' he'd added. 'That's the way it works.'

Meanwhile, the pseudo-attorney's threat had had the desired effect. The owner was wringing his hands and repeating like a mantra, 'I'll settle, *I'll settle!*'

At the time I didn't really care. I was thinking of Harry Houdini — hadn't he been done in by a blow to the stomach? One of his party tricks had been to let people punch him; normally it was like hitting a brick wall, but one day a journalist sunk his fist in before

Houdini could tighten his muscles. And mine were more like papier-mâché at the best of times.

I staggered into the Pizza Parlour to examine my rapidly reddening stomach. To stop the swelling, the owner helpfully gave me a wad of ice wrapped up in a wet towel ('I seen them do it on the World Cup!' he explained). Despite the stupidity of his employee, I felt a bit sorry for him. He turned out to be a Dominican who'd just started up the business; now he was seeing his pizza dreams evaporate before his very eyes. Les led me — still half-bent over — into a taxi and we headed for home.

Next day, a doctor confirmed that the injury was only to the muscles and that my organs had escaped. No broken ribs. The biggest risk had been breaking my legs, he said. I was very lucky to get away with a few welts.

'So where did it happen?' the doctor asked idly. When I told him, his eyes lit up.

'No doubt they'll be hearing from you,' he snickered. He assumed I'd sue. Why the hell not?

In fact, every New Yorker I told about the incident agreed my fortune was made. There may have been no permanent damage. But there was the shock, the pain, the trauma, the downright inconvenience of the whole business.

'Falling down one of those door things? That's the biggest money-spinner in this city,' mused a friend who worked in corporate law. 'Unlike a lot of cases, it's completely their fault. There's no possible argument. Open and shut verdict.'

He thought I should watch some of the cable TV stations during the daytime, when sleazy lawyers advertise for personal injury cases; there's a whole industry based on accidents, with assessments given on toll-free numbers like 1–800-LAWYERS and 1–800-GO-FOR-GOLD. The plaintiff doesn't pay a cent in fees; you merely hand over fifty percent of the take if you win. 'They'd just *love* to hear from someone like you,' he thought.

Others thought I should go for a quicker return. 'I'd go for at least a thousand,' opined Dick, the SoHo sculptor. 'Just go back in to the pizza parlour and ask for three. They'll give you a grand on the spot.'

Even some less ruthless acquaintances thought it was worth a bash. 'Of course, you don't want to fuel this already insane, blood-thirsty, self-consuming legal system,' observed a writer who specialised in health issues, 'but you may as well get a few months' rest out of it.'

I considered the options. Did I really want to wring every last penny from the ordeal? Since they obviously didn't have insurance, the Dominican's pizza parlour would probably have to close. I hadn't been hurt, miraculously enough. Why push my luck? Suing sounded like bad karma, at the very least. 'You may as well put it behind you,' Les agreed.

Lazily enough, I never even went back to get the $100 for the medical bill, or $10 for the taxi ride home. Another assignment cropped up, and I was able to forget about the whole thing. Of course, I never told my New York friends about this piece of Australian wimpishness. They enjoyed thinking about my case so much, I hated to spoil their fun.

Friday Night on

Thursday Island

It was 4 a.m. at a party on a fishing trawler, and a monolithic character named Eddie was telling me about the 'Island of Origin' football series — a tournament for all the Torres Strait islands, including Tuesday, Wednesday and Friday. 'The games get a bit rougher than down south,' he chortled proudly. 'Last grand final, one player broke his neck. Never made it off the field.' Looking at Eddie, it was easy enough to believe: his fists were the size of my head, swallowing up the tinny between his fingers; one tackle from him would pound you into shark chum.

I asked if there were many casualties this year.

'We did some damage,' he grinned, then nodded at the other islanders beneath the yellow trawler lights; several had feet and arms in plaster casts. 'Took some damage, too.'

I slipped off to the fish freezer, where everyone stored their drinks, and found my last can squeezed between two icy sacks full of prawns. Lurching back out to the swaying deck, it occurred to me (not for the first time) what a terrifying bunch everyone on Thursday Island looked. There was one white guy I kept bumping into, who had both front teeth missing, tattoos up both arms and two fresh wounds on his face — one cut over his left eye and the other, like claw marks, dripping blood down his cheek. I'd seen him earlier at the pub, sitting by the bar and flicking his still-burning cigarette butts on to the pool table. Every time he finished a Bundy and Coke — every five minutes — he'd turn the glass upside down with a snarl, letting the ice splash over the counter and anyone nearby. Thinking he was a brawl just waiting to happen, I'd kept a good distance. But here he was on the trawler, six hours of hard drinking later, except for blood still dripping down his face, he was the picture of decorum as he chatted up one of the petite English barmaids who seemed to congregate on T.I. Outnumbered by about ten to one, the women here run the sexual equivalent of the Island of Origin football match every night.

'T.I. really is a hole,' thundered Wendy, the local hairdresser, right in my ear. Her nose was as bright red as a cartoon drunk's. 'But the social scene is fantastic!'

The barmaid disentangled herself from her admirer with practiced ease. She'd taken up bartending on Thursday Island, she said, because there was less harassment than working as a cook on a trawler. 'People keep asking me, with all these men about, how do you choose between them? Truth is, I don't touch any of them. It'd probably cause a riot if I just chose one.'

A more inebriated fellow expat, in her fifties, with a burned-out cigarette butt balanced in her mouth, pressed forward from the murk. 'We're all going out on the boat tomorrow,' she breathed, 'for a picnic by the beach. Why don't you come along? There'll be just three women. And a dog.'

Before I could think of an excuse, two Filipino gals climbed over the boatrails, to a raucous welcome from the party. Time to slip off to my hotel, I decided — if I can ever find it.

'It's not your *average* tropical paradise,' the only person I knew who'd ever been to Thursday Island had told me before I left Sydney. At the Ansett check-in, the baggage attendant was less diplomatic. 'What are you going to that place for? There's nothing there!' she gasped. 'Just four pubs and a meat pie shop. You can't even go swimming. All you can do is drink.'

It was a long story. Back in New York, I'd been contacted by two kayakers who were going to try and circumnavigate Australia. It seemed a suicidal project. Did they know what they were getting themselves into? They swore that they did. They had some publicity and sponsorship for the trip, probably because they were such an unlikely pair. Tony was an Australian, a successful fashion model in the States; Eric was a New York party animal, who used to train with JFK Junior and Calvin Klein. They would make an impressive square-jawed sight in a kayak. It soon turned out that an American magazine was willing to send me back home for a story — if I could ever locate them. They'd started from Sydney some weeks before.

Via a series of obscure messages through Tony's model agency in Sydney, I got a call from a Thursday Island pub. Eric had to shout over some blood-curdling crashes and howls in the background; luckily, he said, he could talk as long as he liked because somebody had head-butted the public phone and it no longer accepted change. 'Come on up,' he said, a little too eagerly. 'It's wild up here.'

The truth was, I'd always wanted to get to T.I. — the end of the line and all that. Somerset Maugham made a point of going there when he visited Australia in 1921. 'I do not think that many people have been to Thursday Island,' Maugham wrote in his short story *French Joe*. 'They told me in Sydney that it was the last place God ever made. They said that there was nothing to see and warned me that I should probably get my throat cut.'

Its reputation, at least, hadn't really changed.

I soon found out why the Ansett attendant had looked at me so strangely. Flying to Cairns took five hours; from there, it was another two hours in a small propeller plane. ('Please sit down the back,' the hostess begged, 'or we won't be able to clear the runway.') Cape York unfurled below, looking brown and bare after the lushness around Cairns. Finally we landed on Horn Island in the sweltering Torres Strait, where a ferry left for Thursday.

The only other passenger was a woman who had been offered a job as a doctor on T.I. She was going to check the place out first. 'I don't think I'm going to fancy it,' she told me hesitantly, wiping rivers of perspiration from her neck. 'I hear it's not … ah …'

' … your *average* tropical paradise?'

'Mmmmm.'

And, when T.I. emerged, it certainly wasn't. The bay was a brilliant turquoise, but there were bilious mudflats instead of beach; scrub where the flowing palm trees should have been. In place of sea-shells glittered shards of broken glass: islanders throw their empty stubbies into the sea, apparently, and the waves smash them and send them back to shore. A peculiar side-effect of this is that everyone on the island wears plastic jelly-babies on their feet, so they can hop in and out of the water at will. And so were the first islanders I saw waiting at the wharf — four huge, pear-shaped figures, with enormous heads of tangled hair, all wearing these cute little pink sandals.

It wasn't the sort of thing to kid them about, though. Torres Strait islanders are Melanesians, and their strong brows make most of the men look, quite accidentally, like they're extremely pissed off. In fact, these guys looked as if they'd happily rip my arms off as soon as talk to me. So I *very* politely asked them where the Federal Hotel was. Their angry expressions dissolved, and they pointed to a spot a mile or so along the waterfront. 'No worries. Hop in. We'll give you a lift.'

They talked for a while in Torres Strait Creole then turned to me. 'You're not looking for those kayakers, are you?'

'Yep. Do you know them?'

'Oh, yeah. Mad bloody bastards.' And they all broke up laughing.

At five in the afternoon, the Federal's public bar already looked like Darwin's dreaded Cage at midnight. It was a functional shell of a place, built for serious drinking. The only decoration was a painted mural, showing a fisherman who had caught two mermaids: he's pushing away the traditional version, who has the upper body of a woman and the lower body of a fish, in favour of one with a woman's legs and the upper body of a giant green cod. A boozer at the bar saw me examining it and helpfully explained, 'You don't fuck a face, eh?' In the corner, half a dozen islanders in stubbies and singlets were standing around a pool table, pushing one another and yelling over the sound of a blaring TV. A couple looked like they were about to lay into each other but were being restrained by some mates.

'It's gonna be a big night,' said Charlie Hawkins, the wiry pub owner who moved here long ago from Cairns, as he manoeuvred me out to the office.

'Things look they can get kind of ... lively,' I said, trying not to sound too overwhelmed. 'Do you get a lot of trouble?'

'Trouble?' he looked at me as if he didn't quite get what I meant. 'Nah. It's all pretty quiet really.'

When I got back into the bar, the two kayakers were there. They were both a bit the worse for wear, sun-scorched and wind-blown. Tony the Australian had planned and financed the expedition; he had a model's sculpted features, but also these wild eyes, like Rasputin's. Eric the New Yorker was stocky, a little melancholy, with a grizzled beard — more like a frazzled Robin Williams. It was only by chance the pair were still on T.I., it turned out. Their electronic Nautilus compass, which guides from the stars, had packed it in, and without it they'd never make it across the open seas of the Gulf of Carpentaria.

As I warily nursed a beer, watching the growing pandemonium in the pub, I must have looked a bit open-mouthed.

'This place intimidated the hell out of us when we first arrived,' Tony shouted over the droning TV. 'I mean, we didn't have anywhere to put our equipment, and when we tried to sleep on the beach, there were all these huge drunken guys staggering about all night.'

'We thought we were gonna die,' Eric agreed.

'But then this butcher who lives next door to the pub said we could stay in his yard. Everyone's turned out to be extremely friendly. Nothing to worry about.'

And the night continued, if not quietly, then without any disaster. The boozing was nothing short of prodigious, and every half hour or so it looked like a major brawl was about to break out. But nothing happened. The arguments were like minor pantomimes, coming to a few shoves and pushes, but with the combatants always restrained before actually coming to blows. Soon the whole place was swaying to a pub band — classic rock with a Hawaiian guitar twang — until the crack of 11.30.

'Last drinks!' screeched the English barmaid, and everyone grabbed three O.P. Bundy-and-cokes a head.

'Take aways!' came the next call, and everyone bought half a dozen Bundy-and-coke tinnies.

'Thursday night's lively,' said Charlie, as I wandered upstairs to my room. '*Friday* night's livelier.'

From the wide pub balcony, I watched the police paddy-wagon make a slow pass by, with some of the boozers jeering at them. But, again, nothing happened. Everyone just went home.

Next morning I padded out to the balcony again and peered through the mango trees to Torres Strait. I couldn't make out the tip of Cape York in the distance, but there were a few of the other islands. The Tuesday islets, Wednesday, Friday — legend has it that they were named by Captain Bligh, day by day, as he navigated towards Timor in his open longboat, having been tossed from the *Bounty* in 1789. The truth is, he probably only named Wednesday. It was the obscure Captain Owen Stanley, on the 1848 survey on HMS *Rattlesnake*, who named the others. In fact, Thursday was originally called Friday, and vice-versa; a minor clerk in the British Admiralty in London swapped them so that the days of the week read more tidily, from east to west.

I went down to Douglas Street to join a nuggetty former schoolteacher named Bill Nelson as he gave his daily tour of the island. Not that there's too much to see: apart from the one stretch of shops, much of the island is taken up by suburban housing for the 3,500 inhabitants. Expensive real estate it is too, with most houses going at around a quarter million a piece. Further building has been banned by the government, driving prices sky-high.

The recent history of T.I. is a shifting pattern of deportations arranged by white settlers. The early Torres Strait islanders were a fearsome bunch, famed for charging passing gunboats in their slender wooden canoes. When Queenslanders finally claimed Thursday, they packed its inhabitants off to a mission station on the mainland and built the four tropical pubs that still sit at intervals along the waterfront. Somerset Maugham stayed in the Grand when he visited in 1921 and wrote the short story *French Joe* there. A few years later, Douglas Fairbanks dined at the hotel with his wife during a round-the-world sailing trip.

By the 1930s, hundreds of Japanese pearl fishermen had moved to T.I., staying until the Second World War — when they too were deported, to internment camps in New South Wales. The memorial to their presence is a serene Shinto graveyard, not far from a fortress built to stave off the expected Japanese invasion. But although nearby Horn island airstrip was bombed in 1942, nobody on T.I. fired a shot in anger.

It was only after the war that the original islanders were allowed to return to Thursday from the mission stations. Even then, there were many restrictions (pubs could only serve whites until the 1970s, for example). Today the Torres Strait is a self-contained nautical community, with islanders slipping by outboard motorboat from one to the other for work and study. The currents are fierce, and I ended up hearing several stories of fishermen being sucked out to the Timor Sea when their engines packed it in, never to be seen again.

The dozen or so others on Willie Nelson's tour were mostly pensioners who had come up through Cape York in four-wheel drives. That made more sense, I supposed, than flying here directly; but most of them only crossed over to T.I. for a few hours, which seemed a pity. Sure, there was technically nothing to do on T.I, but there was a feeling of complete detachment here, a glutinous calm that demanded some time to appreciate. As a grocery store clerk, who was from Brisbane, poetically summed it up, 'This place grows on you. Like a fucking tropical fungus.'

It was probably the perfect setting to interview the two mad kayakers. I met them again in one of the milkbars on Douglas Street (on a section once known as Florie Kennedy's Miracle Mile — according to Eric Hansen, who spent time here in the sixties, it was a miracle if you made it from the back door of the Grand to Florie's boarding house without passing out or being beaten to a pulp). They'd had their Nautilus compass fixed at last, and were getting ready to head due west. To make up time, they were going to cut directly across the Gulf to Darwin.

They had started from Bondi Beach some three months earlier, they recounted, paddling twelve hours a day then camping on the beach. The 3,000 kilometres so far was about a quarter of the total round-Australia odyssey — and by far the easiest stretch, they knew. Just in case anyone is contemplating a similar excursion, here are a few pointers from Eric and Tony:

* What problems should you expect? *Serious* saddle sores. The kayak overturning in heavy surf. Freak waves washing away navigational maps. Once they camped on a sand spit that almost disappeared on the rising tide (they woke up to find themselves with only two metres of land left). Wild pigs chewing holes in the kayak. And talking of tropical fungi, Tony once contracted an exotic growth underneath his fingernails …

* Animal encounters? Dolphins. Sea turtles. Sharks circling the kayak. Giant crocs in the mangroves of Cape York, eyeballing them with sinister intent. Rainbow coloured (and deadly) sea-snakes floating by. And mosquitoes. Millions of them, all along the Queensland coast. Every night they rugged up with three layers of clothes and a net — forty degree temperatures or not.

* Human encounters? Perhaps won over by the lunatic nature of the project, people were pretty helpful en route. For example, after six days straight without seeing anyone, they ran into a coal miner named Finny at Frog Water Sound. He threw them a barbecue of his afternoon fishing catch and force-fed them beer until they passed out on the beach. Passing yacht crews would give them beer and supplies in mid-sea. At the lowest ebb of their morale — near Bundaberg, when everything seemed to be going wrong — a couple of cane-cutters invited them home so they could have showers and a meal of fresh mud-crabs.

* How do you stop from killing one another? Their advice was not to try this with an old friend. 'We've gotten to see each other in times of *extreme* stress,' said Eric, a little warily, 'so we've learned to accept things about each other that might have broken up an older, already formed friendship.' Tony nodded cautiously. 'It's like being Siamese twins.' Eric added, 'Worse than being married.' I got the impression it wasn't easy.

* The big question: why? The because-it's-there sense of achievement; the moments of transcendent beauty on the Reef; and all the time you get to philosophise. Eric: 'Kayaking is like moving meditation. When conditions are good, paddling is a very therapeutic motion, so you start to

feed off your memory and review the events of your life.'
Tony: 'Everybody needs time off to assess things, and a
week at the beach just isn't enough.'

Charlie was right about Friday night on Thursday Island.

'Fancy a XXXX or ten?' The kayakers were up for one last
pub crawl, so we did the rounds. Back at the Federal, all the
nurses on T.I. were showing a new recruit from Melbourne the
ropes. All she had to say for herself was, 'I've drunk too much, I
want to go to sleep,' but the others dragged her along anyway
when the news went round about the party on the fishing
trawler.

The boat was moored at the end of the pier, but you still
had to leap a few feet over the water and clamber up the side.
The new nurse mustn't have been thinking too clearly; she
decided to grip her beer bottle in her mouth when she made the
jump, and she went straight into the side of the boat.

'Oh, Christ, I've chipped my teeth!' she was crying when
they dragged her up the side. Lucky she was in the company of
nurses. 'Bundy!' they prescribed. 'Bundy-and-coke!' They fed her
a medicinal bottle — O.P., of course — chuckling away. 'You
won't forget your first night on T.I., that's for sure.'

And so it went until the first streaks of pink began to cross
the sky. When I finally escaped back to the Federal, I stood on
the balcony, listening to the sounds of the debauch still being
carried across the water by that rotting-mango breeze.

Well, maybe T.I. wasn't your average tropical paradise, I
figured. It was a lot more entertaining than that.

POSTSCRIPT

A few weeks later, I received a message from the kayakers, Eric and Tony. They'd made it across the Gulf of Carpentaria, but only just. It had taken days, battling constant monsoonal waves up to three metres high. They'd managed five hours of sleep each in the whole 120-hour passage. Contemplating the uninhabited Kimberley Coast that lay ahead, they called it quits. You could hardly blame them.

Old World New York

In Jack Finney's time-travelling classic, *Time and Again*, the main character took a suite in New York's eerie, turreted Dakota building so that he could gaze out at the sculpted grounds of Central Park. Since this was one of the few Manhattan views that hadn't changed in the last century, he could mentally transport himself back to the 1880s. These days, you can hardly get near the Dakota for all the tourists trying to photograph the exact spot where John Lennon was shot, and if you stop for too long in Central Park to breathe in the historical aura, you'll probably be run into by someone learning to rollerblade. If you want to make any imaginative leaps into the past, I soon found, you're better off staying downtown.

That's where you realise that, for an island so devoted to Mammon and the future, there's a surprising amount of Manhattan that lingers from the past. You have to approach it like an archaeologist at a well-scoured dig, or an art restorer stripping back layers of paint. The place may be in constant tumult — remaking its entire topography every two decades or so — but on any given day, you can come across some forgotten relic intact amongst the typhoon debris of New York living.

Rarely is this detritus quaint, or even very pleasant. Just down on Tenth Street, for example, sit the Turkish Baths — opened in 1892 and now the last bath house on the island. The guests are almost all old Russians, and the whole place oozes the sort of tineal grime you associate with the shower room floors of the Bondi Pavilion. The only modern touch is the exorbitant fee (US$25 just to get past the snarling door attendant; the same if you want to whip yourself with birch leaves; and twice as much again for a massage from some steroid-powered Georgian weightlifter). Old men sit in corners, clearing their noses onto the floor and spitting down clogged drains. If that sounds gross, just make sure you go on the 'co-ed' days. On single-sex days, the russkis go naked and really let it all hang out.

For more evocative meanderings, the best handbook is Luc Sante's *Low Life*, about the New York underworld of the nineteenth century. It's not a guide in any standard sense, but it's the only way to learn that a few doors away, on the corner of Tenth Street and First Avenue, sat McLaughlin's Bear Pit, where the noble sport of bear-baiting continued until the time of the Civil War (long after most other local bars had turned to rat-baiting, rodents being in much readier supply). How else to learn that the last tenement house standing on Bowery and First Street was once called McGurk's Suicide Hall? The bottom-rung brothel in New York, it earned its nickname from the stream of battered prostitutes who kept flinging themselves in despair from its windows. Such was the building's fame that it was even included in scenic tours of Manhattan for out-of-towners in the 1890s.

Sante's book shows that life in Old New York could be just as nasty, brutish, short and drug-addled as it is in its present incarnation. The waiters at McGurk's carried koshes and chloral hydrate for unruly sailor clients, and if they didn't work there was always the head bouncer, Eat-'Em-Up Jack McManus. In those days, New York wasn't known as the Big Apple — it was the Big Onion or, to Bowery denizens, the Big Smear.

And the city's notorious squalor and splendour have always co-existed cheek by jowl. Still standing only one hundred metres away from McGurk's, at 29 East Fourth, is one of the era's finest buildings: the Old Merchant's House, built by a fabulously wealthy trading family in 1831. Who knows how the venerable Tredwells reacted to the wandering morphine addicts and beggars who trailed past their door? (Much the same way Park Avenue denizens do now, one imagines: by learning to see through them.) Today the Old Merchant's House is Manhattan's only fully furnished home left from the nineteenth century. Uniquely for New York, this gilt-edged world has been preserved as a museum: the austere Puritan portraits, the velvet furniture, the Persian carpets, are all intact. More typically for New York, the preservation has been achieved entirely by volunteer work and donations, as the Old Merchant's House is perennially on the verge of being sold off. Across a vacant lot at number 37 is a mansion built the same year as the Merchant's House: it has been boarded up, burglarised and burned out once every few months for as long as anyone can remember. Which is how the city cares for any fragment of the past that doesn't turn a profit.

To observe the power of commerce, visit New York's oldest saloon, McSorley's, around the corner on Seventh Street. Opened in 1854, it still sports sawdust on the floor and tables hacked raw by graffiti; the kitchen serves corn beef hash, and the Irish waiters will bring two draught beers for every one you order. By night, businessmen line up outside to get in, turning the bar into a hellish maelstrom; but by day it's all but empty. As the winter sun streams through the windows, you can spend an idle moment looking over the boxing photos from the 1890s, hung in dusty abandon on the walls (and if you tell them that the great Yankee Sullivan was actually an Australian whose real name was James Ambrose, nobody will believe you).

Some relics are alive and kicking further south, again because they make good money. Down on Houston Street, the vast 1940s-era dining room of Katz's Delicatessen is still serving Jewish treats as if cholesterol had never been discovered (the lunch special: three hot dogs, a bowl of French fries and sauerkraut for $4.99). A war-era sign reads: *Send a Salami to your Boy in the Army*. Head south down Orchard Street, once the jugular of the Jewish community; the star of David can still be spotted on the sides of buildings, painted over with cable TV ads. Even Little Italy — New York's most ravenous tourist trap — has a bar unchanged since the thirties, called Mare Chiaro (it's at 176½ Mulberry).

Following Manhattan's perverse rule of thumb, the oldest part of the island has its fewest historical traces. The warren of village lanes around Wall Street, built by the Dutch in the 1600s as New Amsterdam, was reinvented in stone for the 1920s and glass for the eighties. Which adds a certain poignancy to tiny Fraunces Tavern: this little building on the corner of Pearl and Broad — overshadowed by skyscrapers on every side — was built in 1762 by the independence-minded Samuel Fraunces, who became George Washington's official cook. He had to flee when Manhattan was taken by the redcoats, but returned in triumph — and served Washington's farewell dinner for his generals in the upstairs lounge. Today the place has a museum, a bar full of stuffed animals and mahogany, and a thriving, pricey restaurant (which serves up, amongst other things, clam chowder from a 1789 recipe and a three-course colonial meal). The only sites of comparable atmosphere are the cemetery near Trinity Church, and the newly-uncovered 'black cemetery', where slaves were buried.

Up until the 1850s, Manhattan's urban sprawl barely extended past 14th Street, and it was not until the 1930s that the skyscraper icons of Midtown came to define 'New York, New York'. Even then, that part of the city has always gleefully knocked down anything that has stood in the way of office space; a few years ago, despite popular protests and petitions from Woody Allen, the city's last Automat was turned into a Gap clothing store. These Depression-era, Art Deco institutions were the first and last word in self-serve: you'd put a quarter into the wall, turn a beautifully crafted silver knob, and your cup would be filled with steaming, watery coffee. A few more quarters and you could choose from a wall full of sandwiches and bagels kept safely behind tiny glass doors. They weren't very good — in fact, they were often stale — but many old New Yorkers used to hang out there. Sadly, not many others were so sentimental, and it went broke.

But still ... in Midtown, there's the foyer of the Chrysler building to examine, the old binoculars at the top of the Empire State, the underground Oyster Bar in Grand Central Station. Wander over to the west side at 46th Street and 11th Avenue, where the 1844 Landmark Tavern stands in Hell's Kitchen. A century ago, it was a waterfront bar of the seediest type, where the unwary would have their beers drugged, and the victims dropped through a trapdoor directly into the Hudson River. Over the years, landfill has bloated Manhattan: the waterline is a hundred yards away now, behind freeways and fenced-off lots. Down at the wharf on 42nd Street, the Circle Line ferries depart for their round-the-island tour, as they have since 1945. Many of the guides are still retired old actors from Broadway, and ham their tours up shamelessly. Sadly, the sound systems are so bad that many of their finest *bons mots* are lost to the wind.

Further north in Manhattan are the residential suburbs that were thrown up in the later nineteenth century. The Dakota, where Jack Finney's character started his time-travels, is the oldest (it got its name because, in the 1880s, it was so far away from the rest of Manhattan that you were said to be living 'in the Dakotas'). But the Upper West Side, like the Upper East, has fewer secret histories, less shameful layers of vice, no ghostly historical life.

High Noon in

Venezuela

In the sun-baked plaza of San Fernando de Apure, beside a concrete fountain adorned with alligators rampant, I met up with the Argentine photographer Eduardo and our Venezuelan *llanero* driver, a truly bovine ranch hand named Juan.

It was well before dawn, and in the steaming darkness Eduardo lost no time telling me what he thought of this country.

'Venezuelans are entirely vacuous,' he muttered *sotto voce*. 'They're vapid. Superficial. Hopelessly Americanised.' Eduardo was a classic Buenos Aires intellectual, short and balding, with a regal silver beard, and his words tumbled out with an Italianate urgency; he nodded at Juan, who was pumping petrol into the Landrover. 'They have no understanding of themselves, or why they do things. They are entirely — ' here he grasped for the ultimate Argentine insult — *'un-self-reflective.'*

Juan, true, was no paragon of intellect. He was nearly seven foot tall, cumbersome, with a neck like a steer's. For the first three hours, he never said a word, just stared ahead at the narrow road that cut straight across the pancake-flat Llanos — the vast, empty cattle plains that were once the heartland of

Venezuela. The sky turned pale; hot air blasted in through the gaping holes where the jeep's doors should have been. Finally, overcome by the tedium, I decided to engage old Juan in conversation. The only scenery had been a few different road signs outside cattle ranches, some called Fincas and some called Fundas, so I asked if there was a difference between them.

'*Si, señor,*' Juan nodded seriously.

'There is?' I asked.

'Of course.'

'Oh, yes?'

'Definitely a difference.'

Eduardo, sitting between us, closed his eyes and slowly sank into his seat. I wondered how long this could go on.

'So there is a difference between a *funda* and a *finca?*'

'*Si, señor.*'

'There is a difference?'

'Certainly.'

Obviously, this conversation could go on forever.

'OK — so what is it?'

'What?'

'The difference?'

'Between …'

'A *funda* and a *finca.*'

'Well … ' Juan pondered this for a minute, 'there are more horses on one than the other.'

Eduardo let out an involuntary groan. '*Ese hombre,*' he fumed when we stopped again for petrol, 'that man does not even know he exists. He's an animal.'

By eight in the morning, the hallucinatory heat had already descended on the Llanos when we pulled into a muddy little village called Mantecal, and entered the Wild West of the tropics.

Slouching on every street corner were clusters of *llaneros*, or Venezuelan cowboys — machetes on their hips instead of six-shooters, thumbs hooked into their jeans, straw hats cocked low over their eyes. While Juan worked on the car engine, I wandered with Eduardo inside the town's main bar — a shed with a sauna-level temperature, no chairs and salsa music distorting over the radio. The few mangy patrons watched us with the same fixed, vacant gaze that the rest of the world reserves for evening television. Meanwhile, the bargirl kept up her end of the show. She sent our morning beers sliding from one end of the counter to the other, without spilling a drop. The question was: did these people naturally act like this or had they just seen *The Magnificent Seven* a few too many times?

Anywhere else in Venezuela, the thought wouldn't be quite so frivolous. It was true what Eduardo said about Americanisation. Since the discovery of oil in 1922, the country has become the most *yanqui*-fied spot in all South America, accepting Cadillacs, fast food and baseball as if, just by imitation, it might become the fifty-first state of the Union. The capital Caracas, where I'd just spent two weeks, was clogged with skyscrapers, toxic smog and eternal traffic jams. But the Llanos were turning out to be a Venezuelan anomaly, a decaying wasteland left behind in a nineteenth century cocoon.

It was the *llanero* mythology that had lured me here, at the tail end of an assignment to this petro-republic. In one way, these remote plains mean the same to Venezuelans as the Outback does to Australians or the Wild West to Americans — they're a legendary frontier, a sacred forging ground of the 'national character', which most people, clustered along the coastline, would never actually visit. But in Latin America, the frontier is also a heart of darkness. The Llanos drives settlers to insanity and suicide; here Civilisation withers and Barbarity thrives.

And we were heading to the very fountainhead of the frontier legend: Hato La Trinidad de Arauca. This cattle ranch was the setting for one of South America's classic novels, *Doña Barbara*, a melodramatic and bleakly sexist work about a *llanero* woman, Barbara, who was gang-raped as a teenager and who spends her life taking vengeance on all men. Combining threats of witchcraft with seductiveness and cruelty, she becomes the de facto empress of the hitherto male-dominated Llanos — until an incorruptible man from the big city awakens her feminine instincts and causes her downfall (she falls into a swamp and is dragged down by poisonous snakes, in a deluge of phallic imagery — a fitting end for a textbook of machismo).

Eduardo had heard that the ranch was now letting people stay overnight. But paying a visit to this peculiar outpost wasn't easy. From Mantecal (we finally prised out of Juan), it would be another eight hours' drive, arrow-straight across the savanna. With little conversational distraction.

And the plains stretched on, hour after hour …

In the wet season, the Llanos are flooded so that they look like an inland sea; in the dry, the sun blasts them into a desert, and classic photographs show the bones of dead cattle whitening on the cracked jigsaw earth. We were travelling between the seasons: the expanse was covered by ponds full of pink birds called coro-coros and the three metre long caimans, known as *bavos*, sunning themselves in the mud. When Alexander von Humboldt passed by in the late eighteenth century, he found 'something awful ... in the uniform aspect of these steppes. All around us, the plains seem to ascend to the sky, like an ocean covered with seaweed.' (Von Humboldt would never forget the Llanos; he accidentally trod on an electric eel here and walked with a slight limp for the rest of his life.) In *Doña Barbara*, Romulo Gallegos was similarly encouraging: 'The *llanura* is beautiful and terrifying at the same time,' he wrote, adding enigmatically that the terror it induced was 'hot, like the great wind of its sunburnt immensity, like the fever from its swamps'.

As we trundled on, the overcast sky pressed down on us like a blanket of wet cotton wool. On the rare occasions when we saw humans, they were asleep. Indians dozed in the shadows of wooden shacks. Semi-trailers were pulled over at the roadsides, their drivers taking siestas in hammocks slung beneath the chassis.

For a break, Eduardo decided to get out and photograph some of the exotic caimans. We left Juan in the car and crept along the side of the road with telephoto lenses at the ready. But whenever we moved ahead, Juan would start the car and follow a few yards behind us. Eduardo frantically motioned for Juan to turn off the engine. He did, but only until we moved a few feet further on. At last, frightened by the noise, the *bavos* flicked up their tails and disappeared into the water.

Under the circumstances, Eduardo took it remarkably well. 'You see? You see?' he declared triumphantly. 'The man is like a mushroom. Barely alive.'

Finally, the gates of the *hato* appeared, opened by three *llaneros* on horseback carrying antique carbines.

After so many hours on the monotonous plains, the ranch house rose like an apparition from Orlando, glistening white and pastel pink, surrounded by swaying palm trees. Closer inspection only added to the disorienting effect. Embedded almost unnoticeably in the masonry were tiny, inch-high figures of Jesus and Mary. There was an elaborate garden, with caged exotic creatures like ant-eaters, chameleons and capybaras (water-going rodents that the local Catholic Church once declared were fish so that they could be eaten on Fridays). A dog kennel had porcelain animals balanced on it. And in the middle of the greenery was an airplane propeller, twisted by an accident into the form of a giant four-leafed tulip, then set on a pillar as a sculpture.

'*Bienvenidos, los periodistas!* The journalists! Welcome!'

Sidling out to meet us was the ranch's current owner, Dr Hugo Estrada. He was in his late fifties, thick-set, silver-haired and bespectacled; his canary tropical shirt and baseball cap gave away an upbringing far from the Llanos. There seemed something over-eager about the garrulous way he shook our hands and slapped Juan on the back. Still, he was a generous host, taking us to the open air dining room, dishing us out great jugs of fresh tamarind and announcing the family scandals with disarming speed.

He told us straight off the bat that he was a doctor in law who, in late middle age, had given up a lucrative practice in Caracas to salvage the ancestral property from disaster. 'My father was responsible for all this,' he said, nodding wryly towards the mansion and its fairytale appendages. 'He was an old man. He liked to write poetry. Saw himself as an artist, a writer like Gallegos. And so he paid more attention to the house than to the farm. That would not have been so bad. But poetry and business do not mix. There was a precipitous decline.'

In the space of a few years, he explained, the property went from owning 18,000 head of cattle to 3,000.

'People who said they were his friends were stealing things from under his nose — cattle, guns, fertiliser, anything! — and he simply did not care. Why would he? He was old. Finally, the family was forced to take legal proceedings to declare him incompetent.' Dr Estrada looked at us both with a peculiar smile. 'There was nothing else we could do.'

All around were signs that the famous heat and loneliness of the Llanos had pushed the old man over the edge. The *pièce de resistance* was definitely the 'Ship of Stones' — a ten metre long hull, built of bricks, sitting there in the middle of the garden with dozens of large turtles inside it. This had apparently been inspired by a famous Venezuelan poem of the same name. Watching the turtles languidly climbing over one another in the mud, Eduardo whispered, 'If García Márquez had invented this place, it would be hailed as a stroke of fantastic genius.'

'My father was a little out of control,' Hugo explained, now almost sheepishly. I had this image of the elder Estrada gazing out his bedroom window at his Ship of Stones as it cruised across the plains — a doddering Kurtz out here in the Llanos, cut off from the rest of the world and exercising absolute power in his small domain. It might not have been quite a descent into barbarity, but it was close enough in his family's eyes.

But then Dr Estrada changed the subject — to his recent trip to Argentina. 'Such a beautiful country, but what a fuck-up. I couldn't believe the inflation when I was there. Or the violence. The crime!' He eyed us both disingenuously. 'Say, neither of you two are Argentines are you?'

Eduardo's expression became fixed — his *porteño* accent was very pronounced, and he knew what was coming. Estrada set off on a stream of Argentine jokes. What's a quick way to make a fortune? Buy an Argentine for what he's worth and sell him for what he thinks he's worth. Did you hear about the Argentine who came to Caracas? He went to climb a mountain so that he could see what the city looked like without him ... I'd already heard these witticisms three times before myself — the canon was invented by Venezuelans to mock Argentine arrogance. Eduardo must have heard them a hundred times, but he endured them with a stoic expression, his knuckles slowly whitening. But Dr Estrada was enjoying himself. After all, where else could we go?

'There is something very strange about that man,' Eduardo muttered, as we were putting our bags in one of the spare rooms. 'It's not just the jokes — every Venezuelan comes out with those sooner or later. There's something fake. And I think he may already be drunk.' I had to admit that Dr Estrada made me uneasy too, especially the way he would stare at you with an expectant look after he made his odd confessions, half-grinning to himself. You had no idea what he was thinking.

Next morning, the good doctor took us to visit the grave of La Señora Fransisca Vazquez de Carilla — the historical woman upon whom Doña Barbara was based.

Señora Vazquez's no doubt sadly defamed history is shrouded in mystery; she was regarded as a witch, and her property known as El Miedo, Fear. The story goes that she was buried here with a fabulous treasure around the turn of the century — but a curse meant that the tomb was not violated until 1986. (Of course, it's said that the two grave-robbers, who found nothing, have since had reason to regret their actions.) Dr Estrada made restoring the tomb his first order of business when he took over the farm. For good measure, he built a replica of a nineteenth century ranch house, and polished up a memorial plaque left by the famous Mexican actress who played Doña Barbara in a 1942 film.

Over the next couple of days, we observed the macho culture that has ruled unchallenged in the Llanos since the Señora's death. Riding barefoot around the farm were small groups of *llaneros*. Like the *gauchos* of Argentina, they became famous as horsemen in the South American wars of independence — *llaneros* were the backbone of the army that Simon Bolívar led from Caracas down through Colombia, Ecuador, Peru and the high Andes of Bolivia. They were a ferocious bunch, living from what they pillaged, using sharpened palm stalks as lances. Haunting *llanero* ballads are now a part of Venezuela's folk history, their lyrics ritually invoking famous knife fights, bouts of boozing, supposed sexual conquests or skill at breaking horses.

But here on the ranch, the *llanero* culture was looking a bit threadbare. Most wore polyester trousers and shirts, with the ubiquitous straw hat (although some preferred construction hard hats for some reason). Despite the staggering heat, a few had on thick woollen ponchos ('Against the rain,' one explained with a shrug). Still, shabby as they were, as horsemen, the *llaneros* lived up to their legend. You could watch them rounding up the longhorn cattle around the ranch with their lassoes, and indulging in an odd branding ritual: for some reason unrelated to efficiency, they swing a bull to the ground by its tail.

Another Old World ritual was hand-milking the cows. A doddering farmer with flaming muttonchop whiskers and great warts over his neck rhythmically chanted each beast's nickname and gently rubbed its back to relax it. *P-u-u-u-ta, p-u-u-u-t-a*, he sung to one — whore in Spanish — as he eased his milking stool into position. To another: *Gold mine ... gold mine ... you're so ugly today, looks like you woke up at three in the morning ...* All morning, his fourteen year old wife gazed on with dreamy, translucent green eyes.('They had to marry when she became pregnant,' Dr Estrada explained. 'Old men marrying young girls is still the custom in the Llanos. She's very happy I hear,' he added, somewhat defensively.)

The big lure of the Llanos — which Dr Estrada hoped would bring some paying guests — was the wildlife. Apart from jaguars, caimans, capybaras and the odd anaconda, there are more bird species in this one province than the whole of North America and Great Britain combined. Driving about randomly, we rode over a shallow crest to find a lagoon full of coro-coros sieving for food, before they disappeared in a graceful cloud. Until recently, flamingo feathers were one of the area's most valuable exports — on one occasion, seven men were killed transporting a single feather shipment before it arrived in San Fernando for sale — but today the birds are protected. Dr Estrada proudly announced that one of his employees had only just been fined three months' wages for catching and eating half a dozen birds.

All this seemed well and good. But after a long day's riding around the property, Estrada wanted to show us one of his own more personal projects: a five metre tall statue of Jesus, imported at huge cost from Italy. Standing there in the middle of nowhere, made of concrete, arms outstretched, it was like the famous Christ above Rio de Janeiro.

'*Muy interessante*,' Eduardo nodded soberly, giving me a sideways glance; he moved off, pretending to take some photos.

Many years ago, the doctor explained, some children on the *hato* had a vision of a figure in flowing white robes, with a halo. It happened many times, but because the figure was wearing a dress, everyone thought it was the Virgin Mary. 'Soon the children began to report that the Virgin had a *beard*,' he said, excitedly. 'And so of course everyone realised that the figure was Jesus.'

I thought this was a punchline at first. But no, he was serious. And there was more. Little statues of angels had been put on each corner of the base, with their faces painted a different shade to represent an Indian, a black, a white and a mix-raced *mestizo*. It was a vision of racial harmony, Estrada said, inspired by a pop record called *Píntame Angelitos Negros* — 'Paint Me Little Black Angels' — which tells how a painter on a religious fresco was asked by God to colour the faces black.

I must have looked a bit baffled by it all, because Estrada changed tack again. He gave me an epic poem he'd written about Doña Barbara, running for twenty-three stanzas, in Spanish and English.

A thousand men I did use
And all of them I threw out,
For none of them ever served
To tie the lace of my boots.

It was a man like my father
That I always really wanted:
Strong, hard, straight and wholesome,
And that ... I could never find.

It was another stifling night in the Llanos, and giant bats were swooping low out of the trees. At dinner, Dr Estrada seemed quite drunk. He was in a sentimental mood, and started to lament the passing of the 1970s — when he was a younger man, the ranch was turning a profit and Venezuela, bloated on petrol revenues, was one of the richest countries on earth. It had the strongest economy in Latin America, and the most stable democracy. But since the oil crash of the 1980s, all the familiar Latin problems had come crashing down — hyper-inflation, devaluation, coup attempts, food riots. Now only a miracle would stop Hato Doña Barbara from sinking further into its slough, Estrada confessed. Opening up the ranch to paying guests was really only a desperate act, the most recent sign of decay.

'In the old days, we *venezolanos* used to be the tourists, not the other way round,' he marvelled. 'The dollar was so cheap, we all just went to Miami to do our shopping. We'd get on the planes with empty suitcases and bring them back full! At dinner, we didn't bother with wine. Why should we? We drank imported whisky. Johnny Walker. Black Label!'

This nouveau riche crassness particularly appalled Eduardo. 'The problem with this country is that the money just fell from heaven. You never had to lift a finger for it. Now everything is in a mess, you have no idea what to do.'

'That may be,' Estrada sighed, looking chastened. 'What we need is another war in the Persian Gulf, to push up oil prices.'

I asked if he intended to keep living at the ranch.

'I will stay because the Llanos brings me peace of mind,' he said, without much conviction. 'I am committed to saving my inheritance. But my wife and children don't agree. They prefer to stay in town, in San Fernando.'

'Oh,' I said. 'I didn't know you were married.'

'Of course,' he shrugged. 'Why not?'

As Eduardo raised his eyebrows and disappeared, Dr Estrada took me by the arm and led me into the dimly-lit house. The air inside was stale. Artefacts were scattered around: a giant tortoise shell, blackened oil paintings, flamingo feathers. On a dresser stood faded photographs from the turn of the century, and a colour snapshot of his family.

'They prefer to look after the company office in San Fernando,' he smiled sadly. 'They say it's too quiet here at the *hato*. They like the distractions of the town.' His expression gave away that the family would really rather be back in the bustling, Americanised capital of Caracas, with its hamburger joints, discos and cinemas showing the latest romantic releases.

As we stood there in the yellow light, watching the great bugs beat themselves relentlessly against the lamp, half a dozen Indian kids had gathered by the door and window, staring at us in fascination. Dr Estrada waved at the bedraggled audience impatiently to go, but they ignored him. Exhausted, he just gave up and sat heavily into a wooden chair, fanning himself with a straw hat, muttering on and on about his ancestral duty. What did the family make of his poems, I wondered, or all the statues of angels and tending of graves? Perhaps they kept their distance from the *hato* for other reasons than boredom. Perhaps they were afraid that the good doctor was already following his father, and that not so long from now he would be building ships of stone in this crumbling outpost on the plains.

The Lease

Meanwhile, back in New York, the tenants in our apartment building were still behaving less like characters out of 'Seinfeld' than *Caligula*. The Scum Upstairs had reached a new pitch of loathsomeness, with their 5 a.m. sparring bouts provoking visits from the NYPD every second night. By day, the charming boyfriend had taken to kicking the pet dog around the apartment; the animal soon turned into a neurotic wreck, and started attacking people in the hallways. The genius girlfriend insisted on mopping the floor with buckets of water, sending rivers pouring into our apartment; she kept going at this until our ceiling plaster caved in. She also got into the habit of spitting on our fire escape. You'd hear her upstairs, sucking her throat clear, then a green oyster would come to rest outside our window ledge.

Why would one put up with all this? Why not find somewhere sane to live? One reason: this was a rent-stabilised apartment, and we'd just gotten our names on the lease — which in New York is like being elevated to the minor aristocracy.

The whole concept of 'rent-stabilisation' is an anomaly in this crucible of capitalism. Back in 1969, a small percentage of apartments in New

York had their rents fixed to stop landlords gouging tenants; by law, the rent could only go up two percent a year. While other rents, particularly in Manhattan, have exploded, these rent-controlled apartments plod along at prices far below their market value. What's more, you get the lease for life. This accounts for the number of ancient Ukrainians and Poles and Germans who have been able to live on in Manhattan, giving neighbourhoods their continuity and traditions. It also accounts for some uniquely New York real estate scams.

On East Tenth Street, we had fallen into one: the extremely common 'illegal sub-lease'.

The story — a familiar one to New Yorkers — went like this. Once upon a time, two musicians named John and Laura move into an old East Village tenement and get their names on the rental agreement. A decade later, they decide they've had enough of New York and want to move to Michigan, to set up a farm and live the bucolic life. Do they give up their apartment in Manhattan, which rents for the absurdly cheap price of $360 a month? No way! The place is a gold mine! They sub-lease it illegally, for $700. They clear $340 a month, all gravy.

Sordid as this may seem, pretty well any New Yorker is happy to pay that. On the open market, the apartment would be worth at least $1,000 a month. This was a bargain — so Les and I snapped the apartment up. All we had to do was deposit the money into John and Laura's bank account every month, and let them pay the rent. The landlord would be none the wiser.

Everyone was happy — for a while. We knew we were paying double, and after a couple of years the arrangement started to grate. We called Laura up in Michigan to ask for a reduction in the rent — to reduce their profit margin, so to speak — but she wasn't budging. Her voice went ice cold. 'Listen, Tony, here's the deal: we look on that apartment as a way to set ourselves up on the farm. If you don't want the place, there's a thousand people who do.' This was quite true, but they were making four grand a year out of us … yes, it began to grate.

✳

Since we'd moved in, the building had been bought by a new owner, one Emannuel Scarlatti. I'd met Manny several times and had to pretend that I was 'John' — so he wouldn't twig to the sub-lease and evict us all, as almost any New York slumlord would.

But Manny wasn't your typical slumlord. He was a real Long Island Italian — a character out of *Goodfellas* — about seven feet tall, with black hair, a black moustache and a black Porsche. And he had a Sicilian code of honour. He hated the building, hated doing repairs. But the main thing he hated, he always made clear, was tenants who *broke his balls*. He'd let people stay illegally if they didn't bother him. In fact, Manny would put up with anything, just so his balls stayed intact.

After a particularly useless conversation with Laura, I decided to go talk to him. It was in the middle of a thunderstorm when I heard Manny was in the building. I found him down with John the Super. They were both just sitting in John's apartment, silently smoking. The TV was on with the volume turned down; a soap opera bathed their sweaty faces in a white electric glow.

I sat down, feeling like I'd come to see the Godfather. 'Manny, there's something I want to tell you …'

Manny just sat there, listening to the story impassively. Peels of thunder were echoing in the background. Finally he just said slowly, 'So Tony — that's your name, right? Tony? — whadaya want me to do about it?'

'I don't know. Can you cancel their lease and give it to us?'

Manny rolled his eyes. 'It's not so easy.' He thought about that.

'Nothing is easy in this fucking city.'

John the Super chuckled. 'Oh, ain't that the truth. Brother.'

'Y'know,' Manny went on, 'I could really get a *hard-on* about all this.'

'You could?'

'Yeah. I could get a hard-on, and evict the both of you. You and this John and Laura in Michigan. But I'm not gonna do that. You never give me no problems. You're an OK guy ...'

'He pays the rent,' John threw in.

' ... so I tell you what I'm gonna do. I'll hand this over to my attorney. See what he says.'

I wondered if telling Manny had been such a great idea.

'Tony, huh?' he laughed, as I was leaving. 'Antonio.' I hoped he was thinking: good Italian name.

About a week later, Manny's attorney came up with a plan. He wrote a letter saying that they'd found out how the place was being illegally sub-leased, and that their 'legal relationship was terminated, as of now'. He sent the letter to us; we were supposed to forward it to Michigan.

It was a bluff. Legally, John and Laura's names couldn't be taken off the lease without a long court case, which in New York could take a year to eighteen months. This fed our most paranoid fantasies. What if they came back to New York and changed the locks while we were out? What if they tossed everything we owned into the street? What if they paid someone to break our legs?

Even if the bluff did work, there was no obligation for Manny to give us the lease. So we sat there with this letter, wondering if it was worth the risk. We procrastinated for days. Finally, we took it away with us on a holiday in Maine. We were in some creepy little Stephen

King town when we decided to post it. We drove up to a mail box in an empty parking lot and just sat there, staring at the box, weighing the letter.

'Let's do it,' Les finally said. I opened the box and let the letter slide in. It closed with a tomb-like thud.

A week later in New York, there were two confused messages on our answering machine.

'Hello … this is Laura … we got the letter … we're … disappointed … you didn't call us to talk to us about it … ah … I don't know what you can do to stop the landlord … evicting you …' Cut.

Second message: 'This is Laura again … we're going to have to change the names on the electricity and gas … if it's no longer our apartment … we don't want the bills in our name …'

We were thunderstruck. They were just capitulating. Not even a whimper. I called them up and told them they had to write a letter to Manny, saying they were terminating the lease. I don't know why, but they just did it.

Manny came through with his end of the deal, as he promised. The lease arrived in the mail. After I'd signed it, I called him up for a talk. He was feeling magnanimous.

'I mean, a lotta landlords would not have been so understanding,' he said. 'I coulda taken everybody to court. It woulda been a bloodbath. But what's the point? You want to sleep easy, I want to sleep easy. Why get a hard-on?'

'Yeah,' I said, getting into the swing, 'why break your balls?'

'*Exactly,*' Manny said.

Hawaii's Last Hula

'You know you've arrived when you see your first naked hippy.'

That was the only advice a friend in New York had given me before I headed off to hike the Na Pali cliffs of Kauai. Somewhere at the end of this gruelling twenty kilometre trail — first carved by ancient Polynesians — was supposed to lie a Hawaiian Happy Valley called Kalalau. It was all a bit difficult to believe, though, at around kilometre eighteen. There I was, clinging to the vertical cliffside, blasted by hurricane-force winds, ravaged by the tropical sun, trying not to slide on volcanic rubble down 200 metre drops into the savage waves of the Pacific and generally feeling like a failed recruit on some Green Beret survival course ... and not a naked hippy in sight.

Oh, sure, there had been the odd clothed hippy, even a couple of barely-clad ones, bounding past like mountain goats in loose sandals, their packs mysteriously light. But the Promised Land of Kalalau never emerged from the series of fluted cliffs that continued ad infinitum into the salty horizon. A magnificent sight, without a doubt — one of the most stunning vistas of the Pacific, even. But by this stage all I wanted to do was lie down in a hammock and drink half a dozen mai-tais in quick succession.

And then I stumbled around a corner and into a burbling, forest-shrouded creek that looked like some Keatsian elfin grotto. Prancing out of the bushes came the messenger I'd been waiting for — a sun-bleached, blue-eyed, wild-haired, ratty-bearded Natural Man in all his priapic glory … carrying a white plastic bucket, his only prop, full of fresh drinking water.

He smiled his beatific white smile, his eyes focused somewhere in the far distance, and said (what else?), 'Aloha!'

I doubt I've been so glad to see a penis in all my life.

The raw charm of the local welcome seemed fitting. Poring over a map one still-freezing spring morning back in New York, I'd realised that the furthest point in the whole USA from the island of Manhattan was the only slightly larger island of Kauai — the remotest, least developed, greenest island of the Hawaiian archipelago. 'When you think of Hawaii,' so the wisdom went, 'you're actually picturing Kauai.' So I figured I might as well go the whole hog. Not only would I make for Hawaii's furthest island, I decided, I'd also head immediately to Kauai's remotest shore — the Na Pali coast, where a millennium-old walking trail was carved to the Kalalau valley.

Before 1778, when Captain Cook made the first documented visit by a European to the archipelago, several thousand Polynesians lived along the Na Pali cliffs. Half a century later, New England whalers and missionaries helped spread diseases that pushed the Hawaiian population into a tail-spin from which it never recovered. But the furthest valley, Kalalau, persisted in memory as the most beautiful hideaway on the island. Jack London wrote a famous short story about it, and as late as the 1920s, several hundred Polynesians still lived there, cultivating coffee on remote terraces. Eventually, the valley became deserted. Until the hippies moved in, that is.

Plunging into my pilgrimage had been simplicity itself. After a couple of days in Lihue — the only town of any size in Kauai — I'd picked up a camping permit for five days, bought a pack-full of supplies and was driving up the island's only highway towards the township of Hanelei, and, maybe ten kilometres beyond it, the start of the trail.

En route were some of Hawaii's most sacred sights: the Coco Palms Hotel where Elvis was married in *Blue Hawaii* and the 'Bali Hai' mountain used as the backdrop for *South Pacific* (can anyone forget Mitzi Gaynor singing 'I'm gonna wash that man right outta my hair'? Ever?) But before long, Kauai's coastline began to look more like something out of *King Kong*, with menacing volcanic mountains looming above the roadway.

It was a little disappointing to find that the fabled Kalalau trail actually starts in a parking lot. After donning my five-day pack, I found the path leading straight up through a tropical forest, and for the first few kilometres, cheery American day-trippers bounded past saying witty things like, 'Gee, I'm glad I'm not you.' But I pretended I only spoke Russian, and soon the trail emerged onto the Na Pali cliffs — a billowing curtain of raw rock pulverised by the Pacific. Higher up, the hillsides look like they've been savaged by a giant claw. Way down below, layers of coral reef poked through the crystal waters of Ke'e Beach, upon whose headland — believe it or not — lie the stone ruins of the ancient Hawaiian hula school.

At this spectacular site, I'd read, acolytes would be sequestered month after month learning the sacred art of hula. For the whole time of their studies they could neither cut their fingernails nor have sexual intercourse. This last was particularly resented; the ancient Hawaiians were the sort of free spirits that Margaret Mead was probably dreaming of, and the first European sailors were astounded to find their boats surrounded by canoes full of gorgeous women. ('In a moment our decks were crowded with young, good-natured girls … uncivilised brunette(s) in a state of nature,' wrote Thomas Manby, mate to George Vancouver, in what one imagines was a shaky hand, 'while the surface of the water around us was covered with some hundreds soliciting admittance. Our bark instantly became a scene of jollity and all was pleasure and delight.')

The trail descended to Hanakapi'ai Beach, the first campsite en route. This seemed a fair approximation of tropical paradise: from my tent, I watched the sun sink below the horizon in the proverbial blaze of watery glory; when the full moon slipped from behind the mountain tops, it was like a giant floodlight being switched on.

DAY TWO: POLYNESIAN TORMENTS

About 100 metres up the first cliff, a sign-post announced that this was how high you needed to be if a tsunami or tidal wave hits. The Honolulu newspapers had darkly advised that Hawaii is overdue for one — in 1964, a quake in Chile started off a wave that killed 61 people on Hawaii; in 1946, a tsunami from Alaska wiped out a whole village, killing 159. If you notice an *extremely* low tide, the advice went, start climbing fast.

On the Na Pali trail, it turned out, tsunamis were the least of your worries. The path stayed way, *way* above the line — zigzagging around sheer headlands, crossing tiny creeks and passing through natural groves of hibiscus and frangipani. Finally, around midday, I found Hanakoa — a deserted village of overgrown coffee terraces, so high that a cloud had permanently settled on it. Every few seconds a fine spray of water would descend from above, like one of the lettuce displays in modern supermarkets (the centre of Kauai has the honour of being the Wettest Place on Earth). According to a small guide book I'd read in a Lihue newsagent, the hardest part of the trail was already over. Why not, I cockily thought, knock over the last leg in the afternoon, and be in Kalalau for dinner?

This may be a lesson in not trusting guide books. Beyond Hanakoa, it transpired, was a different climactic zone. The cliffsides suddenly dried out, the earth turned volcanic red, the trees disappeared and the landscape became almost arid. I felt like an intruder in the Valley of the Giants, surrounded by huge spiked plants like the heads of giant pineapples.

But things really became dodgy when the cliffs began to show the damage wreaked by Hurricane Iniki back in 1992. Swathes of the trail had eroded and slid into the ocean — leaving nothing but a vague outline on a forty-five degree gravel slope. The cliff was like a giant slippery dip, and I could picture sliding, sliding, sliding off the craggy lip of the cliff and down amongst the blooming whitecaps of the Pacific below (later, I found that several people take the ride every year, never to be seen again). Just to add some excitement, the ground was made up of tiny hard pebbles, which acted like ball bearings. The howling dry wind smashed you up against the cliff, or alternately pulled you away from it. To get across, you had to clutch onto the assorted roots and clumps of grass that were still available — and these were few, having been clawed to shreds by other white-knuckled hikers.

Tiny little boats full of sightseers were visible in the blue below, gazing up at the cliffs, no doubt thinking, 'Gee, I'm glad I'm not you.' I wanted to be *them*.

Which is why, when I finally met my naked hippy, I could have kissed him. He politely put the bucket in front of his pudenda before explaining that yes, indeed, I had reached the Kalalau Valley, once the last retreat of the Ancient Hawaiians, now the last hold-out of the Modern Hawaiian-cum-Californian Dream. All I had to do, he said, was walk another mile along the beach and there I could camp amongst the groves, drink of the fresh mountain water, smoke of the wild growing weed, shed my twentieth century restrictive garb and return to the idyllic Polynesian lifestyle.

His actual words were, 'Just head on down that-a-way,' but you get the idea.

DAY THREE: EXPLORING
THE HAPPY VALLEY

When I crawled out of my tent next morning, half a dozen dolphins were arching through the waves offshore; in the surrounding bushes, red cardinal birds were chirping away. Perhaps this wouldn't be a bad new home, I thought — after all, since I'd already sworn I wouldn't walk back, this was it for me, forever.

In the happy valley of Kalalau, I found, all your needs are provided for within a stone's throw of your tent. The mile-long beach lies right outside the flap. At the base of the cliffs, there's a waterfall where everyone comes to shower, wash their dishes and get drinking water (which, rather unromantically, has to be either treated or boiled against leptospirosis; rather like a nasty form of hepatitis, it can be fatal).

The waterfall was also the great meeting place, the town square of Kalalau. The main topics of conversation were how tough the trail was, the weather (pretty well perfect every day, despite fierce winds), and the many trials of nudity. (One freckly woman from Virginia announced, 'I stripped all day yesterday, and now mah butt's as purple as a plum!')

The basic social division in Kalalau, I soon discovered, is between the Naked and the Clothed. Nobody seems to have heard of the ozone hole here. The pecking order is set by just how brown you are *au naturel*, the highest caste being those who looked as if they'd been turned on a spit. These were the regulars, who almost never left Kalalau — the bronzed families you'd run into, excitedly climbing rose-apple trees; the young Tarzan of the Apes types, with hair down to their waists; the old guys as worn as cured leather (including one old codger who staggered along every morning with his plastic gallon-sized vodka bottle).

This semi-permanent population live in caves, tend their vegetable patches, scour the rocks for edible limpets and are permanently shrouded in the sweet, pervasive scent of marijuana. They sit around playing the guitar and have cosmic conversations like one I wrote down:

Hippy Woman: I had a dream last night. Lord Krishna came to see me, you know? He was glowing all gold, and he took my hand, and he led me up a golden staircase ...

White Rasta (knowingly): And what happened then?

Woman: Oh, nothing. I just woke up.

Everyone chortles disbelievingly.

Rasta: Didn't he want to make l-u-u-u-rve to you?

Woman: Does he ... do that sort of thing?

Rasta: Why not? He's Lord Krishna, man! He's got needs just like you or me ...

The lowest of the low in the social order were those who hid their nakedness behind swimsuits. To begin with, I was one of the wretched clothed. But an odd thing happens to people in Kalalau, which sounds like the moral of a Dr Seuss story: if everyone else is naked, then you actually feel foolish wearing a bathing suit. Pretty soon you want to strip off just to stop people staring.

DAY FOUR: THE LURE OF THE LEPER

The main adventure of any Kalalau day was having a swim. The waves were about the size of Mount Kosciusko, but I went in for the ritual dip anyway, got dumped, tossed and spat out. I spent the morning trying to get the sand out of my nostrils.

My blisters having half-healed, I felt steady enough to explore the Kalalau valley, following a river into the mountains above. The trail runs past ancient taro and sweet potato terraces that for centuries maintained a thriving population of Hawaiians. Wild mango and guava trees filled the forest; the air smelled like essence of passionfruit. Soon the waterfalls began, and a string of swimming holes with some of the world's most dramatic views. The mountains beyond protruded like green fingers, and off in the distance the blue Pacific stretched — empty all the way to Alaska.

But even this idyllic spot has seen its share of bloodshed, thanks to the case of Koolau the Leper.

Back in the 1880s, lepers in Hawaii were packed off by the American authorities to a colony on the island of Molokai — a miserable place that was regarded as a death camp. To escape this fate, many came to hide out in Kalalau. When news of this growing group of refugees reached the governor — some thirty-five people were ensconced in the caves at the top of the valley — a party of police was sent to ferret them out.

A cowboy named Koolau took charge of the defence. Despite having lost several fingers to his disease, he was still a crack shot with a rifle. He warned the Americans not to proceed across a narrow precipice; when they ignored him, he picked off the deputy sheriff. Martial law was declared on Kauai, and the Americans returned to shell the lepers' hideout with army mortars. Even so, Koolau killed two more policemen, and wounded a third.

Unable to dislodge him, the police retreated and gave up. Koolau the Leper became a legendary figure on Kauai; Jack London, who spent some time in Honolulu at the turn of the century, immortalised him in an eponymous short story.

DAY FIVE: ESCAPE FROM PARADISE

The only discordant note on this Arcadian sojourn was the knowledge that, on the hike back, I'd probably die a screaming death on a Polynesian precipice myself. Lurking in my little tent I thought of the waves pounding in front, the cliffs pressing in behind, and the wind hammering from above, and felt, well … *trapped*.

But then I ran into a couple of French backpackers limping down to the waterfall. They mentioned that they'd by chance seen a motorised rubber raft pull up to the beach that morning — the 'summer' season of Zodiac visits to Kalalau had just begun (in 'winter', the surf was simply too rough). They'd negotiated with the captain to take them back to Hanelei for $60 a person next morning. I scoffed at this craven cop-out and immediately resolved to join them.

I wasn't the only one who thought this was a good idea. News of the Zodiac visits had spread through Kalalau like wildfire, and some twenty-five people had gathered by the surf. Unfortunately, winter wasn't quite over: the swells were still massive, a sand-bar blocked the way, and the captain could only get the smallest of his two dinghies onto the beach. Our packs would be piled onto this, but everyone else would just have to swim for it. And so we did. The waves kept dumping right on our heads, there was an underwater rip roughly the strength of the Murray River, but anything was better than that hike home.

Grovelling up the side of the rubber dinghy, we came face to face with half a dozen holidaymakers who'd come out on a comfortable half-day cruise and were looking at us with some horror. We grizzled, burned and wild-eyed campers were suddenly back in the eminently civilised world of Hawaiian package tourism. Within a couple of hours, we'd be whisked back to the port of Hanelei, sipping pina coladas and chowing down on shrimp salads; two more and I'd be lugging my sodden pack (it became saturated en route) into the Princeville Hotel, a five-star American Xanadu built into the side of a mountain — aptly described by one writer as 'the place people in Heaven hope to go after they die'.

Decadent? Sure. But it's amazing how guilt-free you can feel about luxury when you've earned it by the sweat of your brow and the skin of your purple butt.

Escape to

Coney Island

I'd only been away a couple of weeks, but when I got back, New York was in the middle of a heat wave. That's the way the seasons work here. Six months of freezing weather, a handful of pleasant days, and suddenly you feel like you're in the Amazon rainforest. Hell of a place to build a city, really.

At least in the Amazon there's a river to jump into, piranhas or no. Here in New York, when the thermometre started to hit forty degrees, there was no relief. The asphalt roadways were reverting to a Vegemite-like paste. The sky turned a dismal beige. It was impossible to walk more for than five minutes without ducking inside an air conditioned café or store for a rest. And then things got really bad, and we had an 'atmosphere inversion': the great bowl of pollution over the city turned upside down, with the brown air sinking to the bottom and the clean air on top. I looked down Second Avenue one day and couldn't see to the end of the block. It was swallowed in smog.

The city spent two weeks on the verge of a collective nervous breakdown. Anyone who could afford to got out of town. Friends spent whole days in their underwear, drinking frozen daiquiris and staring into the A-C unit. Those New Yorkers who were so inclined went wandering the streets, screaming and shooting people. The average murder rate doubled, then tripled.

I figured there must be some escape. Wasn't this city a North Atlantic port? It was time to hop on a subway and make the pilgrimage out to Coney Island, in the borough of Brooklyn.

It was a lucky day on the subway. The F-train ride took only forty-five minutes before it burst from the bowels of the earth and rattled into the end of the line. A few Hispanic kids left on board pressed their noses desperately to the windows, drinking in the scene. The elegant curves of the roller-coaster and Ferris wheel thrust up from the dully sparkling sea like the ruins of Atlantis. Up front was Nathan's Fast Food Emporium — the very spot where the hot dog was invented in 1926.

Nathan's still claims to make the world's best dogs, and at only $1.75 a pop, an over-size wiener with chilli bean sauce was everyone's culinary passport to Coney Island. My mood inexplicably lifted. Sure, the summer sun was still beating down; the beach was a dismal sight, with its garbage and chemical waste and sorry oyster-shell sands; and the dozens of antique booths, bumper-car rings, tattoo parlours and shooting galleries were irredeemably sleazy. But that was all beside the point. This was *Coney Island*. It was an American icon.

While Los Angeles may have Disneyland and Miami Universal Studios, Coney Island is still the archetypal fun park. It took off in the 1890s, when immigrant Jewish and Italian families used to save for a whole year just so they could come and enjoy its wondrous rides. By the 1920s, the place's tremendous popularity made Coney a part of the classic New York landscape in endless cheap novels, B-grade movies and comic books. Some of the magic remains today, despite the utter disrepair and seediness into which it has fallen. In a way, it's still at the heart of the lost American dream — like a rotting piece of Mom's Apple Pie.

I wandered down Sideshow Alley, where a rifle range had drawings of Saddam Hussein and Fidel Castro as targets. 'C'mon!' the vendor bellowed. 'Shoot a Commie for Mommie!' Next door, an ageing tattoo artist had a lion's head freshly drawn onto his bulging brown beer gut; he held up his T-shirt to solicit the admiration of passers-by. A peeling merry-go-round, built just after the First World War, was still turning to the same old accordion tunes. The only concession to the 1990s was the price increase and signs written in Spanish.

The most popular fortune teller was a $1-a-go handwriting analysis by a fifteen year old girl with glittering eyelashes and a red gypsy scarf. Her thirty-second patter was obviously aimed to satisfy anyone in New York.

'This tells me you're gonna live a *very* long time,' she prattled, 'maybe even to ninety. This tells me you're feeling very nervous, but don't worry cos everything's gonna be OK. This tells me you spend your money very quickly, that you spend it as fast as you earn it. That'll be a dollar, please.'

Next stop was the Freak Show. A listless, confused crowd was being addressed by a woman with pink hair and a live anaconda hanging around her neck. Speaking through a megaphone with a thick Brooklyn accent, the Snake Lady invited us inside to witness deformed animals and Siamese twins, the 'Block-head' (who could hammer nails up his nose) and the 'Human Cigarette Factory' (who rolls hundred of smokes with his tongue, since he has no arms). The spiel ended abruptly when a drunk danced from the crowd and grabbed hold of her anaconda.

'Get the fuck outta here,' the Snake Lady muttered, closing up shop. To a tourist with a camera she added, 'And you — no fucking photographs, you hear me?'

I passed up the usual gamut of nausea-inducing rides, but couldn't quite resist the dreaded Cyclone. This was the world's first roller-coaster, and sentimentality is the main reason it hasn't been pulled down (it was underneath its arches that Woody Allen spent his childhood in *Annie Hall*). My enthusiasm was dampened by the zombie gaze of the Indian maintenance men, who looked like they had been spending the last year or two around the hookah, and I wasn't sure if any frame so big should be made out of wood. But the Cyclone had been working perfectly well since the twenties — how hair-raising could it be?

Well ... I don't know how it compares to other whiplash-inducing rides, but there is nothing quite like the sheer, bowel-clenching terror of being in the grip of a machine that has long outlasted its natural life. Glimpsing the roller-coaster's makeshift repairs, which looked like they wouldn't pass inspection in Calcutta, its rusted bolts and cracked boards as they all whistled past — and to be utterly convinced that the ancient cars were about to fly off their fragile timber rails — is to gaze into the maw of destiny.

As I staggered off at the end of the ride, a sign offered repeat rides for fifty cents reduction. Nobody bought it.

The famous boardwalk runs all the way along the Atlantic seashore from Coney Island to Brighton Beach — otherwise known as 'Little Odessa'. For years, Russian refugees came here for their American introduction to wretched tenement housing, street crime and wholesale extortion by the local Mafia. Now of course, they can get all that at home.

The beach took on a more Baltic aspect the further east I strolled: the very air rumbled with thick accents, old men appeared wearing white cardboard nose protectors under their sun-glasses and doughy *babushkas* in thick woollen dresses sat perspiring in the blistering heat. Turning down Brighton Avenue, the sun was blotted out by the elevated railway line overhead. Shops served creamy Russian pastries and a homemade cherry drink from giant wooden vats. Cyrillic signs outside restaurants offered a list of unknown foods for $4.99.

In the Neva Restaurant, where I finally took a seat, there were no windows, the decor was silver lavender and Seventies Revival, and a glittering disco ball hung from the ceiling. With her spattered apron and sleeves rolled up over meaty forearms, the chef wandered through the dining room like the matron in a Siberian mental hospital. And the waiter ticked off my requests as if we were still back in the Mother Country. 'No fish today. No fried chicken. No Coca-Cola. Only one beer: Budweiser.'

As I sat there and picked over an enigmatic bone, I had a bright idea: why should I be satisfied with this ersatz version of Mother Russia? Why shouldn't I see the dreariness and bad taste at first hand? A few phone calls later, I had a small photo assignment. Les wanted to be in on this one. We dug up a cheap package, and set off to a city where even in high summer the heat is the least of people's worries.

Notes from

Leninsky Prospekt

'Not many places bring to bear such gloomy, harsh and strange influences on the spirit of man as Petersburg!' declares the investigator in Dostoyevsky's *Crime and Punishment*. 'It's a city of the half insane.'

On a Sunday evening in Leninsky Prospekt — in the furthest backblocks of St Petersburg's suburbia — *gloomy* and *harsh* seemed like charitable understatements. Gulag-style apartment blocks stretched one after another in every direction. There was no traffic except for a few ancient buses belching clouds of ash. And the only pedestrians were staggering drunks, who were muttering to themselves animatedly or yelling obscenities at the sky, their faces freshly bloodied from brawls or falls. In fact, *Dante-esque* was a description that sprang to mind.

Even more unnerving, we had no idea where we were. Nikolai, a Russian friend-of-a-friend, had asked us to meet him out here. He was arranging an apartment for us to stay in for a couple of weeks; the rendezvous was *stantsia Leninsky Prospekt*, the 'station', so we'd hopped in a dollar-taxi, given the name, and watched for half an hour as we were shuttled along broken highways through indistinguishable suburbs. Eight o'clock sharp, Nikolai had warned us nervously. 'And don't talk to *anybody*. They'll know you're foreigners.' It felt like we were making a prisoner exchange at Checkpoint Charlie, instead of viewing an apartment.

We'd arrived at eight on the dot, but there was no Nikolai. Half an hour later, and the northern sky was beginning to darken. The drunks started to lurch closer. An old man looked like he was about to say something to us; he had a fresh scab covering his eye, and blood down to his collar; a row of military medals hung from his suitcoat pocket; his complexion was as pale as a boiled potato. We stared through him impassively, in that Russian way, and he lurched onwards, babbling a few words at his palm.

'Something's happened to Nikolai,' Les whispered, her natural optimism finally losing hold. 'Let's get out of here.'

But how, exactly? There were no taxis in the suburbs. It was time to start talking, so I pulled out our little Russian phrasebook. A middle-aged woman nearly jumped out of her skin when we approached her; everyone in St Petersburg looked terrified. After some pointing and gesturing, we managed to discover that this was Leninsky Prospekt *bus* station. Perhaps we wanted the Leninsky Prospekt *Metro* station? That was a mile away, down a desolate avenue. After imparting this crucial information, the poor woman turned on her heel and fled.

Who knew where the few buses were heading, so we started jogging along the wide empty footpath, hoping Nikolai would wait for us. More drunks paused to stare at us, flabbergasted. We didn't have to open our mouths to draw attention: we stood out by our clothes, our haircuts, our expressions. When we stumbled across the subway station, it was entirely deserted except for one rake-thin figure silhouetted beneath a street lamp, sucking on a Winston — Nikolai.

He came up to us, his face drawn. 'You're all right?' he kept asking. 'What happened? Nobody saw you?' We assured him everything was fine; his edginess wasn't very encouraging. Finally, Nikolai looked at his watch and peered at the sky.

'Shall we do it?'

'Why not?'

'No reason,' he said, tight-lipped. 'But I must ask you again: as we walk, *please* don't say a word.'

For the next twenty minutes, Nikolai guided us in silence along yet another faceless avenue. In the hazy twilight, I started getting neurotic. What about Nikolai? Could we trust him? What the hell were we doing wandering around this wasteland? Who would ever find us out here? Finally, Nikolai identified one of the looming apartment buildings with a nod.

Facing the central courtyard, a great iron door was hanging loose from its hinges. Inside, the foyer was dark, but the filtered light showed a shattered concrete floor, like a bomb shelter, strewn with mounds of garbage. The smell hit you with a slap — not just garbage but acrid, sulphuric urine. The reek became almost overpowering as we squeezed into the coffin-like elevator.

'Every building in St Petersburg stinks like this,' Nikolai whispered, with a forced smile. 'The basements are full of feral cats. But don't worry; the smell doesn't get into the apartments.'

'Oh, that's a relief,' I said wanly, and glanced over at Les. I knew what she was thinking: this is insane, but we didn't have much choice. For the next few weeks, Ulitsa Ziny Portnovoi 1648, apartment #713, was going to be home.

When I was offered a job to photograph St Petersburg for a small guide book, I have to confess that my image of the city was gleaned almost entirely from the pages of Dostoyevsky. It was a romantic but not exactly flattering picture: he loathed the place passionately.

To Dostoyevsky, St Petersburg was the most 'intentional' city in the world — the modern era's first and most ambitious planned capital, a cold, abstract design without national roots or character. As Solomon Volkov points out in his study of the city, even its foundation in 1703 was, Dostoyevsky considered, a nihilist act, a gesture of cruel megalomania by Peter the Great. The tsar created his Window to the West on a dank archipelago in a malarial swamp; the site was regularly flooded, and boasted a horrific climate that guaranteed months of oppressive darkness and ice. Tens of thousands of serfs are said to have died in the city's construction; St Petersburg was 'founded on tears and corpses', the first urban paradise built on a graveyard.

In *Crime and Punishment*, Dostoyevsky created the most influential vision of the city as a spectral landscape, where inhuman thoughts would breed like fungal cultures and the student Raskolnikov could reason out the axe murder of an old woman. Steaming, stenching, covered with open sewers and lime. It was, of course, a fantastical, nightmarish image — yet there were all the specific street names, the exact corners and precise addresses; you could visit the actual house where Dostoyevsky had Raskolnikov live, with its narrow staircase leading straight to the attic, as well as the old moneylender's home ...

The afternoon before that first trip to Leninsky Prospekt, we sat in the café of the Guten Hotel, watching a clear northern sun sparkle over the distant golden spires of St Peter and Paul's cathedral, and trying to picture the suburban tundra that now spread out forever across the former swamps.

The hotel was one of those Swedish-owned knock-offs that had sprouted up all over Russia, with pink pastel walls and teak sauna-style furniture. We'd paid for three nights here as part of our dismal Aeroflot package from New York, in the hopes that we'd then find somewhere cheap to stay for two weeks longer. Now this was our last night in the bosom of the Guten — we couldn't afford their astronomical day rate, even if they had rooms available — and we were still entirely at sea in St Petes.

Of course, we'd made a few excursions around the city centre, with its glittering palaces and canals and gilt-edged bridges, all the eighteenth century trappings of the 'Venice of the North' and the 'New Rome'. The city's marvels of neo-classical architecture never get a mention in *Crime and Punishment* (Fyodor thought they were simply sad and derivative); it's the cosmopolitan heart of St Petersburg, associated with some of the most famous names in Western culture. (To pick a few: Pushkin, Gogol, Akhmatova, Nabokov, Brodsky; Rimsky-Korsakov, Prokofiev, Tchaikovsky, Shostakovich, Stravinsky; Diaghilev, Balanchine, Nijinksky, Pavlova ...) To us, though, it was downright intimidating. We peered into new hotels that sold rooms for US$400 a night and Faberge eggs for ten times that amount. Every time we hailed a taxi, the driver would bark, 'Tvenny dollars!' no matter what the distance was. If you tried to bargain, they just drove off. The more educated would yell, 'Fugg you!' as they did so.

But the time to make our own way in the city had arrived. In the New Russia, we didn't officially have to stay in pseudo-luxurious Intourist hotels that had been the grist of visits since the 1920s. All controls had been lifted. But what was left? As far as we could tell, chaos. We'd heard that locals might rent out apartments to foreigners for *valiuta*, hard currency. But who could you trust?

Luckily, we had Nikolai. A regular Egon Schiele, you'd have to call him. In his early thirties, he had a withdrawn, monastic air; his face was lean and ghostly under a shock of blue-black hair, and he'd often stare into space for long periods at a time, thinking (you supposed) truly melancholy thoughts. He taught English, and was paid in dollars, so he dressed snappily in Western-made clothes. But you could tell at a glance he was Russian, because of his expression. Something always seemed to be troubling him deeply.

When we'd first met him at his 'favourite Georgian restaurant' — a grim hole that served up gristle on cracked plates — he was particularly troubled by us. We told him we wanted to rent an apartment for a couple of weeks. Did he know of anybody?

He slowly put down his fork and looked us over. 'And how do you expect to survive?' he asked.

'Oh I don't know,' I said blithely. 'We've got a few dollars. We should be able to figure it out.'

'No, really. You don't speak a word of Russian. How do you expect to buy food? How will you get around the city? I mean it, Dtony. How do you expect to survive?'

He spent the rest of the night trying to talk us out of the idea. Petersburg was now a dangerous place. We'd get lost. Mugged. Kidnapped. Did we hear about the woman who'd just been shot between the eyes for her leather coat, down on Vasilevsky Bridge? The tourists slashed up for their Nikes? The mafiosi who held people up in their hotel rooms? How much worse would it be for foreigners out in the labyrinthine suburbs?

'Aren't you exaggerating just a little?' Les asked. She was getting irritated at the scare treatment. 'We manage in New York, so we're not complete saps.'

'I was in New York for six months,' Nikolai said mournfully. 'There you can be anonymous. In Russia, the foreigners stand out like *this*.' He snapped his fingers. 'No, I am sorry, I am quite certain that Russia is more serious for you.'

We were becoming depressed about the whole plan, but the next day Nikolai called us up. His sister, Lena, had an apartment out in Leninsky Prospekt. She would stay at her boyfriend's, and let us use it for US$10 a day. The going rate was $5, but the extra was fine, at least to assuage our guilt. She was a doctor; $10 was the amount she earned a month.

Nikolai still didn't recommend it, but he would show us the place if we wanted to proceed.

Nikolai was right about one thing: apartment #713's double metal doors (each of which had double metal locks) did keep the smell of cat piss out. Instead, the one-bedroom place had a pleasantly musty smell, a fragrance of woollen blankets and mopped tiles and freshly-vacuumed old carpet that reminded me of my grandmother's place back in Chatswood. The decor added to the nostalgia. Every fitting in the house was circa 1940, but perfectly preserved; a single plastic rose sat on the plastic-covered kitchen table; everything looked like it had been repaired many times. In fact, despite the *Blade Runner* look to the outside of the building, the apartment was entirely comfortable. The gas stove worked, and the shower let out a regular trickle of hot water.

There were a few oddities. Everything seemed covered with a very thin film of grease, even the plates and utensils. The glasses were almost opaque. (You had to wonder how the instruments were doing over at Lena's hospital.) Hygiene was a bit of a problem out in the corridors, too: garbage was supposed to be dumped down a great metal chute in the stairwell. The neck was narrow, so a grubby wooden stick was provided to ram it all down. Unfortunately, nobody seemed to have the energy to use it, so everything just overflowed down the stairs, rotting away.

Perhaps this contributed to the distinct lack of neighbourly good cheer. For the first couple of days we scurried around, trying not to run into anybody — feeling a bit self-conscious about it, until we realised that everybody else was doing the same. Nobody nodded in the corridors or elevator — in fact, running into another tenant seemed to be everyone's darkest fear. Out in the courtyard, an empty, overgrown playground, people walked their dogs furiously, skirting the open manholes hidden in the weeds (down below were tunnels with thick rusty pipes, begetting other pipes, for purposes unknown). I once caught an ancient tenant emerging from his iron door: the interior walls were painted a thick, crusty black, like a cave, and covered with medals and pennants. The man blinked at me in confusion, and retreated.

An existentialist once wrote that finding your way around a foreign city is genuine experience, one of the few times when you are so off-balance that you're truly alert. Not one of the famous cities, like Paris or Berlin; it has to be somewhere without any monuments you've seen in photos, somewhere you don't know the language, the customs, even the street plan.

I think St Petes qualified — or at least it did out in Leninsky Prospekt. We spent a day with Nikolai writing down Cyrillic signs, so we could distinguish our building from all the others; we traced the path to the Metro station, counted out the number of stops into the centre of town; and we learned to assume the stony Russian expression from the moment we left our apartment door, into the street and down into the bowels of the earth, to be carried along in the *Metropolis*-style tidal wave of commuters through the series of palatial thirties-era stations. Then we'd finally emerge, like the freed prisoners in *Fidelio*, a stone's throw from the Winter Palace.

The photo shoot was exhaustive, and entirely involved the old city centre, with its 15,000 historic buildings, all crumbling under pastel paint, the palaces, the parks. If the sky was overcast — and a foul-breathed mist fell over the city — we would head for the museums. Photographing here was forbidden, and the rules were zealously enforced by ancient *babushkas* in every room. Les took the task of distracting these harridans while I snapped a few shots; but they were a shrewd bunch, who'd lived through the siege of 1941, and would doggedly chase us through the hallowed halls, bellowing about punishments we couldn't understand. Finally, at dusk, we'd bid farewell to the fairytale city, submerge into the subway and reappear in the geometric concrete wasteland of Leninsky Prospekt.

The schizophrenia wasn't just aesthetic. In the heart of the city, the 'Window on the West' was back in full swing. Any import or innovation to Russia first arrives in the shops of Nevsky Prospekt, and a fistful of dollars could buy almost anything; there were pizza bars where you could pay in any known currency, calculated down to four decimal points (even the wretched Aussie dollar was good here); there were English tea shops; German beer halls; American music stands. Streets were plied by horse-drawn carriages driven by mock-tsarist flunkeys in eighteenth century wigs and finery. Doormen at the Grand Hotel Europe wore white gloves and top hats, fawning before every guest in a manner that might even have embarrassed New Yorkers.

The only catch was that we couldn't afford to eat in the dollar restaurants, and the rubles restaurants were … well, let's say things haven't changed much since the 1930s, when Celine found that the country had the 'alimentary system of a neglected prison … man fills his belly with cucumbers'. And not very fresh ones at that. Aged cow tongue, sawdust sausages, dead lettuce, oceans of oil … But out in Leninsky Prospekt, there were no restaurants, good or bad. But we had a perfectly good kitchen in our apartment. Why not cook at home?

For the first three days, we lived on caviar and champagne — the only food we could find.

The champagne was from Georgia, $2 a bottle, tangy as marmalade; the caviar was $1 a jar, ranging in colour from pale grey to inky black. It was a diet that suited the Cossacks, but it soon began to pale. Out in Leninsky Prospekt, we felt like millionaires with nothing to spend our money on. The shops were empty, except perhaps for a block of plastic cheese. A few valiant street vendors would huddle about the Metro entrance with curd, vodka and flowers; once a kid turned up with a satchel full of imported Italian pasta. Any new arrival provoked a commotion: a truck driver started selling brown onions direct on the footpath, someone turned up with Czechoslovakian beer and was mobbed.

There was a dairy shop around the corner, so we stood in line to see what would happen. While we waited, we practiced our phrases: 'six eggs and milk, please', went something like *shesht yaytsa y moloko, pazhalsta* (which wasn't such a tongue-twister; asking where to get off on the subway went: *pazhalsta, pryedupryeditye myenya kagda mnye nuzhna vikadit*, and God knows what the reply would be). After standing on three more queues (one to get a ticket, one to pay for the ticket, one to wrap), we ended up with the goods. Eggs (which were fine) and milk (sour).

Still, it was absurdly satisfying to be figuring all this out. We found a bread shop, and got a loaf of the famous Russian bread. Soon our horizons widened: what about vegies?

That was the first question I asked Lena when she unexpectedly turned up at the apartment one morning. We felt embarrassed — after all, we were living in her place — and she was just as embarrassed as we were. She was tall, shy, pale and angular, almost hiding behind her thin spectacles. Although she was ashamed of her English, it was near perfect, so we all quickly tried to rise above the sordid financial basis of our relationship. Thus the conversation turned to greens.

'No-o-o-o-o!' Lena cried, appalled, when we showed her a few withered beans we'd managed to buy at the subway station. 'Are you *quite* mad? You must go to the markets of Vladimirskaya!'

An hour later, Lena led us into a cast-iron hall the size of an airplane hangar, crammed with hundreds and hundreds of vendors. It was like a secret food cache run by a Bond villain. There were cheeses, meats, poultry, a dozen types of gherkin; the fruit and vegies from the Ukraine were as plump as organic produce at home: the tomatoes and oranges were like perfect plastic casts, and the carrots seemed to glow orange (which hopefully the fallout from Chernobyl had nothing to do with). The prices were paltry by Western standards, but the only Russians in the place were strenuously over-dressed mafiosi and hard-currency prostitutes. We asked Lena if she wanted to buy anything here, but she just laughed. 'Oh no, this is not for *me*.'

Now the only thing that sent us skulking into the hard-currency stores was water. St Petes tapwater, it's understood, is too polluted for even brushing your teeth with (I saw them repairing a streetpipe on Nevsky Prospekt; it was made of wood). And the Russian bottled water seems more dangerous. It tastes like rust, a sort of iron filings cordial.

As an experiment, I left a glass out overnight. Next morning, it had turned a mysterious orange colour. By the third day, a thick silvery film had appeared on its surface — taking the definition of mineral water to its extreme.

Once they were sure we weren't going to be sucked into some black hole in Leninsky Prospekt, Nikolai and Lena decided to adopt us, and on fine days we went on excursions to Catherine the Great's many palaces out in the countryside. I had to photograph them all, and there were dozens, all beautifully restored (most had been bombed by the Nazis) and surrounded by Chekhovian woods. But after a while, the palaces started to seem absurd. The caked layers of gilt, the polished floors, room after room of antiques and oil paintings, French chests and Italian vases. St Petersburg had managed to out-Europeanise Europe. The extravagance was bulimic.

Back in town one afternoon, we went strolling along Nevsky Prospekt, and passed the Grand Hotel Europe, with its beaming top-hatted doorman.

'Do you want to come in for a coffee?' we asked. Coffee with actual caffeine, we meant.

'No, no, please,' Lena backed away. It was as if we were enticing her to have a root canal. She wouldn't even step in the doorway, to have a look around out of interest. 'These places,' she said again, with a visible shudder, 'are not for *me*.'

I started to feel like Lena and Nikolai were ghosts in their own city. During the referendum of 1991, when the name was changed back from Leningrad, they'd both been away. It had been a heady act of symbolism, but neither of them were terribly pleased about it, although not out of any sentimentality for the Communist era.

'To me, this city is still Leningrad,' Nikolai said as we continued along Nevsky. 'Look at it: it's a disaster. The buildings are collapsing. Our water is poisoned. The air is filthy. People are virtually starving. When these problems are fixed, *then* we deserve the name St Petersburg. Until then, we'll always be Leningrad.'

St Petersburg is honeycombed with valuable 'house-museums', and we went to visit every last one. There was Pushkin's aristocratic mansion, with a letter announcing his intention to fight the fatal duel for his wife's honour. Dostoyevsky's last apartment was perfectly preserved, with the solid oak desk where he wrote *The Brothers Karamazov*; by this time he and his wife had pulled themselves out of bankruptcy and enjoyed a certain fame within literary circles. The rooms were comfortable and cosy. The clock in his study was stopped at the exact moment he died.

But the most affecting house-museum belonged to the poet Anna Akhmatova.

Upstairs from a cluttered courtyard, in an annex to the former Sheremetiev Palace, her apartment was a series of long, thin rooms, all painted an institutional palette of greys. I couldn't find a thing to photograph. But in this drab setting, there were gathered a small number of almost embarrassingly intimate odds and ends — tiny paintings, notebooks, personal photographs — from her symbolic life. As an aristocratic young poet, Akhmatova recorded St Petersburg's Silver Age before the First World War: reading in the Stray Dog cabaret, travelling to Paris, befriending Diaghilev and Modigliani. Her first husband, the poet Nikolai Gumilyov, was shot by the Bolsheviks in 1921; Punin, her lover of ten years, and her son were arrested in the Great Terror of the 1930s; both were released after her pleading letter to Stalin, but her son was soon re-arrested and sent to Siberia. In 1946, after a British diplomat dropped by her apartment for a visit, she was expelled from the Writer's Union, her house was bugged and she was followed in the street by the KGB.

Just as the future ripens in the past,
So the past smoulders in the future …

Although she could have left Russia after the Revolution, Akhmatova stayed on, she said, to 'bear witness'; no matter what happened, St Petersburg was her home. The apartment's bareness has its own meaning. Akhmatova's most famous poems, *Requiem*, about the Terror, and *Poem Without a Hero*, a coded autobiography, were too dangerous to be kept on paper. They were memorised by a few friends and the manuscripts burned on the iron stove.

Finally, I left Les drawing in the Summer Gardens and decided to go and find Raskolnikov's house.

It was a more spurious mission than usual — visiting the home of a fictional character — but irresistible. Unfortunately, the street address in the book had been changed three times in the last century; people sent me one way, then another, around the area that had more or less been the Haymarket, until I eventually found a grey building on a grey street not far from a grey-watered canal. A very old woman was sitting in the gutter nursing a somnolescent ginger cat, which looked much better fed than she did. She seemed to know what I was doing in this unassuming street, and nodded to the top floor.

A dark gabled window poked from an attic. That was the 'closet-sized' room where Dostoyevsky had housed his nihilistic superman. Apparently there really were thirteen steps to the room; word had it you could really count the 730 steps around to the address of the moneylender he went to visit with the axe hung in his coat; even the stone under which Raskolnikov hid the pilfered goods existed. But now that I was standing here, this address seemed much less real than the room I had in my head. In fact, if any modern day location was close in spirit to 'Dostoyevsky's Petersburg', obviously enough, it was Leninsky Prospekt.

Wandering back along one of the canals, I realised that even the most splendid parts of central St Petersburg were starting to depress me. I didn't much like Leninsky Prospekt, but it seemed more concrete than this historic, pretty, almost touristic shell. The distorted alleys of the city had even begun to seem more sinister than the suburbs — at dusk, you saw shadows around every corner, like a de Chirico painting.

St Petersburg was popularly held to have been cursed at its foundation (Peter's first wife, Eudoxia, pronounced that it would one day stand empty). Dostoyevsky used to dream that a fog would lift the whole 'rotten, slimy city' with it, 'leaving behind the old Finnish swamp'. It reminded me a bit of *The Last Wave* — regarding another act of imperial hubris almost two centuries later, on the opposite side of the globe ...

For Russians, no matter how cosmopolitan and sophisticated St Petersburg became, it could never shake its image as an isolated frontier on the Gulf of Finland: on the border between order and chaos, peripheral, uninhabitable, on the verge of crumbling into oblivion. And there was a deadness to the city now. Moscow is so much more bustling and energetic. In fact, it's hard to believe that anything so dramatic as the 1917 revolutions ever really occurred in St Petersburg; difficult to picture John Reed running with the Red Guards through the Winter Palace (and nearly being lynched as a *provokator*).

It's been a steady downhill slide for the city since then. Lenin quickly moved Russia's capital to the Slavic Moscow. With the murder of Kirov in 1934, Stalin set out to destroy the city's cultural elite. Then came the 900 day siege in the Second World

War — Hitler wanted to blast the birthplace of Communism from the map, Carthage-style — when some two thirds of the population died from starvation. No sooner was the war over than Stalin singled out the 'hero city' for more repression.

Could St Petes have suffered more even if it had been cursed? In time, it has been ground down to little more than a provincial centre, a beautiful ruin slowly decaying on the marsh.

Not to mention, *a city of the half insane* ... 'Just think of the climate alone!' cries Porfiry.

We watched August come to an end, and the weight of northern fog, darkness and drizzle rolled down upon the city. In Leninsky Prospekt, it seemed that more and more people were muttering and wailing in the street every day. Even to us, with our cushion of dollars, the atmosphere was starting to become oppressive.

We'd sometimes stumble into open displays of emotion. Once, running from some rain, we ended up in a café with a wedding reception, where the vodka-soaked guests were singing and flailing about in Cossack dances. But the demonstrations became rarer as the shadows grew longer. Down in the subway, the ubiquitous blank expressions began to seem like profound sadness. Les began to freak out about the old women, who would just stare at her sullenly. 'I try to stare them out, but they never look away,' she whispered. 'They *hate* me, I know it.' We even grew sentimental about the New York subway, wishing that some panhandler would wander by, start yelling about his service in Afghanistan or wanting to sell chewing gum or ... *anything*.

I think we were going a bit mad ourselves by the last morning. The idea of negotiating an international airport was vaguely terrifying. We had to leave before dawn. Nikolai lined up a friend to give us a lift for some dollars, to make sure a taxi driver wouldn't mug us en route.

At the airport, there was still a customs check for leaving the country: very few foreigners were flying Aeroflot, so officials were going through their luggage with a fine tooth comb, finding anything they'd bought and inventing fabulous sums as 'excise duty'. Through a glass wall we could all watch the poor sods ahead of us getting an old-style Soviet interrogation. One Midwesterner, who had bought a valise full of caviar, was saddled with US$400 bill. He argued with the officials for a full hour, but they just kept smiling back; eventually he handed over everything he'd bought and stormed off. The whole thing was obviously a great scam for these two customs officers.

By the time they got to us, the flight had already been delayed for two hours. First we had to empty our pockets. I pulled out a wad of rubles — about $45 worth — I'd hoped to change back to dollars, but there was no bank at the airport. The customs officers rubbed their hands, almost salivating at the sight.

'Ah! Is not legal to take rubles from Russia.'

'Can we exchange them?'

'No exchange.'

They shrugged and opened their palms. Their smiles said: *you know how it is.*

'Well, they don't deserve them,' Les muttered. I looked around. The glass wall was only nine feet high: on the other side, rows of old women who'd come to see off relatives were staring blankly away into space. I took the rubles, threw them over the glass wall, and watched them float down like dirty brown snowflakes.

For a few seconds, everyone just kept staring. And then a party began. *Babushkas* began laughing and snatching the notes from the air. The two customs officers went pale, veins standing out on their foreheads. Soon even they started giggling. They didn't even bother going through our bags, they just waved us on.

There was obviously no use dealing with the half-insane.

The Personals

One of the more eclectic Manhattan institutions is a place called the Lifelong Learning Centre. Year after year, it offers cheap three-hour courses on how to dance the cha-cha, abseil, cook Chinese food, write historical novels, become a famous movie director and much, much more. Flicking through the handbook one day — it arrives as junk mail in almost every household on the island — I noticed Course Number 296 on Personal Ads: how to write an alluring ad, how to reply, how to screen out the crazies, reject the losers and snare the desired. It was given by Lynn Davis, 'the country's leading expert on the Personals'. And included in the modest $50 course fee would be a copy of her remaindered classic, The Guide to Personal Ads.

I thought: the world needed to know the latest in the eternal quest for soulmates — so I gave the centre a call.

The receptionist was certainly encouraging. 'But your accent's lovely,' she told me. 'You just talk and those women will come rolling along ... ' Seduced by flattery, I arrived on time at the Upper West Side schoolroom where the course was held. A motley group of students were perched under neon lights, suspiciously picking chewing gum from the wooden seats. To my left was a seventy-one year old man with inch-long brown fingernails, who constantly fondled an obviously unused clipper. To my right was a wide-eyed woman in her thirties who had just resigned as a fashion designer for *Vogue* — or at least that's what she said.

Most of them were middle-aged divorcees who had placed ads before, with disappointing results. 'I keep getting the wrong sort of reply,' complained a bouncy Jewish lady in an olive jumpsuit. A younger, rather shrewish woman announced that her current relationship was on the skids and she needed to draft an ad before it broke up. Meanwhile, a dapper 'TV writer' with a grey goatee was taking the chance to chat up his neighbour. Of course, this was the subtext of the whole course: *it was an excellent chance to meet other singles in a 'supportive environment'*. Why waste a minute?

'Personal ads are an art form,' Lynn Davis declared as a prelude to her three-hour lecture, delivered at breakneck speed. Davis herself, to quote her most oft-used personal ad, was 'mid-forties, nurturing, into mega-vitamins and Renaissance Europe'. She sometimes made strategic use of the adjective 'Rubenesque'.

The perfect personal ad has four basic components, we were told: the description of one's self; the description of who you're after; the reason; and (this was the key to a successful piece) the 'Add-A-Little-You' Section. This latter will distinguish your ad from the hundreds of others that clutter the pages of magazines, vying for the attention of your perfect mate.

To stand out, Davis continued, every ad needs a line of poetry, a wild idea or a fantasy. You Write the Script, I'll Be Your Leading Lady. Burnt By the Queen of Diamonds, mourns another, Looking for Queen of Hearts. But the 'Add-A-Little-You' Section mustn't be too clever, or the results become unpredictable. For example, Seeking Unicorn Rides in Central Park drew some unsavoury responses. Seeking Someone to Share the Other Half of my Pastrami Sandwich attracted only Jewish suitors, while changing this to 'egg salad' lured only Gentiles.

Another crucial decision was where to run your ad. *New York* readers were mostly Upper West Side yuppies, for example, who describe themselves as 'CEOs with Armani style' and look for marriage based on strict racial and demographic rules. Meanwhile, the *Village Voice* had a more free-wheeling bent. 'GBM 6'4" seeks GWM 4' or shorter for night shift love.' 'SWM seeks Asian women for oral sex during lunch hour (I'm serious!)' 'Busty bi-curious lady needed for vampire couple.' 'A School For Naughty Boys: Call the Professor Now!'

Someone brought up the serious problem of honesty in ad-writing, wondering why so many 'Brad Pitt look-alike' guys and 'drop-dead gorgeous' gals were still out there in the singles market. 'You can say what you like about yourself, *within* the art form,' Davis assured us. Extensive studies in the field have shown that men knock five years from their ages, women five pounds from their weights. These days, almost all ads simply demand photos — a trend Davis pooh-poohed as too blatantly superficial.

But the dangers of deception went much further, she warned. Remember that ads asking for an older person may be prostitutes, or worse, college bums looking for a Manhattan crash pad. Watch out for salespeople placing trick ads, and (casting a merry smile at me) don't forget that people from other countries gain US citizenship if they marry an American.

New York being what it is, many students admitted to being worried about safety, and Davis spent some time explaining how to avoid 'peripheral people'. Personal ads, with their 'screening processes', were actually a *safer* way of meeting people than just hanging out at the corner watering hole, she said — using as her authority not *Looking for Mr Goodbar* but an actual police officer, Captain Boltz, ex-hostage negotiator for the City of New York. 'People who use the personals are a little sharper and better educated than average,' advises this fellow Boltz. 'They tend, as a group, to be more stable.'

'After all,' Davis added cheerily, 'your friendly axe murderer doesn't need to use personal ads to find a victim.'

The TV writer was dubious. 'I know a journalist who writes some beautiful replies to ads,' he muttered, 'but after five minutes face-to-face, anyone can tell he's off his rocker.'

Since nearly everyone who answers your ad must be rejected, Davis explained the tactful procedure: first tell the 'loser' to ring again in a week. Then, if he/she persists, explain that in the meantime an old flame has been rekindled. If this fails, DON'T say that 'people as fat as you usually have emotional problems'. DO say, 'I've enjoyed talking with you, but I don't feel we are right for each other.'

As the discussion was wrapping up, the woman in the olive jumpsuit rather rhetorically asked about AIDS and modern dating. Was there anything in a personal ad that might ... y'know ... improve one's chances? For once, Lynn had no easy answers. 'Look for the phrase "in good health",' she shrugged.

The censor snorted again. 'Once we only had to worry about a lonely and meaningless life. Now there's the problem of a painful and early death!'

And on this sombre note, the pupils scattered into the Broadway night.

Belize: Deep Cover

in the Caribbean

The first thing I saw on leaving Belize's international airport was a bar with the sign: *$45 ALL YOU CAN DRINK*; on the door, another read *Conserve Energy, Be Apathetic*. The ethic was in full swing as the taxi crawled along a palm-shaded river and into Belize City. Peeling wooden terrace houses were lined up along the waterfront, looking like they hadn't been repaired since Hurricane Hattie hit in 1961 — or maybe the hurricane of 1931, which killed about one fifth of the population. Open sewers flowed lime green; the sun-baked streets were eerily deserted.

'Does anybody live in this place?' I wondered out loud.

'Queenie's birthday, mon,' explained the taxi driver, whose name appeared on the license card as Big George. He seemed profoundly depressed to be working on a public holiday. 'No traffic today. Lizzie's damn birthday.' To cheer himself up, Big George told me one of the highlights from the Queen's only visit to Belize, in 1985. For her dining pleasure, she was served the local delicacy of gibnut, a large Belizean rodent. 'And do you know the damn headlines in London? QUEEN EATS RAT

IN BELIZE!' He laughed about that one for the rest of the ride, occasionally muttering to himself, 'Oh, shut up, mon, shut up!'

In the Bellevue Hotel, right on the swampy foreshore, a photo of Her Majesty was tacked on the brown lino wall, with a note to say that she had stayed here on her state visit. It was a little hard to credit. The rooms were tiny and steaming hot; the air conditioner roared like an airplane engine, and shook the walls. I slipped up to the bar, which had a view through chipped louvres of the river mouth and a ship's mast dedicated to Baron Bliss. He was an English aristocrat who fell sick on his yacht here in the 1920s; the locals treated him so decently that he willed Belize his entire fortune (as a result, there's a Baron Bliss national holiday and boat race every year). Ceiling fans were jerkily rotating; a damp, salty breeze drifted in through the slats; an obese American sat in the corner, eating bacon rashers.

Out on the murky brown water, a mysterious scene was unfolding, which I followed through a telephoto lens. An ancient, twenty-foot steamboat was being surrounded by a dozen wooden canoes. The captain was wearing a spotless linen suit and wide-brimmed hat; the canoeists were in loincloths and carrying spears. The steamer was clearly in trouble. People in sunglasses were frantically bailing. Suddenly the captain jumped out.

Here at the Bellevue, the Creole bartender had shown no inclination to serve drinks, but she didn't mind filling me in on the film shoot — Conrad's *Heart of Darkness*, she said. Directed by Nicholas Roeg. With John Malkovich in the lead. The boat wasn't supposed to sink, but they were using a genuine antique steamer they'd found up-river. This was the third time it had gone down, apparently, which was making a mess of the schedule.

Belize City was obviously the perfect location for the shoot. It's such a colonial relic, all the set decorators would have to do was change a few signs from English to French and it was instant Belgian Congo, circa 1890. And the rest of the country didn't do a bad imitation of tropical oblivion, either.

Of all the malarial corners of Central America's Caribbean coast, the Commonwealth of Belize (known until 1980 as British Honduras) is perhaps the most obscure. In fact, its defining trait for centuries has been its sheer irrelevance. 'If the world had any ends,' Aldous Huxley wrote in his 1934 travel journal, *Beyond the Mexique Coast*, 'British Honduras would be one of them. It is not on the way from anywhere to anywhere else. It has no strategic value. It is all but uninhabited.' To many, this has been precisely its attraction. Back in the 1600s, English pirates used the coastal islands, or cayes, as bases from which to plunder Spanish ships, easily losing pursuers in the maze of treacherous off-shore reefs. Belize soon became the first Caribbean hideaway, a land where anyone could elude persecution or a shady past.

Exiles and cast-offs from around the globe have washed up on its muddy shores: British mahogany loggers and their African slaves; Confederate soldiers fleeing the US Reconstruction; refugees from the Mexican race wars of the 1850s; East Indian soldiers deported after the Great Mutiny; sporadic boatloads of Garifuna people, the descendants of shipwrecked Nigerian slaves and Carib Indians; even Mennonites, of a religious sect vaguely related to the Amish, who came to carve colonies from the wilderness. The combination has made this the most relentlessly eccentric part of the British Empire: a largely black, English-speaking corner of Central America, all but forgotten by London and the world.

In an irony Huxley might have appreciated, Belize's irrelevance guaranteed its only resource: nature. Contained within its borders are vast swathes of virgin rainforest, endless savanna and mangrove coasts — the greatest variety of animal habitats north of the Amazon basin. In recent years, this has transformed Belize into one of Central America's 'eco-tourism' hot-spots. With only 210,000 inhabitants, it boasts twenty-five nature reserves (including the world's only jaguar park). Offshore, the Barrier Reef is second in size only to Australia's. Add to that the 900-odd Mayan ruins only now being disentangled from the jungle and you get an idea why Belize is being 'discovered'.

Well, semi-discovered. The most popular T-shirt sold in local markets still reads *WHERE THE HELL IS BELIZE?* And the so-called eco-boom isn't yet so much an industry as a Monty Python venture.

This had been fairly obvious back in New York, where I had been amazed to discover that the country actually had a travel office — located on the top floor of a sleazy 34th Street hotel above Madison Square Garden. The elevator door opened onto what seemed an abandoned ballroom from the 1930s. There were mouldy fixtures and rotten ceiling plaster and a damp, torn-up carpet. The light sockets were empty, raw wires brushing my shoulders. Armies of pigeons were nesting on the windowsills. I wandered along the sepulchral hallway, thinking there'd been some mistake. But no, there was a metal door with several buzzers: the Tourism Authorities of Mozambique, Senegal and Belize.

The office stank of cigar smoke, as did the director, who was sitting behind a vast wooden desk. He was actually Scottish, around fifty, with greasy shoulder-length hair and a silver-streaked goatee; his three-piece suit looked like it had been in moth-balls since the fifties.

I explained how a company in London had asked me to edit a guide to Belize — news that the director took in with a flicker of a smile. Of *course*, the Belizeans would be interested in having a book done on their country, he informed me. The government Tourism Authority could also arrange some unique Belizean accommodation while I did my research, and put me in touch with local experts. More than happy to oblige. I should just drop by at the offices in Belize City and meet my contact, a Creole woman named Miss Charlotte.

'Just one thing. Do watch out for yourself. Belize is, in general, a harmless sort of place. But use your wits, eh?'

A couple of hours in Belize City and I saw what he meant. Going out by day meant facing a parade of high-fiving Rastas trying to sell exotic substances from South America; by night it meant certain mugging. Big George the taxi driver was in a boom industry: only the unhinged dared walk even a hundred yards after dark.

Like everybody else, I holed up each night in the Bellevue bar, sitting beneath the rickety ceiling fans, drinking potent rum punches and generally feeling like a character in *Casablanca*. The flotsam drifting through this watering hole all seemed to have hair-brained schemes that gained credibility in the overpowering heat. Life may be more sedate now than it was back in the 1980s, when you might have been asked to run guns to El Salvador or fly a Cessna full of marijuana into Texas, but I met several drunken archaeologists heading off in search of a secret new dig, three Israelis planning to build their own yacht to tour the Caribbean and a Japanese chap who was bicycling from Alaska to Tierra del Fuego. Nobody had the heart to tell him there was still no road through Panama.

In the daylight hours, I tracked down the select group of writers who for one absurd reason or another were living in this city. First on my hit list was an urbane local academic by the name of Colville Young. An expert in the local patois called Belize Creole, he dryly suggested the true spirit of Belize could be found in its proverbs.

Delicately peeling a mandarin, he quoted a few examples:
* Fowl caca white an tink e lay egg (the chicken shits white and thinks it has lain an egg, used to describe a person who is self-important)
* Fishaman neva say e fish 'tink (a fisherman never says his own fish stink)
* Ax me no question, I tell you no lies, if you ax me again, I spit in your eyes (which could be on Belize City's coat of arms)

Second on the list was Emery King, an American who was shipwrecked in Belize back in the 1950s on a sailing trip from Florida, and stayed on. A corpulent character with a straw hat and a Cuban cigar clenched between his nicotine-brown teeth, he'd just worked a few days as an extra on *Heart of Darkness*, as a typhoid victim. King was the closest thing Belize had to a historian, amateur or otherwise. 'No country escapes its foundation,' he opined loudly, when I met him in a restaurant. 'The United States was founded by Puritans and it still shows a strong conservative strain. Your own Australia has its penal history, and I understand there is still a rebelliousness lodged in the psyche. Belize was founded by buccaneers, and an element of anarchy is always just below the surface.'

Emery looked half-pirate himself, but he was generous with his information. He slipped me a paperback called *History of Belize* — the only extant account of early colonial life here, from a manuscript found by accident in the British Library. It was the first-hand report of a young Scottish logger, who made his fortune pulling mahogany from the swamps with his African slaves. Apart from Boy's Own adventures — one day the narrator's betrothed, visiting from Britain, was kidnapped by Mexican bandits — the book recounted the establishment of Belize City in 1640 by the pirate Peter Wallace, who had served with Sir Walter Raleigh on his disastrous Orinoco expedition. At different times, the Belizean community included Blackbeard Teach and the ubiquitous William Dampier (and I'd like to believe that old Selkirk/Crusoe paid a visit on the privateering circuit).

Handing me the book, Emery's eyes narrowed; wasn't I planning, he inquired, to meet with *Gordon*?

It was the first I'd heard of him. But Gordon was the fellow I should talk to, apparently, if I really wanted to learn about the great wilderness of Belize — its secretive wildlife, its exotic fauna, its most ancient, chthonian customs. The man lived far out in the Maya Mountains, apparently, running the first, most proper, most important 'eco-lodge' of all. He wasn't quite a universal genius, it seemed, but the man was knowledgeable. Immensely knowledgeable.

My contact in the government, Miss Charlotte, was in Belize City, but no matter how many times I dropped around to her office or telephoned, she never returned a call. When I mentioned this to Emery, he poked his cigar over towards the corner table, where a full-bodied Creole matron was hunched over her plate, and whispered, 'You see that woman? That's your Miss Charlotte there.'

I went up and accosted her, and she nearly choked on her beans. Oh yes, she knew I was here to write about her country. No, she wasn't avoiding me. In fact, she had a fax confirming that I had a visit lined up at Ambergris Caye, the premier tourist destination of Belize. When should I leave? Why, tomorrow.

Gordon would have to wait, but it was probably just as well, I thought: after Belize City, I could do with some Caribbean horizons. At the riverside dock next afternoon, a high-powered motorboat bounced across the waves amongst the tiny cayes — pronounced keys — that were former buccaneer haunts. It wouldn't have been a bad spot to hang your bandanna — white sands, translucent waters, swaying palms, just the right change of pace after a hard few months' looting and pillaging. But the boat kept going past all the most pleasant beaches, skipped the relatively charming little hotels, and dropped me off at the resort Miss Charlotte had lined up — a place all by itself, cut off at the tip of the island, ominously called Journey's End.

As I walked down the private marina, the sun was sinking over Tahitian-style thatch cabanas, but nobody was around; set back in the scrub like a ruined temple was a squat, three-storey hotel block, also completely deserted. Great pools of water lay on the bare concrete around the pool, left over from the recent rains, while a couple of attendants were trying to drain them. It was soon clear why. As I checked in, a few mosquitoes flitted onto my arms; by the time I got to my room, there were a dozen buzzing around my ears. By nightfall, the air was thick with the creatures. You could see them in billowing clouds around the lights, like a single living mass, palpitating and blood-crazed.

I'd bought some insect repellent that had been tested by the British Army, so powerful it melted plastic. But even that wasn't enough. As soon as I stepped outside, the mozzies came on in kamikaze waves, biting through clothes, finding any square of unlathered flesh — ear-lobes, eyelids, in between toes. In the restaurant cabana — decorated for a Polynesian luau — three mosquito coils were placed beneath every table, to little effect; the waitresses were wandering about slapping their legs with the menus. The hapless guests were all doubled up over the tables, scratching their ankles raw.

And then a peroxide-haired Englishwoman appeared like an apparition by the table, thrusting a hand towards me. It was Agatha, the resort manager. 'Oh, you've had such bad luck!' she cried. 'We *never* have insects like this.'

I tried to escape, but Agatha would have none of it. 'You *must* talk with Randy. He's our P.R. man.' Then her voice lowered. 'I have a plan: you can dine in the gaming room.' She furtively ushered me behind a doorway, into what might have been a meat cellar lined by poker machines. It was the only part of the restaurant with air conditioning, and it was ice cold. But there were no mosquitoes, so to warm up I ordered a rum and coke, and knocked it back. Then another.

Presently Randy opened the door, carrying a plate of inedible fish in glue sauce. He was an elderly English gent, bald and frail, with shaking hands; he apologetically handed me a satchel full of P.R. material, then sat back dejectedly. 'Damned if

I'm going back out there,' he muttered. His sweat-streaked face shone yellow in the neon of the poker machines.

Two double whiskys later, Randy's hands were steadier. 'Listen, who did you say you worked for?' he asked in a low voice. 'D'you know if they have any openings?'

This seemed a bit odd, coming from the P.R. man. 'You're leaving Journey's End?'

'Too right. But don't tell Agatha. Did you know they're trying to sell the place? Christ knows who'd buy it. Some poor bloody Yank's interested.' He snickered mirthlessly at that. 'Good luck to him. I'd go tomorrow if I could. Journey's bloody end.'

I bought him another drink. 'A book on Belize, hey? You wouldn't believe what goes on in this place. Not one good cook in this whole country. Lazy blighters, the Creoles. Insolent little beggars. You ask them to do something, they just stare at you. The rudest people on earth. And mosquitoes? This happens every year. Don't believe a word that woman says.'

As if on cue, the door swung open and Agatha appeared. We both froze, smiling fixedly at her. 'Randy dear —' she eyed us slowly, one to the other '— you're wanted in the other room.'

'Right-ho,' Randy sighed, easing himself off his stool. He held open the door for a second on his way out — a heaving tropical deluge had begun, less like rain than a waterfall. 'More rain, more bugs,' he sighed, then slipped away.

It was time to head inland. Back in Belize City, I picked up a garish blue four-wheel drive jeep and started driving west. The gravel road passed by scrappy Caribbean villages one after another. They didn't look like much but they had entertaining names, like Double Head Cabbage, Go-To-Hell Camp, and Pulltrouser Swamp.

Miss Charlotte's next Belizean highlight was a jungle 'health resort'. I was put in 'the Tree House' — a room about four times the size of our apartment back in New York, built fifteen metres up in a giant banyan. It had huge beds, a CD player with four foot high speakers, and dozens of twisted sculptures made out of bones, spears, spikes and bark. I thought they were oddly violent: part Southwestern kitsch, part voodoo apparatus.

Even after a bath in some thick jungle oil, I couldn't seem to relax, so I wandered back down around the grounds. One of the attendants was screeching like a cockatoo into his talkback radio. Business was slow this week, he explained, so the workers had begun communicating by animal cries.

Then, out of the bushes, flitted the woman who ran this place, Miranda. She was made up like a jungle hippie doll. Four feet tall, dark and slender, she wore a white translucent robe with nothing underneath. Whenever she moved, her dozens of golden bangles and piles of necklaces jangled like a percussion section. But any ethereal effect was shattered as soon as she opened her mouth; her high-pitched voice and American accent grated like fingernails on slate. 'I hope you're com-for-ta-ble,' she said. 'We like everyone to be com-for-ta-ble.'

Miranda proudly explained that her elaborate operation had been one of the first hotels in rural Belize. From this detached spot, she had watched the country's growing popularity with First World dropouts. One visitor after another tossed over the rat race and tried to set up little empires down here. It was no wonder that Peter Weir came to Belize to film Paul Theroux's *Mosquito Coast*, she said.

'You know, I fell asleep in that movie — but that Harrison Ford character was so true to life. People like him come here all the time. They look at me, and they think running a hotel in Belize must be easy. They look at the Belizeans, at how undeveloped the country is, and they start thinking they're God. They tell me all the amazing things they're going to do, and I just listen and go: *yeah, yeah, I'll believe it when I see it.*

'Almost all of them end up alcoholics,' she said in wide-eyed wonder. 'There's just nothing else to do down here, so everyone who opens a hotel or a bar starts drinking. A *lot.*'

As for sunny Miranda, she made sure she never touched a drop. Instead, she kept sane by putting flowers into cow skulls and making those twisted sculptures.

Next day, smelling of jojoba oil and seaweed shampoo, I plunged on towards ground zero for Belize's eco-boom: the Maya Mountains, where rainforests swirl along the Guatemalan border, full of rainbow toucans, jaguars, tree frogs and gibnuts, as well as the greatest concentration of Mayan ruins in Central America.

The hub of all this is San Ignacio, a sweaty village sitting on top of a ravine, so that it looks like a British hill station in India. Throughout the green ranges beyond, cabana-style 'eco-lodges' have spread like lice. To the chagrin of many Belizeans, almost all are owned and run by North Americans, mostly from California — even Francis Ford Coppola has one up there.

Back in Belize City, I'd asked Miss Charlotte to make sure I could spend a couple of days with the legendary Gordon. ('You're going to stay with that guy?' Miranda asked as I was leaving her place. 'Sheesh. Good luck! He scares me.') But first, I was being put up in a five-star lodge nestled above the Macal River, called Chaa Creek. After the string of loopy hotels, the anonymity was luxury. In the mud cabanas, cool breezes wafted from the luscious river valley, Guatemalan tapestries covered the walls. And although there weren't any mosquito nets, nothing more meddlesome than a flying beetle came into the room.

It was Saturday night, perfectly clear and still, with a full moon blazing. Almost everyone at Chaa Creek had crawled into bed, listening to the chorus of tree frogs. But after a few celebratory Belikin beers, I was in no mood for sleep.

'So what do you get up to in the rainforest on a Saturday night?' I asked a couple of the off-duty staff members, Raúl and Rafael, who seemed as strangely wired as I was.

The pair looked at each other a little maniacally. 'Perhaps — a midnight canoe ride? Into San Ignacio? It's not hard to arrange. The river runs right past our doorway, no?'

I staggered down with them to the riverbank, and watched them drunkenly pull out three narrow canoes. I wasn't sure they knew what they were doing, but figured it was too late to back out now. Within minutes of pushing off from the bank, the rainforest had closed in around us; bats swooped down from towering trees; the vines stretching along the riverbanks quivered in the moonlight. Unfortunately, I'd neglected to mention that I had no real idea how to steer a canoe, so I kept spinning around in currents and crashing into the shore; caught up in the trees, I was convinced that giant anacondas were about to drop down onto my neck. Raúl and Rafael were way ahead. After a couple more fortifying Belikins, they had started practising their howler monkey impersonations — letting out blood-curdling shrieks that echoed across the water.

Finally, I saw the sky start to glow in the distance. Lighting up the jungle darkness in a blinding electric arc was the San Ignacio bridge, accompanied by the comforting throb of … disco.

It was like entering a low-budget remake of *Apocalypse Now*. At 2 a.m., the jungle town was hopping. We hid the canoes behind some bushes and staggered up the dirt road — into a shanty nightclub called the Blue Angel, frequented mostly by wild-eyed citrus workers and the last few British soldiers posted in Belize. A band was belting out cacophonous Punta music, the local rage, and Creole couples were grinding their pelvises together to the rhythm. A guy in a purple tuxedo with yellow ruffles caused some lecherous hoots. Prostitutes in blonde wigs teetered by on high heels. A bottle spun slowly through the air, announcing a drunken scuffle on the fringes of the dance floor.

'Party gettin' *wild* tonight,' the barman advised us darkly, pointing to the chicken wire covering the second-storey windows: it had been put up to stop brawlers throwing each other out. Rafael reappeared from a tour of the crowd, looking ashen-faced; someone had taken a swing at him for no particular reason.

'It's the full moon shining,' Raúl explained. So after one more home-brewed rum we piled the canoes into the back of an ancient pick-up truck, and bounced off back to our haven in the forest.

Out here on the Guatemalan border, nothing was over-organised. The only Mayan artist I could find was copying ancient designs for his pottery out of a dog-eared schoolbook. A popular local attraction was visiting a farmer named Antonio, who had discovered a cave full of ninth century Mayan pots in his backyard. For a few dollars, he led me with a flashlight into the silent, muddy hole to end up in a cold, pitch-dark ceremonial room, where the only sound was my own heart beating.

Even visiting the most famous archaeological ruins, you could still feel like Stewart Granger. I took the eroded four-wheel drive route to the ancient city of Caracol, sliding and sprawling for hours through the rainforest. When the first pyramid emerged behind hanging vines — it was still overgrown and unkempt — there was nobody about to spoil the illusion that I'd discovered the site myself. Stone stelae and Mayan courtyards protruded from the undergrowth; from the top of the Caana Acropolis, you could look out over the jungle canopy and imagine this as a city of 180,000 people at the time of the European Middle Ages — one of the great rivals to the city of Tikal before a mysterious disaster shattered the Mayan civilisation.

The crucial time had arrived. Coming back from Caracol, I turned down another dirt road back in the Mountain Pine Ridge, and pulled up at yet another cluster of cabanas nestled in the rainforest. But this would be different. Chez Gordon.

A skeletal figure in shorts and Indian sandals sauntered down a leafy path, scratching his scraggly beard, then stiffened when he saw me. At last I was meeting the great man. He strode purposefully over and clutched onto my hand for grim life, saying how very, very, very pleased he was to meet me.

As soon as I looked into Gordon's beady eyes, I could tell that everyone had neglected to mention one thing about him. The man was a complete maniac. 'I hope you'll find inner peace in our home,' he said, before adding with a penetrating look, 'You know, we're of the Bahai faith — myself and my young family.'

Soon his wife Jilly bounced out — a frail, colourless, bird-like creature — with her two kids. All I wanted to do was shower off the mud from Caracol, but Gordon and Jilly buttonholed me for hours to explain the details of every shrub and beetle within five hundred metres. Apparently the pair had abandoned their lives in California a decade ago to build with their own hands this 'educational eco-resort' in the middle of nowhere.

I tried to keep the look of horror from my face. In another era, this pair might have become missionaries. Instead, they had become eco-zealots. Which would have been fine if they weren't such insincere, highly-strung prats. Gordon especially made my skin crawl. After every bland pronouncement about nature or the universe, he stared at me with this defiant, self-righteous gaze, as if challenging me not to admire just how environmentally-correct the place was. It was eco-this and eco-that, the same way McDonald's bandies its prefix for McNuggets or McShakes.

And I was caught like a rat in a trap: it turned out there wasn't another guest in the whole place, and hadn't been for weeks.

Time for eco-dinner arrived, so I was sat amongst the extended family on the porch, with nothing stronger to fortify me than some watered-down guava juice. Gordon started on a monologue, and his two spotty kids would nod eagerly at each juicy fact. It was like staying with the Flanders family from 'The Simpsons'.

'Do you know what we're eating tonight?' Gordon asked the table.

'Yucca!' chirped one urchin.

'The staple food of … ?'

'The ancient Maya!'

'And of course the modern Maya,' Jilly corrected firmly. 'They are the same people.'

'Tony,' Gordon turned to me. 'Do you know how the Maya grind the yucca?'

'No, Gordon. Can't say that I do.'

He was in the process of explaining it in graphic detail when the table froze. A toxic stench was wafting over us.

'Skunk!' squealed one urchin, pointing under the floorboards.

'This *never* usually happens,' Gordon assured me, as the table broke up in chaos. It was a brilliant opportunity to escape, and I beat a tactical retreat to my cabana.

But this was going to be a big night for Belizean wildlife. I'd just crawled into bed and was about to turn out the light when I froze. Up on the wall was a six-inch long scorpion. It was quite a paragon of the species. Black as sin, glistening like polished metal, its barbed tail slightly raised and looking for all the world like it wanted to slip in between the sheets.

I tried to think fast. What's your best weapon against a giant scorpion? The first object I laid hands on was Emery King's *History of Belize*. The critter put up quite a fight (the paperback barely covered its flailing legs and stinger), but the job was done. I slipped the impressive corpse under the bed, feeling a bit guilty at slaughtering the native fauna like that, and thought it best not to mention it to Gordon.

But next morning, when I staggered out to the eco-bathroom, there was another six-inch scorpion sitting in the sink.

This time, I decided to take the two fossils down to breakfast. Gordon perused them with this fixed, serious expression, then explained unflappably that the Belizean scorpions, unlike their cousins in Arizona, are not normally lethal. 'It's more like a very, very, very bad bee sting,' he shrugged. 'It's the price you pay for staying in the rainforest.' A few minutes later, Jilly turned up with a little earthenware pot. It was a mix of garlic and ground chilli peppers — an ancient Mayan remedy to ward off the visitors that could gather by the dozen in thatch roofs (although, of course, it *never* usually happened).

I was already packing. The place was infested — a brilliant excuse to get out of there.

'Well, I hope you enjoyed your time with us,' Gordon said, as I loaded my bags. His smile was even more rigid and, I knew, entirely false, as was his studied air of complete calm.

'Wonderful, wonderful,' I lied, assuring him he'd get a jolly write-up in the book I was editing. He was wound up like a spring inside, and I thought another word might set off some Jonestown-style mass-suicide in the jungle.

This country was starting to take its toll on me. So this was the latest phase of neo-colonialism, I feverishly thought — waves of emotionally disturbed First Worlders trying to save Belize from Belizeans, mouldering away in the rainforest, slowly going insane. And I would be encouraging them; hell, maybe I was one of them. Now I needed some r-and-r, neo-colonial or not. Surely there was some straightforward stretch of beach where I could just relax for a couple of days before heading home?

A few days later, at the end of the Hummingbird Highway, I came to rest at Placencia, a fishing village on the Gulf of

Honduras. If the rest of Belize was slow, this place was in suspended animation. Main Street was a single footpath running through the village, where even bicycles were forbidden. You could eat at a Creole restaurant called Brenda's, where the waitress' vast swaying hips nearly knocked customers out of their seats. Maybe this was the sort of place old travellers mean when they liken Belize to 'the Caribbean before it was ruined'.

But even here, the flotsam had settled. Tentacles Bar, at the end of the wharf, was littered with the shabbiest expats I'd met so far: men with ballooning beerguts and moth-eaten beards, women with sunken red cheeks and vacant eyes. A sign over the bar read MEN AND SHIPS ROT IN PORT and on the evidence, it was true.

So this was the elephant's graveyard for the refugees Miranda had spoken about — the shore where the dreamers finally washed up, bloated and broken, after all the great plans had collapsed. But the same soporific calm that drives long-term residents to dementia was just what I was finally ready for. I took a cheap room in a place called Kitty's: the only decor was a few dozen conch shells, and the clientele never strayed more than one hundred metres from their hammocks. The punishing daily routine was to wake up for the sunrise, have some coffee at seven, breakfast at eight, read for a couple of hours, have lunch at one, take a long siesta, enjoy a Belikin in the afternoon and have dinner after sunset. Everyone was asleep by nine.

Well, you could begin to see why this might not be such a bad place to rot after all.

Lost in Harlem

If I had to choose the most doltish thing I've ever done in New York, it would have to be the time I took an unplanned tour of Harlem at three in the morning.

It was the sort of mistake that anyone could have made, at least in my condition. I'd been out at a bar on the Upper East Side, celebrating a friend's promotion to contributing editor of *Rolling Stone*. *Rolling Stone* writers being such sober pillars of society — Hunter S. Thompson is amongst the magazine's patron saints — the evening had gone on later than was strictly necessary. I lost count of the number of martinis that had been physically forced upon me. Luckily, I'd kept my presence of mind.

Sure, I'd spent every red cent I had, but I made sure I still possessed a token, so I could hop on the bus downtown. When the time came, I went out into the freezing wind tunnel of Second Avenue — this was darkest January, just after a huge snowstorm, so I was scrabbling over mountains of dirty ice — and to my great relief saw a bus at the stop.

I leapt on, deposited my token, and promptly fell fast asleep.

The bus driver shook me awake outside a bus depot. Turned out we were in Harlem, right by the East River. I must have caught the bus on First Avenue, which runs uptown, not Second, which would have taken me straight home. At 3 a.m., this was something of a problem. The driver patiently told me I'd have to walk a half mile to the west to get another bus downtown. I looked out the window: the streets were utterly bleak and desolate. No cars. No taxis. Remarkably few street lights. None of the heart-warming, twenty-four hour grocery stores and bars of other residential areas, no scurrying pedestrians coming back from clubs or parties. Just looming public houses, empty lots, burned-out shopfronts. And more pyramids of ice.

I confessed to the driver that I didn't have a cent. She just looked at me pityingly — another idiot foreigner — and wrote a note on the back of a transfer ticket. *Route 151 driver: Please give this man a ride downtown. He is lost and has no money.*

'You be all right,' she said, as she opened the door. A blast of arctic wind hit us in the face. 'Just walk kind of fast.'

Harlem may be a metaphor for New York's urban blight and racial tensions, but by day it's perfectly safe to visit. On Sundays in the past, I'd called in to the gospel masses at the Abyssinian Church on Malcolm X Boulevard and the southern-fried brunch at Sylvia's, the Museum of Black Culture, the market by the 125th Street subway station. Harlem has some of New York's finest architecture, and community-run tours show it all off to tour groups every day. I'd been there at night once, when I went to 'amateur night' at the Apollo Theatre (where performers like Ella Fitzgerald and James Brown first had their starts). Two African diplomats from the United Nations had decided to 'guide' me on the visit; they'd gone down the wrong street, we nearly got mugged, and the whole bunch of us were scared out of our wits. The pair from Madagascar swore they'd never go anywhere near Harlem again.

This time, as I shuffled into the 3 a.m. darkness, I was too exhausted to be scared. The first thing I noticed was that the mountains of snow were bigger up here than downtown — short-changed on every public service, Harlem is also the last place the city gets around to clearing up after a storm — and I had to grovel on hands and knees over some of them, tobogganing clumsily down the other side. The frozen avenues sparkled in the orange streetlamps like rivers of glass. It must have been about ten below zero, and I thought of an old Jack London story set in the Yukon — where it got so cold you could hear your spit crackle as it froze in mid-air. Maybe, I thought hopefully, the night was just so godawful that everyone was staying indoors?

This unfortunately wasn't the case. I soon noticed a figure separate from the shadows and start walking alongside me. A squat, meaty guy, in a long coat. Not looking real friendly. He just sort of peered at me and asked, 'What you doin here?' It was too weird to see a white person wandering alone at this time of night; I think he was genuinely curious.

'I got on the wrong bus. I was trying to get downtown.'

He snorted at that. 'Yeah, you sure got on the wrong bus.' We trudged on for a while, listening to the chalky crunch of the snow underfoot. 'Sure, the wrong bus.' There wasn't another soul in the whole silent street. Eventually, he prodded the bulge in my coat pocket. 'What you got there?'

It was my plastic camera — the $15 Chinese-made Holga that took most of the photos in this book — and I took it out to show him. He took it with a disappointed air. Shook it in his ear. The thing makes a cheap plastic rattle. 'Plastic shit,' he muttered. 'What else you got?'

'What do you mean?'

'What else you *got*?'

I turned to him and laughed — genuinely. 'I haven't got a cent, man. Not a single cent.'

He looked taken aback by that. For good measure, I showed him the transfer ticket the bus driver had written on. He didn't read it. The whole scenario was so bizarre, I think, that he just figured I was telling the truth. And really, why else would a white person be wandering around Harlem at 3 a.m.?

We scrabbled over another mountain of ice, while I guess he was wondering what to do. Finally, he just handed me back the plastic camera and turned away.

'Okay, bro,' he shrugged. 'You get outta here.'

Soon I'd made it over to First Avenue, where there were a few cars and shops, then Second Avenue. The bus came. The driver looked at my ticket and was half-tempted to throw me off, but it was too cold, too late, and my accent too obviously foreign.

Back down at Tenth Street, there was still some activity even at 5 a.m. I was elated — I'd made it back to the city I recognised. It was only then that I was struck by how unpleasant things could have gotten in Harlem — if I'd wound up bobbing in a hessian bag in the East River, say. I leaned up against a garbage dumpster outside the Second Avenue Deli to catch my breath. And then I heard over a megaphone, 'Hey, you! Come out of there!'

A police car had pulled up and had me in a spotlight. I couldn't believe it. People skulked in the shadows of our street every hour of the day. What were they going to do, arrest me? I went over to the car and said as politely as I could, 'Uh, sorry, officer. I got lost in Harlem.'

'You got lost in Harlem doesn't mean you can loiter in the street.'

'I live just here … ' I pointed helpfully.

'You *live* here doesn't mean you can loiter in the street.'

He gave me the same pitying look as the bus drivers and the guy I'd met in Harlem.

'Now get the fuck home,' the officer said, 'before we fucking lock you up.'

And this sage advice I took.

Australia: Loose in the Top End

1 THE ONCE AND FUTURE FRONTIER TOWN

Far North Queensland is a lot further than it used to be.

Back in the early eighties, when I first hitch-hiked up from Sydney with my plastic Woolworths tent, Cairns was still a remote tropical outpost marinating in a humid soup; Port Douglas had two pubs, a meat pie shop and not much else. In Cape Tribulation — a place hardly anybody had heard of — you could camp in a private recess in the rainforest and walk straight down to the placid Coral Sea every morning. People lit small campfires by the beach at night, and visited from tent to tent; there was a grocery store for food, a freshwater stream to wash.

There was no shortage of odd characters. I particularly remember a megalomaniac Scotsman named Duncan, who'd decided to create a youth hostel in the jungle. He'd convinced two dozen wandering backpackers to build the place for him, in exchange for bed and board. I think they were all glad to have some sense of purpose up there. I remember feeling vaguely envious myself.

On that trip, my goal had been to get up to Cooktown, which had a talismanic status as the wildest port of the North. I tried to hitch there, but never made it. This time, I decided to rent a four-wheel drive and finally complete the Queensland odyssey.

Of course, there'd been some radical changes up in the base of Cape York. Cairns had its international airport now, its casinos and shopping malls, high-rise hotels and bus-loads of tourists ('they're like little wind-up toys,' one old publican sighed, shaking his head). Port Douglas had its huge marina, dolloped in pastel pink and greens, and looking like somewhere in South Florida. ('This town reminds me of Key West in the 1950s,' an elderly American lady confided, 'before it was spoiled.' A local waitress was less generous: 'You can smell the greed here. It's just money, money, money.') Cape Tribulation was as pristine as ever, thanks to all the World Heritage and National Park protection. But it was eminently civilised. Camping was no longer allowed by the beach — far too destructive, sadly. Instead, I ended up in one of the new eco-lodges, where cabins of polished Queensland timbers opened directly onto the greenery. All perfectly pleasant, but not exactly what I was looking for. The question was: just where did the Far North start these days?

I felt like I was getting warm as soon as I hit the Cape Trib-Cooktown road. The tank-like Toyota four-wheel drive bounced through tunnels of virgin forest, ploughed across shallow rivers, dragged its bulk up and down forty-five degree inclines and almost ran over a yellow-bellied black snake asleep on the road. In the village of Bloomfield, I dropped by at a fish-and-chip shop, only to learn that the proprietor had been shot in the head — apparently suicide. The man who ran the caravan park next door was sceptical of the story. 'People are always getting shot in Cape York,' he shrugged. 'They're always playing with drugs and guns.' As I was leaving, he grinned. 'Don't worry, mate. We only shoot each other.'

But I knew the Far North was really beginning when I pulled up at the Lion's Den pub — a long tin shed that was built in the 1870s and has drifted along, alone on that dirt road, ever since. In the back room, a decrepit piano sat beneath bull horns and captured snakes kept in spirits; in the front room, at the original wooden bar, three guys were just as pickled. They'd spent twelve hours driving back from a fishing trip somewhere in Cape York — 'I'm paralysed from the waist down!' the driver kept roaring — and were arguing about what booze would best get them back down to Brisbane. In the end, they decided on a dozen tinnies of XXXX in the back seat and two litres of rum in the front. The last thing I saw was their car leap-frogging off to the south, the clutch obviously giving the driver a bit of trouble.

To break the silence that filled the room, I struck up a conversation with the only other people at the bar — four artists who'd dropped out here years ago to run small farms. The traditional inhabitants refer to such folk as 'ferals', but they were the most normal people I'd met since I'd arrived in Cairns, and after a few more beers I felt half-feral as well. In their spare time, Tania was a potter, Nigel photographed, Karen painted, and this bloke Pete with a silver beard, hat and open shirt ... well, Pete was getting back to jewellery-making after two decades growing, uh, 'cash crops'.

Over the next few hours, they told me stories of survival without power, dodging death adders in their cellars and the vagaries of trying to grow your own food in the tropics; I regaled them with stories of surviving New York without central heating, dodging muggers in the subway and the vagaries of living from freelance writing. In a lull, we checked out the graffiti scratched into the raw wall.

'Eighty-eight must have been a good year here,' I noted, looking at the dates.

'Yeah,' Tania nodded, playing a few dead notes on the ancient piano. 'But which century?'

'Eighty-eight was a terrible year,' Pete threw in. 'I got busted in '88.'

'Eighty-*nine* was a good year,' his girlfriend added. 'You got out in '89.'

As we pondered this, a gecko dropped from the ceiling right on the buckled wooden floor between us. Like a bright green plastic toy, it looked about, startled, then darted off.

With the world's oldest rainforest, its strings of secluded beaches and coral cayes, the 150 or so kilometres from Cairns up to Cooktown may be the most postcard-perfect corner of Australia. But until recently, the rest of the country has regarded it with some disdain. Venturing beyond Cairns became synonymous with falling off the edge of the known world — either physically (it was all but inaccessible) or figuratively ('going troppo'). And if you look at its history, you can perhaps see why.

For centuries, stray explorers — Malays, Chinese, Portuguese, the Dutch — drifted down the coast of Cape York, dodging the coral claws of the Reef, marvelling at the uselessness of the land and the Aboriginals' utter lack of material wealth. When the first English tourist, Captain Cook, dropped by, he wound up having to stay awhile when the *Endeavour* ran aground. For the next hundred years, the Far North was largely avoided. Then, in 1873, the aptly named Irish prospector James Venture Mulligan struck gold inland from the estuary where Cook had once berthed. Overnight, Cooktown became Queensland's busiest port, and the gateway to history's most wretched gold rush.

Thousands of miners traipsed off into the uncharted bush, only to be cut off without supplies by the summer monsoon. Loaded down with gold dust, many drowned in raging rivers. Others starved to death, and skeletons were found still clutching their precious ore. Having initially shot most inland Aboriginals on sight, the miners soon found themselves being picked off one by one by tribesmen. And the copper-skinned Merkins (as they were called by the settlers) were more ruthless than the coastal Gugu-Yalangi Aboriginals. Accustomed to long droughts, they supposedly practiced cannibalism on a regular basis, breaking captives' legs to stop their escape until dinnertime arrived.

Every story from the North was a tragedy of operatic scale. There was the notorious case of Mrs Watson, who put out to sea from Lizard Island in the only floating object she could find, a *bêche-de-mer* fishing pot, with her young son and a Chinese servant, when she was afraid Aboriginals were about to attack. Their corpses were found on another island, along with Watson's diary detailing how they died of thirst. Then there was the 'Normanby Woman' — a young white girl who had been brought up from childhood amongst the Merkins. Rescued against her will by the Queensland police, she refused to talk or eat English food. The authorities forcibly dressed her in European clothes and strapped her onto a horse to move her.

Unfortunately, the horse bolted, injuring her seriously; the mysterious woman expired some days later, and doctors agreed that she willed herself to die.

The burghers of Australia's southern cities shook their heads at tales like these and dismissed the Far North as a den of dementia. The sentiment lingers. A station worker I once met in Darwin put it succinctly: 'All the black fellers up North Queensland, they're all normal enough. But the white fellers' — here he rolled his eyes — 'they're all mad as cut snakes.'

Coming from someone in Darwin, that was some recommendation.

Which century? It was a question I pondered again once I finally trundled into Cooktown and had a celebratory XXXX Gold — the 'champagne of beers' — in the Middle Pub.

Hanging over the bar was a mural painted by some Michelangelo of the North to pay off his tab. It depicted Cooktown in its glory days of the Palmer River gold rush, when there were ninety-four pubs and 35,000 miners, few of them teetotallers. Returning prospectors blew their pouches full of gold dust in a single night on the town, chasing women like the legendary Palmer Kate, passing out on drugged whisky and waking up penniless in the mangrove swamp. The mural caught it all — the men with their waist-length beards, in cabbage tree hats and overalls, drinking, fighting, carousing. And when I looked down from the mural to the pool room, the scene looked pretty well the same.

Huge cattle station workers with floppy hats and waist-length beards knocked back drinks at a rate of about one every sixty seconds. Two shirtless regulars placed huge bets on the pool table, then started to yodel. Their girlfriends were both passed out drunk at the bar. The guy at the next stool, who was passing through from Perth, had been arrested the week before for drunken driving and had his licence suspended for six months. He'd already settled into pub life, and wished he had a camera to record all the brawls he saw here. 'One poor bastard was lying down under the bar after a fight, and some bloke just walks in off the street and kicks him right in the guts! All these different-coloured liquids were running out of his head. They had to fly him to the hospital in Cairns.'

'They call that the Animal Bar,' winced the beleaguered council official, Vince — a portly, jovial, profusely sweating character I met later in the Lounge. 'But you're not interested in a place like that.' He looked at me askance. 'Are you?' Vince was hoping Cooktown would live down its reputation as Australia's last stop. He hoped it would turn into the next Port Douglas. Personally, I liked Cooktown fine as it was.

Down south, Queenslanders have been almost as keen as Americans to tear down historical buildings, but here in Cooktown, detached and forgotten, the memories were everywhere. The three surviving watering holes (to avoid confusion, known as the Top, Middle and Bottom pubs) were amongst a string of turn-of-the-century buildings poking between the palm trees in the main street. The bank still had the original mahogany teller's desks; over at the Historical Museum, one of the best in Australia, sat the *Endeavour*'s anchor and Mrs Watson's makeshift boat. Old black and white photos hang framed in the baker shop, the real estate agent, the milk bars. It reminded me a little of towns in the US South, cured by the heat, clinging to memories of a distant past.

After a few days in Cooktown, I was beginning to think you had to be a card-carrying eccentric to be allowed to live inside the town limits. There was Myrna, who had abandoned her life in Sydney to set up the guest-house where I was staying. She'd built a huge tent in the backyard to breed butterflies; they had wings the size of hubcaps, which hummed when they flew. Most people had nicknames like bushrangers — 'Yankee John' or 'Lightning Ted'. The most famous local drunk was 'Mango Bob', who was named after his homemade fruit liquor. He could be found in the Bottom Pub, having been barred from both the others; when I met him, two Aboriginal kids were sitting at his feet, chanting, 'Mango Bob's mad! Mango Bob's mad! Give up beer, Mango Bob!'

I paid a visit to the man who's done most to save Cooktown's collective memory, although his own early days here he'd just as soon forget.

A fastidious, soulful old German, Hans Looser wore a precisely-trimmed moustache and immaculate white singlet; his house was just as neat, with a crocodile skin stretched over the lounge from his days hunting salties. In 1950, while he was still in Germany, Hans had read in a guide book that Cooktown was one of the great ports of the Antipodes, so he decided to leave the rubble of post-war Europe behind and move here with his wife and son. He arrived about six decades too late. On the downward slope since the gold dried up in the 1880s, Cooktown had shrunk from 35,000 inhabitants to 350.

'I thought: oh my God, what did I do wrong in my life to end up in a ghost town like this?' he remembered, as he served tea. 'But we had no money. We had to stay.' He wound up working on the railroad and doing other odd jobs.

Hans drove me out to his pet project, the Cooktown cemetery. When he first saw the site, it was completely overgrown; bushfires regularly swept through, and black fungus covered the headstones that hadn't already been knocked over. The memory still offended him. 'I thought: By God! The pioneers deserve something better!' Summoning up his Teutonic sense of propriety, he restored the cemetery piece by piece. As the hot, dry wind blasted across the graves, Hans pointed out the headstones of Cooktown's first settlers, who usually died of diphtheria, typhus or brawls. 'So young,' he sighed at one family's tomb. 'So young.' A wave of melancholy seemed to come over him, and he confided that he was getting too old now to maintain the cemetery himself. Nobody else in Cooktown has shown much interest in it. Worse, a visiting professor from a southern university had chided him for using concrete to repair the gravestones.

'That made me real angry,' Hans spat. 'If it wasn't for me, all this —' he waved at the wind-blasted terrain — 'would be gone.'

2 THYLACINE DREAMING

'There's *no* other animal that craps like this!'

At Jowalbinna homestead, Percy Trezise was triumphantly showing me his collection of turds: kept dried in little white bowls, they were a mess of undigested bones and hair. Next exhibit was the plaster casts he'd made of footprints in the mud of his yard. 'D'you see how the dingo print is neat and compact, and these ones are splayed?' He held up a particularly big print. 'Look at that. Size of a bloody stubby holder.'

Thylacinus cynocephalus. The marsupial wolf, or Tasmanian Tiger. The last known example died in Hobart Zoo in the 1930s; larger specimens were found that stood four feet high, with tiger stripes and jaws like a steel trap. Sightings have been reported all over Australia since then, but none have ever been confirmed. Now Percy was convinced that marsupial wolves were alive and well and on his property at the base of Cape York Peninsula.

To be honest, I wasn't so sure I could tell the difference between a dingo turd and a potential Tasmanian tiger's, but Percy's enthusiasm was contagious. About seventy years old, he's a warm, bubbly character with a great sense of humour. Wandering about in his shorts and long socks, chain-smoking with a long cigarette holder, he was like a hard-living version of Captain Manwaring from 'Dad's Army'. It was easy enough to suspend disbelief: out here in Cape York, anything seemed possible.

For the last thirty-odd years, Percy has lived out here, finding Quinkan rock art in the wilderness, writing about local Aboriginal legends and illustrating a series of children's books with his luminous, naive paintings. Now he's set up a 'bush camp' on his property, which makes it easier for people to visit. Even so, dropping around took a little planning.

The route from Cooktown is the old Battle Camp Road — the same route miners took in the 1870s to get to the Palmer River gold fields. Back then, it was a walking track with markers cut onto the gumtrees every few hundred yards. It hasn't improved much, and it was a bruising drive through the rugged mountains and down into the interior of the Cape. To make matters worse, a crazy Frenchman kept painting over the only sign at a crucial junction, and I took the wrong turn — luckily a passing jeep from a cattle station set me right, otherwise I might still be up there.

Within just a few miles of the lush tropical coast, the landscape was transformed into the raw, dry, monochromatic Outback of myth. Red dirt roads. Fields full of ant-hills three metres tall. Trees packed with pink galahs. Grey kangaroos pausing to watch. The road ran through several vast cattle ranches, including Battle Camp station — scene of one of Australia's largest pitched battles, between miners and some 500 Merkin warriors in 1873. As recounted by Hector Holthouse in *River of Gold*, a barking dog spoiled a dawn ambush on the miners' camp, so the Aboriginals attacked in formation. Wooden spears were no match for breach-loading Sniders, the Magnums of the nineteenth century. Never having seen guns, the Aboriginals were reported to have stuffed grass into the gaping wounds of fallen warriors.

It was near dark when I finally reached the turn-off to Percy's place. The road was almost bare rock, making top speed fifteen kilometres an hour. So it was a relief to see the orange glow in the distance of what was — surely — the Jowalbinna homestead? But instead of welcoming electric lights, it was a long line of flames crackling toward the road ahead.

In my somewhat addled state, I tried to figure out what to do. I remember being taught at school that if you're stuck in a bush fire, you should just stay in the car. What happened if the petrol tank blew up I wasn't sure. There wasn't much choice but to press on, so I barrelled towards the flames, the orange glow flickering above the dashboard. Then the bush barbecue was cancelled as suddenly as it had loomed. The road veered away into the darkness, and I could grope on in high beam.

I finally crawled into the bush camp — about twenty tents rigged up in a clearing, with a corrugated iron roof on stilts as the dining hall. When I told one of the archaeologists about my stuntman debut, she wasn't too concerned. 'They burn-off on the property every night, mate. It's all controlled. The dew puts it out in the morning. So I wouldn't lose any sleep over it.'

Next dawn, I was jolted awake by the inevitable chorus of kookaburras echoing up and down the towering gumtrees around the camp; soon after, a winged horde of sulfur-crested cockatoos joined in. The camp's guide, Tony, a local Aboriginal, was already up and about, and had started the campfire. A cheery sort in a Free South Africa shirt, he soon whipped up a great mountain of eggs and bacon with some billy tea.

There were half a dozen guests, and we all piled into another four-wheel drive to check out the Quinkan rock art. This vast collection of Aboriginal galleries was only uncovered in 1959, when a deaf mute road construction worker, taking a lonely lunch break, stumbled onto one at Split Rock. The next year, Percy Trezise came up with the writer Xavier Herbert; Percy bought a slice of the surrounding land and turned it into an open reserve. Some 1200 galleries have been found since — only a fraction of the assumed total riddling the vast, unexplored Cape York Peninsula.

'We've only found ten percent of the art,' guessed Rochelle, the archaeologist from Melbourne, as we hiked along a track at the foot of red sandstone escarpments. 'The country is just so remote. You have to walk in, carry all your water, hunt for food. But the paintings just turn up everywhere.'

Hidden in crevices throughout the steep cliffs were ochre catfish, wallabies, kangaroos, possums. In the farthest cracks were the tiny, human-formed Quinkans — evil spirits who creep up in the night to steal your kidney fat. (Which seemed an odd thing to pilfer, until I found out that the kidneys are what Aboriginals prize most in their own game.) The Quinkans are still so feared that local Aboriginals burn fires next to their camps all night; certain branches, when lit, would let off a machine-gun rattle, to keep the Quinkans away.

Finally, in a gallery high above a valley of dense bush, was the drawing of a four-legged animal. 'It could be a dingo. But you see how the back legs are shaped?' Rochelle asked, following the full, rounded curve. 'Percy believes it's a marsupial wolf.'

That evening was when I dropped around to the Jowalbinna homestead — an open air painting studio, crowded with canvasses for an exhibition coming up in Sydney — and Percy showed me over his evidence.

Percy's theory was that marsupial wolves have always lived in the Daintree rainforests, but that a string of sixteen poor monsoons in the North has driven them out in search of food. From the size of the prints, he believed that a female was now on the property, roaming about with one of its young in the pouch.

Scientists in Cairns had looked at him askance. All he needed was one clear photograph … and so he'd set up an elaborate homemade camera rig to snap the wolf in the wild.

'I messed around with electronics,' he explained, as I helped him set up a bait of raw steak in the bushes about five yards from his porch. 'But it always bloody failed at the crucial moment. So I went back to gravity ... which is always bloody there!'

His previous photographic efforts certainly showed a large, four-legged creature, but the flash had burned the details out, so that I couldn't tell if it was just a big dingo. Percy's new photo rig was simple: when the wolf pulled the steak, a rope released a wheel beneath the camera. The weight would pull down on a wire that would then release the shutter. The camera was pre-focused on the spot, and a trio of flashes pre-set.

The night before, the camera had gone off around midnight, and he'd found fresh tracks — 'like a bloody lioness'. Tonight she'd be back. 'I'm living in anticipation,' he chuckled.

Next morning, I dropped by at the homestead again for a steak and egg breakfast. Percy was excited. He'd been woken up at 3 a.m., he said. The bait was gone, and there were tiger tracks. But he wasn't going to jump the gun and claim victory.

'The camera might've gone off, but that doesn't mean a bloody thing,' he observed, tossing the chops on the fire. 'Did I load the film correctly? Did I set the flash properly? Once it went off and I rushed off to get the film developed — and a bloody cane toad had got itself caught up in the string ...'

It was time to go, and I wished Percy good luck with the photos. But he hardly needed the moral support. After all those years working with Aboriginal legends and paintings, this was a discovery that was entirely his. Empirical evidence, in a sense, was beside the point; he knew the tiger was there, no matter whether the photo turned out. It was a spiritual need.

The tiger felt like his totem. Percy's tiger dreaming.

'I'm living in anticipation,' he grinned again, as he waved goodbye at the gate.

3   TIWI   TOURING

When I first signed up to go hunting and gathering on Bathurst Island, north of Darwin, I vaguely hoped there'd be time to ease into things slowly — pick a few edible nuts, perhaps, or dig for some wild roots. But on the first morning there, two Tiwi Aboriginal guides turned up on my doorstep with rifles and axes, all set to take me catching a four-legged dinner. Ready or not.

'First we pick up some Tiwi people,' announced Bosco, as I cautiously picked my way over ropes, billy cans and sacks of flour on the minibus. He was a beefy character with an unshakeable grin; the driver, Theo, was a more sombre type, with a shock of bouffant white hair, like Little Richard's. 'Then we head out bush,' Theo nodded laconically. 'Chase up some tucker.'

I cleared my throat nervously as Theo pondered the menu.

'Might catch some possum. Wallaby. Bit of goanna. Some carpet snake, maybe.'

I must have looked a bit hesitant about the last one, because Bosco thumped his thigh and beamed even harder. 'Oh, carpet snake's beautiful, mate.'

This was the end of Bush Camp month, when Tiwis head out into their traditional country and eat native foods; thanks to their small-scale company, Tiwi Tours, visitors like myself could now come along for the ride. For the next half-hour, we drove around picking up Bosco's extended family — brothers, sisters, an aunt, the in-laws and at least ten little kids who all screamed at the top of their lungs in Tiwi. A four-wheel drive full of Theo's relatives decided at the last minute to follow us. Finally we were all roaring down a straight orange road carved into the endless bushland of Bathurst.

Hunting and gathering, I can now report, goes like this: first you stop at the wreck of a four-wheel drive by the roadside and pick up some shards of mirror, to peer up into hollow logs for animals hiding there. Then, take your axes and buckets and hike off into the country of the Tiwis' skin group, or clan. The Top End bush looks entirely different in every season of the year. This was July, the height of the Dry, and swathes of gumforest had been freshly burned off. Vibrant green cycads were already poking like feather dusters through the black dirt, while clouds of smoke eerily drifted across the flat landscape.

Our instructions? Find a hollow tree. Listen for contents. Chop it down and get ready.

On our second attempt, an animal bolted out in a grey blur. Fast, sure, but it never had a chance against the lightning Tiwi kids. Soon Mary Margaret, who was wearing a Bob Marley shirt, had it dangling by the tail. She swung the possum above her in a great arc and whacked its head onto the trunk.

'Ah, one possum won't go round,' Bosco shook his head at the critter now curled in a bucket. 'Not for this mob.'

Two more trees came down, both empty, until Mary spotted a swarm of insects around the top of a trunk — bush honey, the perfect dessert. There was only one problem: this was a hardwood tree. It took about two hours of us all hacking away before it fell (and I was heartily put to shame by the Tiwi women, who slashed at that trunk like Canadian lumberjacks).

It was all a bit much like hard work, especially as the winter sun was now high in the sky, hitting thirty-five degrees. We rinsed off in a waterhole — taking care no crocs were about — and then went off to the Tiwis' regular bush camp for lunch.

The idea, Bosco explained, was to throw the possum onto the fire for a while, then peel off its blackened skin. That would go with damper. But even as he was going over all this, the multitudes were getting hungrier. 'One possum won't go round,' Bosco shook his head again. 'No way, mate.'

And so we did the only logical thing: broke out the ham and cheese sandwiches.

Lost at the very top of the Top End, splaying out on maps like a giant Rorschach blot, the two Tiwi islands are rarely noticed by the outside world. Even friends in Sydney had never heard of Bathurst and Melville; when I explained at a barbecue where I was off to, one wit joked I might be 'hunted and gathered' myself. And flying towards them in a light plane from Darwin did feel like slipping off the fringe of the continent. The Beagle Gulf glistened below like taut blue vinyl; the islands were a plush green, separated by the fast-flowing Apsley Strait. A vast virgin coastline alternated between croc-infested mangrove swamps and great white beaches, stretching for mile after mile without a single moving person. Inhabiting this entire expanse are only 2,000 Tiwis.

Isolation has always shaped these islands. Although the mainland is only eighty kilometres away, dugout canoes rarely survived the journey, so the Tiwi culture and language developed separately from other Aboriginal groups. Early Dutch explorers found the Tiwis hostile and warlike. When the British set up a military camp on Melville in 1824 — the first settlement in northern Australia — it lasted less than five years thanks to Tiwi sieges and tropical disease.

As a result, the Tiwis largely escaped the first, scorched-earth century of Australia's colonisation, when Protestants extirpated any Aboriginal belief they could find. Catholic missionaries only arrived in 1909, bringing with them a less cruel, if still paternalistic, mission rule. The Tiwis were returned control of their own affairs in the 1970s; most crucially, since they have never been moved, their land rights have never been disputed.

This healthy sense of possession may be why the Tiwis are such an outgoing bunch — despite their once-fearsome reputation, they now bill themselves as the 'Friendly Islands'. It's a quality the Land Council is hoping to promote now that Aboriginal-guided tours have taken off in Australia and abroad. The islander-owned company, Tiwi Tours, has begun offering camping trips into the bush led by local guides with young trainees. Profits go into a health program and cultural fund for the islands.

And the idea is taking off. After all, white bread sandwiches aside, visiting the islands could be the most intense cultural experience the Territory has to offer.

The plane touched down in the main settlement on Bathurst, Nguiu (pronounced noo-yoo), where government houses on stilts were lined up in neat rows; in front of them, groups of Tiwi women were sitting in circles, smoking and playing cards. After dark, families stayed outside around open fires, watching TVs on extension cords. I spent the night listening to coconuts thudding down from trees and a series of screaming arguments in the distance. ('Domestic disputes are very public here,' I was told later. 'That takes a bit of getting used to.')

If the town was a little disorientating, it was nothing compared to the next couple of days in the bush with Bosco and family. Left to my own devices, I could have appreciated the scenery — all the virgin eucalyptus and casuarina forests, with their flaming outcrops of grevillea, wattle and red kapok. But with the Tiwis, it was as if I was seeing the bush for the first time. Apart from showing me how to catch possums and find bush honey, they explained where to dig for wild pumpkin, and how to treat the orange nuts of the samia palm — which are deadly poisonous when eaten straight, but after being left three days in running water, then cooked, taste like ricotta cheese.

And as with any journey, the unplanned encounters were the most memorable. Walking with Bosco silently through the bush, we came across a cluster of the famous Pukumani burial poles — ironwood shafts, about three metres tall, carved and painted with geometric patterns. You can see these in the Darwin Museum, but the experience is nothing like finding them with the pale smoke drifting through the gumtrees. Bosco explained a little about the Tiwi burial ceremony — how the body would be wrapped in bark, and mourners expressed grief by violently beating their chests and heads; relatives would then walk away, never looking back, in case the dead person's spirit chase and haunt them. But that was the old way, Bosco added hesitantly. The Catholic church had been making Tiwis use coffins; there was a local push to return to bark, but the matter was unresolved.

I thought of all those barely-used houses back in Nguiu. The government put the Tiwis in boxes while they were alive — and the Church wanted them in boxes even when they were dead.

✳

I headed out to the east coast of Bathurst where, hidden in mangroves, Barra Base Fishing Lodge is owned by the Tiwis and run by mainland fishing guides. Picking me up at a broken-down dock was Geoff, whose peeling nose and hairy chin jutted sharply from beneath sun-glasses and a cap. As we navigated in a motorboat, a three metre saltie lay sitting by a bank with its mouth wide open, sunning itself. It took one look at us and disappeared like a bullet.

'You wouldn't believe what I've seen crawl out of that water,' Geoff cackled, in a slightly deranged, Jack Nicholson fashion that seems to be cultivated in the Outback. From the open air wooden bar of Barra Base, fishermen watched the sun set over one of the most pristine beaches on earth, knowing that nobody in their right minds would ever take a dip. Another croc approached the lodge, and as darkness fell you could only see its red eyes; like something out of *Peter Pan*, it was still there, watching and waiting, when I got up the next morning. Three dolphins arched by in the distance, and Geoff said he'd seen teams of sharks cruise a few feet from the shoreline.

About a mile away, a family of Tiwis was camping out, so Jodie took me to be introduced. She was the only woman at the base — a chain-smoking ex-air force vet, who spent her spare time bottle-feeding an orphaned baby wallaby. The Tiwis were cooking up yam roots, and gave us a few to try (they tasted almost like coconut). Two middle-aged sisters, Edwina and Delia Puawtjimi, said they were about to set off mud-crabbing, and didn't mind if we tagged along, so we motored over to a grey expanse of mudflats and helped them dig away at the earth.

Delia was obviously the expert. She poked in holes with a stick, coming up dry several times before she finally hit pay-dirt: a huge orange claw came snapping out of the clay at her.

'Baby crab!' Delia announced, pulling out one by the body. It was followed by another ('Mother crab!'). Then she revealed an orange monster whose carapace was a foot across. 'Father crab!' As the patriarch's vast pincers swivelled to take a piece of her, she just flicked it away. 'Cheeky one!'

One snap from even the baby crabs' claws might have broken a finger, but Delia and Edwina hardly paid attention. Holding the crabs from behind, they gently folded the claws forward to be tied; the crabs simply obeyed, as if they were hypnotised. A leafy branch was tossed over them in the bucket. 'Make 'em sleepy,' said Delia.

Afterwards, encrusted in mud, we sat around in the shade with some cans of lemon soda. Delia told one of the best stories of recent Tiwi history, about how her uncle helped capture the first Japanese POW on Australian soil. When Japanese Zeros were heading to bomb Darwin in 1942, they strafed Bathurst first; when one of the fighter pilots crashed, Delia's uncle took him prisoner using only a stick for a weapon (one of the Catholic brothers radioed Darwin to tell them the attack was on the way, but nobody believed him).

Edwina talked about her own travels. She'd helped her husband give up the grog seven years ago, and ever since has been lecturing on alcohol abuse in Aboriginal communities all over the Outback. Women are particularly powerful on the Tiwi islands — unlike mainland Aboriginals, for example, men here can't hold ceremonies in secret. And the women do everything they can to take their families on regular trips out bush, away from the temptations of Nguiu, where alcohol abuse, domestic violence and poor quality commercial foods are common. Thanks to the women's vote in the Land Council, the town's one pub, 'the Club', is closed on Sundays, and for the whole of Bush Camp month in July. Now they were picking up their few last meals.

Which brought up the subject of one of the Tiwis' favourite delicacies. 'Edwina, mate,' Jodie said conspiratorially. 'How about some mangrove worms, eh?'

'Yuwurli? No worries.' The worm hunt was on.

We all piled back into the motorboat, picked up Edwina's husband and son, then headed down a tiny inlet. Minutes later, I was sloshing through foot-deep brown mud in a dense mangrove swamp, clutching onto rotting tree roots to keep my balance and nervously looking about for wandering crocs, while the Tiwis bounded agilely ahead, hacking away with axes at black roots.

Delia let out the first joyous cry — 'Yuwurli, Yuwurli, Yuwurli!' — and pulled out a long rubbery slug from the tree root.

White, fat and covered with clear mucus, it came out with a truly sickening slurp. Delia smiled, threw back her head, and dropped it down her throat like fettuccine.

I wish I could write that I tried one of these delicacies myself, but I'd be lying. I just couldn't face it. Jodie, however, was made of sterner stuff, and she gulped a decent-sized worm. Later, back at the base, I asked her what was it like.

'Oh, mate,' she screwed up her face. 'A bit like mud, eh? A bit salty. A bit like an oyster.'

Geoff overheard and just cackled. 'You want to know what they're really like? Foot-long crocodile snot.'

It was time to get out of the mangroves and back into the bush.

Picking up the guiding role were a young Tiwi trainee named Jamie, looking cool in psychedelic Rasta clothes and wrap-around shades, and Anthony Venes — a wiry Territory character with a bone-dry sense of humour, who was hired to set up the tour company. (The Land Council lets a non-Tiwi manage the operation, he said, because complicated clan obligations would make it almost impossible for a Tiwi not to lend out vehicles to relatives, grinding tours to a halt.)

We bounced off in the four-wheel drive to the northern coast of the island for the climactic camping experience. The landscape felt utterly remote and otherworldy, deserted and strangely prehistoric; even the flocks of cockatoos were screaming overhead like pterodactyls. Soon, fiercely orange sandstone bluffs appeared, fringed with spidery pandanus trees. This was the very edge of Australia, facing out towards Indonesia, and it felt like it.

Once again, left to my own devices, I could have appreciated the unearthly setting; but with a Tiwi guide the islands felt like an entirely new universe whose rules I didn't understand. Jamie decided to teach me the basics of spearfishing — but as we were stalking through the ankle-deep water, he suddenly grabbed me. 'I almost stepped on a stingray. They're all around us. Hundreds of them.' I couldn't see a thing, but I had to carefully follow his footsteps out of the murk. Just to make me feel even more helpless, we stopped to examine some huge tracks in the sand. They went into the trees and didn't come out.

'So, uh, Jamie — what do we do if we see a croc?'

Jamie pondered this, before revealing the Tiwi tactic. 'We see a big one, we run.'

We'd come back empty-handed, so Anthony cooked up the traditional white Australian steak and vegies on the campfire. As the sun sank into the Timor and the sky turned the colour of ruby grapefruit, Jamie began to lose his good cheer. 'I could've been back in town right now,' he muttered, looking nervously about. Whenever he came here as a kid, he said, a witch had given him bad dreams, until one of his relatives made her lift the curse. 'She's still there, that witch,' he said bitterly. As we rolled out our swags to sleep under the stars, Jamie built a huge fire so close to his head that it almost burned his hair; like the Aborigines back in Quinkan country, he kept it going all night to ward off bad dreams and spirits.

Even in a week, it was pretty clear, I'd only had the barest glimpse of the Tiwi world.

The Great 'Green Card' Lottery

Americans have some strange ways of deciding who should live in their country, and the strangest of all is the annual 'green card' lottery — a sort of mail-in bingo that randomly distributes 55,000 US work permits to citizens of specified countries. The logic is that certain nationalities are under-represented in the slow-burning melting-pot that is the Land of the Free. There's no shortage of Mexicans, Canadians, Chinese, Indians, Colombians and English, Congress reasons. But what of the Bolivian, the Marquesas islander, the Liechtensteinian, the lonely Ethiope? What, indeed, of the Australian?

It all began when a friend in Sydney forwarded a tiny newspaper ad about the lottery. We were based in New York on journalist visas, but a green card would be a definite upgrade: it meant we could work for Americans, and stay as long as we liked. To get a hold of one through normal channels is legendarily difficult (friends have paid from US$4,000 to $10,000 to lawyers with no guarantees, and suffered interminable angst). According to the ad, for a mere US$100, an Attorney at Law in California would handle our entry in the lottery — which meant, basically, that he would write our names on an envelope and post it for us.

The lawyer's name was something reassuringly American, like Robert F. Zimmerman. There was a picture, too. Grinning, curly hair; heart-warming yet a no-nonsense go-getter; he looked like a Jewish Elvis.

We felt a bit like saps paying Robert F. Zimmerman to write in for us, but it seemed somehow luckier. Of course, this was entirely illogical. Millions of people go in the lottery every year — 4.5 million, to be precise — and about 500,000 of them get the extremely simple instructions wrong. But apart from avoiding such mishaps, a lawyer can't improve your chances. Each letter (and you're only allowed one) is given a number in a giant computer somewhere in Virginia, and winners are randomly selected. It's mind-boggling to imagine the amount of work that goes into this (results are always months late). It's even more distressing to think how small the chances are of winning. Of the 55,000 green cards available to those 4.5 million, some 260 are reserved for Oz.

Still, whatever Zimmerman did, he did it right.

I've never won a thing, even a raffle at the school fête. But Les has always been a pretty lucky person. One dark November evening, I opened up our mail box to find two letters from Robert F. Zimmerman, Attorney at Law. Mine was pathetically thin. It read like junk mail: 'We have some bad news and some good news. The bad news is that you were not selected in this year's green card lottery. The good news is that you can try again next year ... ! Just send a check for $100 ...'

But Les' letter was good and fat. When she opened it: 'Congratulations! *You* Are A Green Card Winner!' What's more, I was also a winner, thanks to my 'derivative status'.

As we'd understood it, the promise of the lottery had been that, if you won, you'd get a green card, guaranteed. No questions asked, no holes barred. Illegal immigrant or whatever. The reality turned out to be more complex. In fact, the whole green card process seems designed to convince you that the United States is in such a mess you wouldn't want to live here anyway.

First, Zimmerman wanted an extra US$1,300 to handle the case. We decided to do the paperwork ourselves, but we needed the notification documents he had received directly from the State Department. We spent hours on the phone to California trying to get these papers; his minions seemed reluctant to give them up, but finally, after much spirited cajoling and pleading and railing, Mr Zimmerman gave up and sent them along.

It turned out that we still had to file numerous documents to support our 'application' for a green card. The swathe of instructions seemed illogical; couched in bureaucratise, they seemed to contradict themselves. To get some information, we sat on the phone to Washington, going through hour after hour of recorded telephone messages. Finally, we got to speak to an actual human being at the State Department. She was shocked that we hadn't filed the application already. There were only 55,000 green cards being awarded, but 100,000 people had actually been notified that they'd won (apparently many people don't follow through after winning). And those 100,000 could theoretically all have spouses and children, who would be given green cards by right! File immediately or you could miss out entirely, that was the message. No, there was no guarantee of anything.

That freaked us out. We went straight to an immigration lawyer on Madison Avenue — great wooden doors with polished bronze handles, plush carpets, long thin tables — and forked over our $1,300. Then we set about getting the documents needed for our application. A medical check-up, to prove we didn't have syphilis, TB or were criminally insane. Photographs signed and registered. Letters from employers and banks to prove we wouldn't become wards of the state. And we had to be fingerprinted, so the FBI could run a security check on us.

The lawyer didn't do a thing but rubber-stamp the documents and file them. Couldn't have done it without him, though. Which is why the law has such a fine reputation in the US.

The day for the interview rolled around. We dressed ourselves up and took a cab down to the great Immigration and Naturalization Service (INS) building in Federal Plaza, lower Manhattan.

On the few times I'd passed this bureaucratic ziggurat, it had always been a terrifying sight. Even at eight in the morning, a line of around one thousand people would already have formed at the front door, snaking along the metal barriers set up for them; many, I heard, had been there since 4 a.m. They were the poor sods without official appointments. But as winners of the lottery, we had privileges. We were allowed to slip in the side entrance. Sure, they made us wait in the hall for two hours — just to let us stew — but that was nothing compared to the sheer pitch of anxiety everyone else seemed to endure.

Finally our number came up, and we were ushered behind closed doors. We were extremely lucky, I think; our interviewer had an unexpected streak of humanity left in him. He reminded me of the taxi driver, Big George, I'd had in Belize City, with a perfectly spherical head, like a basketball. He seemed even more nervous and confused than us, and kept misplacing documents. But soon he had us stand up, raise our right arms and swear to tell the truth, the whole truth and nothing but the truth. Had we ever been in prison? Had we ever used drugs? Had we ever been members of the Communist Party? Had we ever conspired to kill the President of the United

States? Questions like that; answers not hard to guess. It was tougher keeping a straight face.

Mr Belize just had to check the documents were in order, then he broke into a genuine grin and shook our hands.

'Welcome to the United States,' he said, with his Caribbean lilt.

Les, as I said, was always the lucky one. She got her green card through the mail in about six weeks. As for me, I had a problem.

A letter arrived saying that the 'green card centre' in Texas had rejected my fingerprint as too blurred — they need a clear digit to appear on my card with the photo and signature. It was a formality, but I had to go back to Federal Plaza and do the print again.

Thus began a new, bleaker phase of the saga. The first appointment I had to change, because I'd already lined up an assignment out of the country. The second date fell at the same time as I was offered another assignment, on a safari to Africa (believe it or not). The notice was 'final'; I cancelled the safari.

Things had gotten a lot worse at Federal Plaza, possibly because the US government at the time had no money. I didn't have to stand in the queue of thousands, but I did have to stand in a queue of hundreds. It wasn't an inspiring experience. Maybe Lou Reed had this place in mind when he wrote his line about the Statue of Bigotry: 'Give me your tired, your poor — I'll piss on 'em.' Everyone else was either Latino, Indian or Asian; few could speak English; security officers would go up and down berating people loudly; overweight white lawyers would elbow their clients into the front of the line. We downtrodden bastards just stood there, taking it. What else could we do?

When I finally got inside, Room 1102 looked like Saigon airport before the fall. Crowds of applicants were wandering in despair.

Lawyers rushed back and forth. A family of Brazilians was weeping, as their lawyer stared at the ceiling.

The INS workers were even more hysterical. One obese clerk was yelling at people to stand behind a white line or he wouldn't serve them. The veins were popping out of his neck. None of the new immigrants understood a word he said. I barely could myself.

After a while, this guy just leaned back and repeated, 'Fucking jerks! *Fucking* jerks!'

My window was run by a woman who looked surreally like George's mother in 'Seinfeld'. I was studiously calm and polite, so she'd do a good job and I wouldn't have to come back. She took my fingerprint four times, just to make sure.

A week later, I got another letter. My new fingerprints were perfect, but they'd forgotten to get me to *sign* them. I'd have to come back again in six weeks. Gee, I thought, glad I cancelled that safari.

This time, the appointment was in the depths of January. Ten degrees below freezing. The queue was no shorter, even at 8 a.m. Everybody in the line was paralysed with cold, teeth chattering, noses running, fingers turning blue.

I tried to cheer myself up. In Russia, people must go through this every day, just to get bread.

George's mum was solicitous when I staggered in. 'Ooh, that's a pity,' she said, when she pulled out my old prints to sign. My fingers were so stiff that I could barely work the pen.

By this stage, I was convinced that I was trapped in some never-ending loop, doomed to keep returning to Federal Plaza in perpetuity. I was wrong. A few weeks later, the green card arrived through the mail. No fanfare. Just a plain envelope. The card announced in big letters that I was officially a 'Resident Alien' — with all the sense of belonging that such a charming title implies.

But you know the strangest thing of all? The 'green card' is pink. Pat Buchanan will have to fix that.

Tierra del Fuego:

South American

Gothic

The end of the world was nigh and I was feeling pretty blasé about it.

Somewhere down below, veiled by anonymous clouds, lay Tierra del Fuego. For centuries, this dank archipelago has been the definition of remoteness: it's the storm-battered tip of South America, the last shred of land before Antarctica; even the name has a storybook ring, as if it lies only partly within this earth. But getting this far, twentieth century style, had been suspiciously mundane. I'd simply hopped a flight in Buenos Aires and watched as four hours of flat, hide-brown pampas unravelled down below. In the grim military dustbowl of Rio Gallegos, just across from the Falkland Islands, the aircraft had been taken over by a tour group of Argentine matrons, all dressed in pearls and fur coats and noisily brawling for space in the overhead lockers. After travelling 11,000 kilometres across two continents, I was losing the illusion of Going Where No Man Has Gone Before.

Then we arrived. The ponderous 737 snapped into a dive, broke through the blanket of clouds — and kept on plunging, straight towards a sea of snowcapped mountain peaks. It seemed we were manoeuvring like a fighter jet; glaciers flashed by, forests, alpine lakes full of turquoise milk. As I clutched my seat and tried desperately to enjoy the view, the plane skimmed across the Beagle Channel and thumped to a halt between two expanses of churning black sea.

The Argentine passengers erupted into a round of applause — a disconcerting habit after regular landings, but this time I thought the pilot deserved it. ('We have the second most dangerous runway on earth!' a resident told me proudly later; winds off the Strait regularly hit 150 kilometres per hour, and are savagely uneven. 'But our pilots have great practice: they have to land here during winter blizzards.')

It was oddly gratifying that arriving in the world's southernmost town could still be hair-raising. No matter how many commuter flights arrive in Ushuaia every day, nature has the last word: Tierra del Fuego is the same dismal, mist-shrouded extremity that has been dreaded by navigators for nearly 500 years.

The Land of Fire received its evocative name from Ferdinand Magellan in the early sixteenth century, when he saw mysterious flames dancing in the darkness of its shores (the crew thought the fires were souls in hell, so not surprisingly no landfall was made). Early mapmakers assumed Tierra del Fuego to be the northernmost tip of the great Antarctic continent, a place where the laws of nature did not apply. Only after the first Dutch sailors rounded Cape Horn in the early seventeenth century was it found to be a cold, windswept archipelago — a jigsaw of uninhabitable specks scattered around a central island the size of Tasmania, called the Isla Grande, or Large Island. Place-names along these treacherous coastlines betray the despair of early mariners: Cape Punishment, Cape of Storms, Desolation Island, Last Hope Bay. And pulling ashore was considered all but suicidal, for fear of wild Stone Age peoples who plied these icy waterways in canoes and who had lit the fires Magellan saw.

The gloomy image of Tierra del Fuego was confirmed by Charles Darwin's 1834 account in *The Voyage of the Beagle*, and by a string of writers who visited only in their imaginations. Poe, Coleridge, Verne, Melville, all developed the idea of Tierra del Fuego as hell-on-earth. Bruce Chatwin strung the gloomy tradition together in *In Patagonia*, and added his own sombre verdict, likening the town of Ushuaia to a tomb.

My own peculiar obsession with Tierra del Fuego dates back ten years, to a barbecue in Bondi Junction before I first headed off to work in South America.

In the 1960s, one of my uncles spent some years as a wool classer on the great sheep *estancias* in the northern half of Isla Grande (the island has been divided by nature between the mountainous, thickly-forested south and the barren, flat north; modern politics has divided it rigidly east-west, between Chile and Argentina). The farms, which were larger than some European nations, had been set up at the turn of the century by the British. Then, in the best colonial tradition, the pioneers brutally wiped out the Fuegian Indians of the plains. 'I don't know where it is,' my uncle recalled, as he threw some more Argentine sausages on the grille, 'but I kept hearing about a photograph taken on a farm in the 1890s. It's of bounty hunters in Tierra del Fuego, who are posing with a set of human ears strung along a wire. These grisly bastards were paid a pound sterling for each pair of Indian ears they brought back from the *campo*. And the caption on the photo says that the bounty hunters were *Australians* ...'

On my first trips to Tierra del Fuego, some years ago, I never found that photo, but on the way, plenty of equally gruesome stories turned up. A century ago, individuals from every corner of the Empire came to Patagonia to work (regardless of their nationality, they were often referred to as 'British'.) The fascinating — and frustrating — thing was that there were almost no documents: history was passed down by folk legends, rumours, intimations. And now in Tierra del Fuego, you could still meet many of those wandering pioneers who all seemed to live to fabulous ages and remain entirely lucid, as if preserved by the chill Fuegian air.

On this trip, I was researching a novel; what I was looking for was a particular atmosphere. I don't know anywhere else that can get your historical imagination buzzing like Tierra del Fuego. In the remotest corners, the colonial era seems unchanged: houses are left to rust and decay; people wear the same fashions as in the 1920s; farms operate much as they did at the turn of the century. The settlers on Tierra del Fuego were all Europeans, with little signs of Indian blood, so there is an eerie familiarity about it all, as if it could be Australia or the US a century ago. These pockets of the past drift on, undigested by the present — so I planned to hire a car, get out into the *campo* and delve into this fissure in history.

✱

A century ago, the settlement of Ushuaia was the only refuge from Tierra del Fuego's storms, evolving from a lonely missionary outpost to a desperate prison camp for Argentina's most recalcitrant anarchists. Today, pumped up by tax breaks and high wages, the town is the island's beachhead for the twentieth century — a cross between a Klondike-style boomtown and a cut-rate Vegas.

'We've got streetlights now!' the taxi driver announced proudly, as we negotiated the harbourside streets that had been paved since my last visit. 'And look at the docks. *Es una maravilla!*' Gleaming white boats were lined up, ready to ferry tourists out to the Beagle Channel, where clefts of rock were inhabited by penguins and sea lions. The taxi driver was one of the new wave of immigrants from Buenos Aires — a cosmopolitan, fashion-conscious and neurotic bunch (B.A. has more psychiatrists per head of population than Manhattan, and probably as many designer stores). I'd spent a few days there before heading down south, and had been surprised at how chaotic it was becoming.

'Do you think you'll go back?' I asked.

'What for? So I can be robbed in the street? So I can be choked by bus fumes? So I can work my *cojones* off and not even feed my family? No! For me, Ushuaia is a paradise.'

Here we go, I thought suspiciously — another created Eden. In the blinding sunlight of 10 p.m., I strolled along Ushuaia's main street, past a gilded bust of Evita Perón, signs saying *Las Malvinas Son Argentinas* ('The Falklands Are Argentine') and a neon billboard for the Tropicana sex show. Crowds of South American shoppers jostled for electronic goods produced by the Japanese-owned factories on the outskirts of town. Teenagers tooled along the streets on giant all-terrain motorbikes. Businessmen sipped espressos in Italian-style *confiterias* and barked into cellular phones. Maybe this was the Argentine paradise, I thought, but it was all a little appalling.

Not every resident is so enamoured of the new Ushuaia. I rented a room in the home (designed after a Swiss chalet) of Luis Alanis, the manager of the local government radio station and a descendant of one of the original pioneers. 'Ten years ago, everything was *tranquilo* in Ushuaia; everyone knew everyone else,' he said carefully. 'There was a sense of solidarity that's now being lost.' He was worried that settlers were no longer coming with any sense of commitment; many just wanted to make money and get out. 'It's the old conquistador mentality. Looking for El Dorado. It doesn't help the social fabric.'

Still, Ushuaia, despite the thick commercial gloss, hadn't lost its innate grandeur. Lying in bed in my room, I could watch the black clouds roll across the Beagle Channel, deposit their rains, then disappear in an instant. The lounge window looked onto the jagged granite outline of Mount Olivia; normally it looked sinister and threatening, but a light dusting of snow had given it an almost benevolent, alpine look. Luis' two young daughters spent hours staring at it in silence, as if they were hypnotised.

Was there anything left of Old Ushuaia? Even the museum here was Scandinavian style, with its anchors and whale bones laid out in minimalist displays and experimental jazz music piped over the air. I'd almost given up, when I came across a waterside restaurant called Volver, whose interior was still papered with the original newspaper sheets from the 1930s (War in Abyssinia!). The only other customers were a nerdy American biologist and his elderly aunt. They were retracing Charles Darwin's journey, and were about to go sailing for two weeks on the Beagle Channel. As I downed a plate of mussel stew, the old lady nonchalantly chatted about how the two of them intended to sail around Cape Horn. It made my own plans seem pretty pale.

'It's my last cruise,' she smiled, 'so I wanted it to be dramatic.'

Her nephew took her hand and whispered, 'Don't say that; it won't be your last.'

'Yes it will,' she said primly. 'My last cruise ever.'

'Oh, don't be morbid.'

'It's not morbid. Just the truth.'

They went on like this for some time, clinging to each other like incestuous lovers. It was much more in the spirit of old Ushuaia than anything else I could discover.

Luckily, the feeling of being at the end of the world is preserved just outside Ushuaia's town gates, in Tierra del Fuego National Park.

There was an English student named Isolde at the guesthouse. Isolde's personal cross was that she looked a bit like a walrus, whiskers and all, and because people were unnerved by her appearance, she had become quite dour, even by English standards. But she had a uniquely valuable asset — a two-person tent — and so I gladly agreed to join her for a hike in the national park.

Starting off at a shrine to the Virgin of Luján, the patron saint of Argentina, a trail headed into the primeval Magellanic landscape, which looked even more forbidding than the Icelandic moors. The few gnarled trees grew at forty-five degree angles with the prevailing wind; the unprotected trails had become ribbons of sphagnum moss and mud. Out here, every Fuegian element regularly hit at once: cataclysmic winds, sprays of cold rain, and bursts of sparkling sunshine that lit up the red firebrushes across the crags. Once, frozen sleet poured from an almost cloudless sky.

'I mean, Tierra del Fuego's a bit of a disappointment, don't you think?' Isolde said as we battled along. 'It's not *that* spectacular, really.' She had travelled the whole of the Andes, and on a sheer majesty scale, the end of the world was relatively anti-climactic. I tried to argue that it was the atmosphere you get into — the feeling of being somewhere utterly savage. I wasn't even sure I believed it myself, as the cold drizzle pelted our faces and filled our boots.

We ended up at Bahia Lapataia, where sheer mountains drop into the Beagle Channel; a whale skeleton was laid out neatly on a field; the rocky shore was littered with mollusc shells. It was after 9 p.m., and Isolde was all for camping right there, but I cajoled her into carrying on while it was still light. Another trail led right along the waterline, which my little map said would lead to a further bay of great obscurity — and thus, I reasoned, even more raw beauty. The remoter the better was my argument, if you're going to be in Tierra del Fuego.

Perhaps the trail did lead somewhere, but we never found out. After an hour, it descended down to the rocks; soon we were hopping from one mollusc pile to the next, and the tide was coming in quickly. Drizzle came down; freezing waves lapped up and soaked our legs; it was getting dark; we wouldn't have time to go back, even if the trail wasn't already below the waterline.

'Well, this is marvellous,' Isolde announced, with a grating note of triumph. 'We're about to get swept out to sea, I expect.'

The only option was to start grovelling up the hillside, pulling ourselves up along the rich carpets of grass. There was an indentation about ten yards up, between two arthritic claws of beech; you could lean back there without feeling too much like you'd slide back down into the oily waters.

'I don't see how we'll get a tent up here,' Isolde observed.

'No, I don't think we will.' I was too tired to care any more. 'Let's just hope it doesn't snow.'

'Snow? But it's December.'

I couldn't resist telling her about Sir Joseph Banks' visit here in the summer of 1770, en route to Terra Australis, when he got caught in a snowstorm with his assistant Solander and a handful of Cook's crew; a couple of the men who had tucked into the rum supply succumbed to hypothermia and died. 'Well, thank you very much,' she muttered, as we wormed into our sleeping bags and gnawed on some damp cheese and bread. 'Last time I go camping with an Australian.' She pulled out her tent and wrapped it around her.

It started getting light again at about 3 a.m.; it had hardly rained during the night, thankfully, and the sky was now a brilliant dark blue. I felt like death and was chilled to the bone, but that seemed to make the view more vivid. The landscape felt Wagnerian, haunting, unbelievably remote. There's a heightened sense of reality here, an almost perplexing clarity — which is why Tierra del Fuego takes hold of people and never lets go.

I don't know if Isolde agreed. She didn't say a word as we trudged back out of the park; we'd planned to stay a couple of nights, but somehow, without discussion, agreed to skip it.

I had a theory: thanks to its gloomy image, Tierra del Fuego is one of the only parts of the world where rotten weather is not only appropriate, it's almost pleasurable. But when I mentioned this to Captain Hector Monsalve as we were navigating the Beagle Channel, he exploded into a tirade of Argentine curses.

'Yes, sure, Tierra del Fuego is famous for its foul weather. But it's even worse than they say! You get maybe fifteen decent days in a year. If it's sunny and perfect all day, it's a miracle.' *El Capitán* was from Buenos Aires, and sunshine wasn't the only thing he missed. 'Ah, *las minas*, the girls! Especially in summer! Down here, you never glimpse a leg, a thigh. Maybe on one extra-hot day there'll be a woman in shorts, but otherwise … ' He rolled his eyes and bit down hard on his pipe.

True, the morning had been particularly grim. The leaden sky oozed rather than rained, fog blurred the shoreline, but the *Tres Marias*, a fishing vessel converted into a small tour boat, had chugged out of port anyway. Looming from the channel's inky, kelp-filled waters were rocks crowded with sea lions, penguins and cormorants. Monsalve moored near one tiny island and pulled up a wicker trap holding some king crabs. They looked like giant red spiders; their long spindly legs scratched at our shoes.

While the captain cooked up lunch, I went for a walk on the island with two other passengers, hyperactive Italians who had driven 5,000 kilometres through Patagonia and had been pushed by all the space to an ecstatic pitch. Out here, there was not a single tree for protection; even the path seeped freezing water. And the most sodden corners were piled high with shells that had once served as wind breaks for the Yahgan Indians — Tierra del Fuego's 'canoe Indians', who lived naked in this punishing weather, smearing themselves with seal fat to keep warm.

When the young, unknown naturalist Charles Darwin stepped ashore here 160 years ago, he was horrified by the Yahgans' powerful smell and frenzied, gutteral grunts. Darwin's *Voyage of the Beagle* recounts how four young Indians had earlier been kidnapped by Captain Fitzroy and taken to England, where one died of smallpox and the others, dressed up in silk finery, their table manners properly polished, were presented to the King and Queen. On their return to Tierra del Fuego in the Beagle, they quickly discarded their European clothes and reverted to their old ways. Later explorers reported meeting Darwin's favourite, Jemmy Button: he would climb on board, comb down his hair, ask for English trousers and a coat, then dine with them as if he were still at St James Palace in London.

On this particular day, the wind and rain drove us back onto the ship, where the captain served king crab and cracked open a jug of wine. The Italians charged their glasses and we toasted — what else? — the weather.

The next morning dawned so still and warm that I caught myself wondering why Ushuaia had no outdoor cafés. But it was time to head north. I bribed the two hyper Italians with a good bottle of Argentine red to drive me to Rio Grande — leaving behind the magnificent mountains and forests of the south for the flat, barren, endless pampas, which looks disconcertingly like the remoter backblocks of New South Wales.

Objectively speaking, this is one of the world's most tedious landscapes, where the relentless wind drove early settlers to madness and suicide. But it's also perfect sheep country, and by the turn of the century became an outpost of the British Empire; even as late as the 1930s, English was the lingua franca, the pound sterling the main currency. The farmers' lives were the chilly equivalent of the Malayan rubber planters described by Somerset Maugham — with their bevy of local servants, their six-month leave back to England once every four years, the men working long hours, their wives driven to distraction by boredom.

Since then, a long decline has set in, but descendants of the British pioneers still run isolated farms. Bruce Chatwin wrote about their eerie dislocation in the early seventies, and things haven't changed much. Although they may never have been near the motherland, these Anglo-Argentines speak perfect English, discuss the latest cricket tests and send for magazines with titles like *Royalty* that rehash the imbroglios of Charles and Di.

The gateway to all this, however, was a half-formed oil town by the frothing Atlantic called Rio Grande, where I had to spend the night. When the Italians roared off, the dark streets were deserted. An old *gaucho* on crutches was leaning into the wind, a ghostly figure in his wide-brimmed black hat and baggy *bombachas*. I slipped into a *parilla*, or barbecue restaurant, where lamb was the only item on the menu, and the few diners sat in silence, listening to a tango on the radio. The melancholy accordion suited the loneliness of the plains, its strains rising and falling with the relentless wind outside.

Next morning I set off in the world's most expensive hire car along roads that ran like feeble wagon trails into the treeless pampas. Driving along in that desert monotony, you lose track of place, or time, or speed. Without realising it, I was pushing the car too hard. The tyres bounced along the polished stones, until they hit something the wrong way. I spun, out of control, and twisted off the side of the road; for a second I thought the car was going to turn over. It thudded to a rest, the engine died, and I leapt out, gulping down the cold air. There wasn't a sound except for the wind, not a sign of life. It would have been a poor location for a serious accident.

An hour of dust-eating later, I spotted the red roof and white walls of Cullen, an Irish-Argentine *estancia*. Although this was the first day of shearing, Errol and Barrie O'Byrne, the two brothers who managed the farm, insisted that I stay the night. Errol was thin and more reserved than his brother; peculiarly, he had an Irish accent, while Barrie sounded Scottish-German (in conversation you'd look from one to the other and think they were making the accents up). Inside, the farmhouse reminded me of *All Creatures Great and Small*: worn leather armchairs, mahogany dining table, cricket trophies on the mantelpiece. Only in the drawing room were there signs of the New World — fangs of a local fox, an antique silver knife belonging to the famous Patagonian *gaucho* 'Facón Grande', a set of Indian arrowheads.

A third brother's wife, Mónica (a blond Argentine), cooked up mutton pieces on a potbellied stove, and we sat around the fire swapping stories about the first British settlers and the last Ona Indians. While the Yahgans of the south died out slowly from disease and missionary paternalism, these tall nomads of the plains were often hunted down and killed to open the range for sheep stations. The legend persists of the pound sterling bounty paid to workers for each pair of Ona ears they came back with. One manager, Alex MacLennan — nicknamed the Red Pig for his ruddy face made ruddier by constant boozing — preferred to do the butchering himself. News of the slaughter barely reached the outside world; there were attempts to remove the Indians, Van Diemans Land-style, to another offshore island. The result was the same as in Tasmania: decimation.

Mónica, although she had been born in Buenos Aires and had the *porteña's* meticulous grooming, had become the most zealous collector of gruesome stories. She recounted the history of *una estancia maldita*, a cursed farm, nearby. The first manager brought his family there from Scotland in the 1890s. When his wife contracted typhus, he rode off to find a doctor; it was the dead of winter, and it took him three weeks to return. He found not only his wife dead from the disease, but also his two daughters and brother. The farm's second manager saw his three sons go off to fight on the British side in the First World War: all three were killed. Finally, the third manager, in the 1920s, watched his daughter go insane; she set fire to herself in the kitchen, and burned the *estancia* house to the ground.

Mónica had a dozen of these bleak tales. 'There are so few of us here in Tierra del Fuego,' she explained. 'The only way to keep the stories alive is by telling them to one another over again.

'Of course,' she admitted, 'there's not much else to do here.'

Barrie chuckled mirthlessly at that. 'You know what we say about Tierra del Fuego? It's a shit-hole, but we're used to it.'

On the opposite side of the Magellan Strait, the Chilean town of Punta Arenas was shrouded in storm clouds and memories.

A century ago, before the opening of the Panama Canal, this was one of the busiest ports in the Americas. Now, the warehouses were rusting, the sailor's bars empty; a few drained men sat staring into their glasses, wrapped up tightly in coats and scarves like Yorkshire miners. The capital of Patagonia felt like London in a sodden February — at the height of the Great Depression. In the plaza, a military band was playing dreary anthems that dissolved in the wind, while Santa Claus posed for photos with two llamas. Down by the shore, I tried to make out Chilean Tierra del Fuego across the strait.

Back when the sheep companies ran both the Argentine and Chilean sides of the Isla Grande, crossing the border didn't require a passport. But ever since tensions escalated between the two countries in the 1970s — the pope had to adjudicate a dispute over some mollusc-covered islets in the Beagle Channel — life has become more complicated. To get to the Chilean side, I'd had to fly off Tierra del Fuego and re-enter via Punta Arenas.

I didn't mind. I needed to come here to do some more research. For a week I cajoled librarians into giving me material, slept on oily sheets, battled colds and tried not to be poisoned by aged meats. I found what I was after, but somehow all the musty evidence taught me less about the Far South than a meeting I'd had near Punta Arenas some years before.

One frozen dawn, I'd taken one of the petrol workers' buses due east along the Strait. Eventually, the driver pulled up and gestured out at a ruined string of buildings. 'This is it,' he announced. 'This is the San Gregorio farm. You get out here.'

The bus roared off, and I was left alone on that ghostly dirt road. One shattered building said proudly *Founded 1879*. Another said it was a bakery. Another a worker's club. Behind them, half-sunk into the black waters of the Strait, emerged the rotting skeletons of two transport ships.

These were the last remains of a powerful rural dynasty, which for nearly a century had ruled this corner of the south like a Latin royalty. The people of Punta Arenas were still in awe of the families' vast wealth and black legend. Don Mauricio Braun had been a key player in the demise of the Fuegian Indians on Tierra del Fuego; patriarch José Menéndez had called on the Argentine army to crush a labourer's strike on his land in the 1920s, resulting in mass executions of workers. The farm, San Gregorio, became a thriving little village as these great landowners intermarried their children, worked with British capital and managers, and prospered like robber barons.

Since then, the empire had collapsed, but Alfonso Campos, an eccentric heir, was still trying to run the family *estancia*. In Punta Arenas, they spoke about him in hushed, bemused tones, as if he were a cross between Count Dracula and Jim Carrey, but insisted I should go out and talk to him. Now, at San Gregorio, there seemed little more to greet me than dust and wind. I poked my head into the Theatre, which had once held shows for workers and management; the windows were shattered, the chairs all torn out. A few sheep bones were piled in the fireplace.

An old peon materialised at my elbow. He was short and powerful, with a brushed moustache and watery eyes bulging from beneath his beret. I told him I was here to meet Alfonso; without a word, he marched directly towards the open horizon of scrub. Onwards we stumbled, until a gabled mansion rose from the pampas. Thin poplars — the first trees I'd seen for days — surrounded it like the spars of a fortress. 'La casa de familia,' the peon nodded, and turned away. The family house.

Nobody answered at the oak front door, so I tried the rear, where a servant lady was taken aback. It was early, she said, and Señor Campos was still bathing. After a moment's hesitation, she let me wait inside. The family home was a gutted museum: sparsely furnished and bitterly cold, its bare wooden floors creaked at every step. Paint peeled in great sheets from the ornate ceiling. I took a seat in the living room, listening to the death croaks of a grandfather clock.

When Alfonso appeared, he wasn't quite what I'd expected. The descendant of the dreaded sheep barons looked like an absent-minded history professor. He was about thirty-five, and seemed to have put his woollen jumper on back to front. Streaks of shaving cream lined his neck, and his wet hair kept getting in his eyes. I apologised for arriving so early and making him rush his ablutions, but he would hear nothing of it. In a fit of distraction, Alfonso shook my hand, dashed from the room, and just as suddenly returned.

'I'm just back from Australia myself!' he told me in perfect English, as if to explain his confusion. 'Sheep buying. Have you eaten? Stay for lunch.'

As a family of guests arrived from the neighbouring farm — red-faced farmers from less aristocratic stock than Alfonso — the scene became increasingly detached. Drinks were served in the sitting room under the frowns of ancestral portraits as we listened to crackling 1930s records on a hand-wound gramophone.

A mutton lunch was laid out in the icy dining room, with seats so far apart we had to yell to be understood. Roaring dully in the background, as ever, was the wind: a storm was whipping up from the Strait and bending the trees like wicker canes.

Inevitably, the conversation turned to politics and the now-defunct Pinochet dictatorship. 'You shouldn't believe all you hear about the Pinochet years,' the visiting farmer said in a smug patter. 'We *chilenos* like to joke with foreign journalists. We used to tell them that people would be shot in the afternoon, and they believed us! They wrote it in their newspapers.' He shook his head at the gullibility.

Alfonso awoke from being lost in thought. Things had gone wrong for his family, he said, when the Socialist President Salvador Allende nationalised the Patagonian farms. A blunt letter arrived at San Gregorio in 1970, giving them two weeks to quit before handing over to the workers.

It was a disaster, Alfonso lamented. Intoxicated by freedom and wines taken from the family cellar, the peons had slaughtered prize breeding stock for mutton stew. Fences were left unrepaired, accounts were lost, sheep chewed up the vegetable gardens. (Isabel Allende fictionalised such a takeover in *The House of the Spirits*). As the ultimate disrespect, the bust of Mauricio Braun was carted out to the *baño*.

After the 1973 coup, General Pinochet had returned the *estancias* to their original owners, and the landowners of the south would not hear a bad word against him.

I steered the chat to the more distant past. What about the bloodstained family history? 'All lies,' Alfonso laughed indulgently. 'Rumours spread by enemies.' The tales of Indian slaughters were complete fabrications; even the massacre of anarchist workers in the early 1920s was 'vastly exaggerated'.

(That whole gory episode had been all but forgotten until the 1970s, when the Argentine historian Osvaldo Bayer pieced the story together again. He was able to show that the long-running strike was settled by the military with a bullet to the heads of hundreds of captured peons — including the *gaucho* leader Facón Grande, whose slender knife I had seen at the

Estancia Cullen. Earlier, in the mansion's library, I had been allowed to examine the leather-bound farm records of the time. The yellowing pages were simply left blank, until the short entry *Strike Over*.)

The lunch ended with a tour of the old shearing sheds, all the while being buffeted by the now gale-force winds. Faded agricultural show prizes hung from the rafters — the latest dating from the 1960s, since even under military rule the damaged farms had never been able to recapture their previous glory.

Many in Punta Arenas had said that it was a pity the farm had been caught up in politics, since the Campos side of the family were the only ones to pay decent wages. But such pale sympathy hardly mattered to Alfonso: consumed by bitterness, he could only see the end of an empire. Pinochet's bloody coup was already ancient history; the dictatorship's repression had been invisible, a myth, hidden in the distant capital and as easily denied as the events of a century before.

'The Socialists set out to destroy the farm,' he muttered, staring at the baby-blue prize ribbons. 'One hundred years of work ruined in a day!'

The wind was now so strong that it was difficult to stand upright. Alfonso brushed the hair from his eyes and shuffled back into the cold, empty mansion.

Tropical squalor is quite different from squalor in colder climes. In the tropics, you may have your millions of insects, your festering sores, your stenching sweat, but the monsoons always pound down to wash the more offensive sights and smells away. In the cold climates, people tend to go out less, wash less, change less. Air goes stale. Circulation ceases. Grime builds up. Becomes true filth.

I got to ponder this distinction on the Chilean side of Tierra del Fuego, in a place called Rusffin — which was, I think, the closest spot in the Americas to the year 1897.

Getting there took some application. I'd hired a car at Punta Arenas, and taken it across the Strait of Magellan in the middle of a storm, on a ferry modelled after a landing craft from the D-Day assault. While some parts of the Argentine side have leapt into the modern world, the entire Chilean side has withered. The ferry leaves people at the only town, Porvenir (Future!). It looked like an abandoned mining camp, the dirt streets lined with houses of corrugated iron, chimneys drooping. A few pasty inhabitants wrapped themselves in blankets and stood smoking in doorways. Animal hides flapped on the clotheslines. The population was declining with every passing week.

I dropped by on Carlos Ozuljevich, a town councilman I'd met on a previous visit. He had been depressed then; now he declared Porvenir 'dead', and said that he planned to abandon it himself as soon as possible. 'The only foreigners who visit this side of the island,' Carlos added delicately, 'are *unusual* people.'

He went with me around the corner to visit 'the old Croat', a well-known local astronomer who had built an observatory tower on top of his house. He was a bit like Steptoe, this Vlasov: skeletal, cranky, all but toothless, surrounded by scraps of antiquity. At any given time, you could find wooden ship's figureheads, iron street signs from Santiago, parts of old merry-go-rounds, all piled up in his workroom. This visit, I wanted to talk to him about the ozone hole. Everyone was in a panic about it in the Far South. Farmers reported savage sunburns, increased eye cataracts, sheep going blind, chaotic bird migrations, rabbits running mad. One peon explained how he would only wear white clothes to ward off the sun's harmful rays.

But as with everything, old Vlasov was contrary. 'The ozone hole is not a *bad* thing!' he screeched when I asked his opinion. 'It's a *good* thing! The same with this global warming! How can it be a *bad* thing for us in Tierra del Fuego, when we're all shitting ourselves from the cold nine-tenths of the year?'

He'd obviously given the ozone hole a good deal of thought, as he started scribbling away on a blackboard with outlines of the atmosphere and the angle of the sun's rays at this far latitude, with a few arithmetical jottings in the margins.

'Look at me, I'm a physical wreck from the weather. My ankles bloat up like tree trunks. It's horrible to look at. God, how I wait for the ozone hole to expand! Do you think I'm worried about a little sunburn? At my age? Don't be idiotic.'

Then he ordered us out of the house.

As I drove south along the wretched coastline, the decades simply dissolved.

In this part of the island, there were no hotels, no petrol stations. Wild *guanacos* elegantly leaped the rotten fences that once enclosed multitudes of sheep. I was listening to the car radio from Punta Arenas. One by one the stations began to disappear. Finally I had nothing but Latino rap music crackling away. Soon that faded into silence as well.

The isolation was a bit intimidating, but the archaic Fuegian solidarity (lamented as lost by Luis Alanis back in Ushuaia) still protects wandering travellers out here. An old settler in a pickup truck sold me petrol when I ran low. And when I stopped by at Estancia Cameron — still functioning in the way San Gregorio must have once done — the peons insisted I join them for lunch in their wooden dining hall.

It was a scene straight out of Dickens: an obese cook, his apron covered with gravy, strutted back and forth from a bubbling black pot, while the shearers silently wolfed down great chunks of mutton. That was their diet for breakfast, lunch and dinner, except on Christmas Eve, when they got chicken (and then they felt oddly dissatisfied). Sitting next to me was a character who looked like he'd as soon slit my throat as talk — until I asked him about the day's wool clip. Then his scarred face broke into a cherubic grin. 'There's nothing more beautiful than to shear sheep,' he said. 'It's the reason God put me on this earth.'

Everyone was so amiable that I decided to keep driving south, towards the foothills of the Andes. This, I congratulated myself, was one of the remotest places on earth, one of the last frontiers in the Americas. It was almost dark when I pulled up to the only *estancia* for many miles, to see if I could find a bed.

This was Rusffin — which turned out to be less like Dickens than *Deliverance*.

The *patrón*, or boss, was slumped unconscious across the kitchen table, with a bottle of wine in his hand, but his enormous wife said I could sleep in the dorms. She handed me over to the cook — four feet tall, deathly pale, and dragging a club foot — who headed off across the courtyard, muttering sarcastically all the way. 'Oh, yes, we love visitors here ... we treat them with great respect ... we're like the Hotel San Moritz here, friend ...'

His kitchen was where I began to ponder cold climate squalor. The benches were black with generations of grime, while a dog was slavering over one of the cooking pots, eating lumps of congealed fat. Half-gnawed pieces of raw mutton, stolen by the cats, were mouldering in every corner of the building. 'Would you like a bit of dinner?' the wormy little cook was grinning. 'Look how the dog enjoys it ... he's got taste, that one ...'

He led me to a disused storage room, where a mud-caked sheepskin was pulled over some wooden boards as a bed. I was going to crash out, but he started tugging on my arm again with that endless smarmy patter.

' ... you can't sleep now ... come and meet my friends ... we love visitors ... I wouldn't offend them ... I like your hat ... would you give it to me as a present? ... what about your watch, then? ... you wouldn't have a map would you? ... we have no idea where we are, poor bastards that we are, out here in the *campo* ...'

The half-dozen shearers were all squeezed into a windowless room, lying two to a bed and all blind drunk on warm white wine, which they sucked from tetra-packs. A mosaic of Playboy cutouts covered the nicotine-stained walls. Somewhere next to a wood stove, framed by drying clothes, was a television set and VCR. One glassy-eyed shearer, who could barely stand, put on the evening's entertainment: an American soft-porn flic called *Blood Games*, about a female baseball team that goes berserk and turns on the men in a small country town. 'Look at the arse on that thing,' he kept muttering, clutching himself. The others were staring at me with vague snarls.

I don't know if it was exhaustion or the perfume of rotten meat, but I was starting to get paranoid. I'd been blithely motoring about like Bertie Wooster out here in the middle of nowhere; now I was trapped with a bunch of drunken desperados. After bowing out politely, I escaped to my storage room and wedged my pack up against the door (what was Spanish for 'boy, ah'm gonna make you squeal like a pig'?)

Next morning, the shearers were still curled up two to a bed. I slipped out without saying goodbye; it was just a little more frontier than I could take.

Epilogue

Spring has crept up on us again — announced, as ever, by the roar of jackhammers. New York is back on its cycle of endless motion: city workers are tearing up the street, laying new pipes, repairing the potholes created by winter freezes; businesses everywhere are re-painting, re-working, re-naming, re-locating. With an almost Parisian flourish, the trees along Tenth Street all sprouted tiny white flowers overnight — except for the one in front of our building. Turns out John the Super poured gallons of poison down a rat hole at its base, which killed off the roots. One of his New Year resolutions, he told us.

Still, change is back in the air. A few weeks ago, we even figured out a way to evade the Scum Upstairs, at least temporarily — by sub-leasing a second apartment in the building. It's a bare shell of a room, but the sense of *liebensraum* is overwhelming — almost agoraphobic. 'You should sit for a while with a cardboard box over your head,' suggested one droll acquaintance. 'To ease yourself into it.'

And so it goes. Sometimes you have to wonder if it wouldn't be more logical to move out of this city. Securing the most basic elements of existence can be absurdly difficult — renting an apartment, finding work, arranging health care, catching the subway, coping with the weather . . . just walking down the street can be exhausting.

But even the sense of constant crisis helps addict people to New York. The truth is, you fight so hard to get a foothold here, you can't just give it up and walk away. You'd have to be crazy.